THE BEAUTY OF
AMERICA

To our friends, Jean and Robin,

With the hope you will visit us.

Peg and Hank Weymer
November, 1986

THE BEAUTY OF
AMERICA

Keith Lye and Eric Inglefield

Crescent Books

New York

Photographic acknowledgments

Arkansas Department of Parks and Tourism, Little Rock – Robyn Horn 100 top, 100 bottom, 101; J Allen Cash, London 141, 142 left, 142 right, 143, 238; Chicago Convention & Tourism Bureau 111; Bruce Coleman, Uxbridge – Gene Ahrens 44, 119, M Timothy O'Keefe 174, Charlie Ott 215, Joe Van Wormer 210 bottom; Colour Library International, London endpapers, 7 top, 7 bottom, 8–9, 9, 10, 12–13, 14, 15, 16, 17, 19, 20, 21, 22–23, 24 top, 24 bottom, 25, 26, 27, 28, 28–29, 32, 34–35, 36, 37, 38, 39, 40–41, 42, 43 top, 43 bottom, 45, 46, 48–49, 53, 54–55, 55, 56–57, 64, 65 top, 65 bottom, 66–67, 68–69, 70, 72–73, 75, 76, 77, 79, 80–81, 82, 84, 86–87, 88, 93 top, 94, 95, 96–97, 103, 107, 108–109, 112, 120–121, 124–125, 132–133, 135, 138–139, 145, 149 top, 151, 152, 153, 154, 155, 157, 158, 159, 160–161, 162–163, 165, 166–167, 169, 170, 171, 172, 175, 176, 178, 182–183, 184, 185 top, 186–187, 189, 190 top, 191, 192–193, 199, 201, 202–203, 212–213, 217, 218, 221, 223, 225 top, 225 bottom, 226–227, 229, 231, 232, 233, 234–235, 236, 237, 239, 240, 241, 242–243, 244; Michael Dent, Richmond 30 top, 30 bottom, 31, 52, 78 top, 150, 156, 168, 173, 177 top, 177 bottom, 179, 180, 181, 185 bottom, 194, 198, 200, 204, 205, 206, 207, 220, 221; Department of Economic Development, Jackson, Mississippi 93 bottom; Jennifer Feller, London 41, 71, 99, 190 bottom; Florida Division of Tourism, Tallahassee 89; Georgia Department of Industry and Trade, Atlanta 83, 85; Greater Cleveland Growth Association, Cleveland 104; Richard & Sally Greenhill, London 110 top, 128; Robert Harding Picture Library, London – Moore & Moore 51, 140, Walter Rawlings 50; Eric Inglefield, London 58, 66, 67 bottom, 98, 219; Iowa Development Commission, Des Moines 122 top, 122 bottom, 123; Kansas Department of Economic Development, Toplka 129 bottom; Las Vegas Convention 214; Michigan Travel Bureau, Lansing 105, 106; Missouri Division of Tourism, Jefferson City 126, 127, 129 top; Nebraska Division of Travel & Tourism, Lincoln 130; North Dakota Travel Department, Bismarck 137; Oregon Department of Transportation, Salem 208, 210 top, 211; Pennsylvania Bureau of Travel Development, Harrisburg 48 top, 48 bottom; Pennsylvania Dutch Visitors Bureau, Lancaster 47; Picturepoint, London 110 bottom; Margaret Saunders, London 33, 78 bottom; South Carolina Department of Parks, Recreation and Tourism, Columbia 80; South Dakota Division of Tourism, Pierre 131, 134, 136; Spectrum Colour Library, London 90, 91, 92; State of Nevada Department of Economic Development, Carson City 216; State of Wisconsin Department of Development, Madison 114, 115, 116, 117; Tony Stone Associates, London 209; Sun Valley Company, Sun Valley 195, 196; Texas Tourist Development Agency, Austin – Michael Murphy 146, 147, 148, 149 bottom; Virginia State Travel Service, Richmond – Brent Cavedo 74; West Virginia Governor's Office of Economic & Community Development, Charleston – Gerald S. Ratliff 59, 60, 61 bottom, 62, Ron Snow 61 top.

Title spread: Maroon Lake and Maroon Bells, near Aspen, Colorado (Colour Library International, London).

First English edition published by
Deans International Publishing
52-54 Southwark Street, London SE1 1UA
A division of The Hamlyn Publishing Group Limited
London · New York · Sydney · Toronto

Library of Congress Catalog in Publication Data
Inglefield, Eric.
   The beauty of America
   1. United States – Description and travel – 1960-
– Views.   I. Lye, Keith. II. Title
E169.02.152   917.3'0022'2   82-2529
ISBN 0-517-37866-3   AACR2

This edition is published by Crescent Books
Distributed by Crown Publishers, Inc.
g f e d c

Printed in Italy

Contents

America and the Americans

According to legend, the Ute Indians who settled in the Rocky Mountains in what is now Utah and Colorado were once a tribe of giants. One day, during a hunting expedition long ago, a band of braves left behind one of their number to stand guard while they went off to look for suitable prey in the surrounding grassland. As time passed and the braves failed to return, the tired loyal sentry at last lay down to rest in the grass. Slowly he was transformed into the well-known landmark known as Sleeping Ute Mountain, which clearly shows his silhouette. As for the forgetful hunters, it appears that they so offended the Great Spirit that they and all their tribe were reduced to the size of ordinary people.

This story illustrates the propensity of the Indian peoples of North America for explaining the landscape and relating themselves to it. Thousands of years ago, they spread over the vast kaleidoscope of territory which we now call the United States, resourcefully adapting themselves to the nature of the land, finding sustenance by hunting, fishing, and farming, and by gathering wild berries and fruits from the rich vegetation. In their closeness to the earth they found identifying names for the natural features that marked the landscape, sometimes using straightforward descriptive labels such as *Maco Sica*, literally meaning "bad land," for the barren, eroded wastelands now called the Badlands of South Dakota. Alternatively they chose a more poetic phrase, such as their name for "Mirror of Heaven Springs" in Michigan, or a more elaborate simile, such as the well-known "red rocks standing like men in a bowl" which they applied to Utah's Bryce Canyon. Everywhere features of the landscape were interwoven with religion and mythology, as the story of Sleeping Ute Mountain bears witness. There were also several legends associated with that eerie monolith of rock known as the Devil's Tower, which soars above the plains of Wyoming. According to one of them, the Devil used the tower as a drum to create terrifying crashes of thunder during the severe storms that occasionally lash this part of the High Plains, while another tells how the tower was raised up by the Great Spirit as a platform to save a group of Indian girls from an attack by bears, after which he took the girls up into the sky and transformed them into the stars of the Pleiades.

The inventiveness of the Indian legends that offer an interpretation of the landscape finds an echo in the exaggerated, jocular tales devised, it is said, by the white pioneer lumberjacks in Minnesota's forests in the late nineteenth century to record the astonishing exploits of the superman Paul Bunyan and his blue ox, Babe. The flavor of these stories can be judged by the one which tells how Paul gouged out the great gash in the land now known as the Grand Canyon by dragging his pickaxe behind him as he walked.

Although these legends have their charm and appeal, it is the first-hand observations and explanations of geography and geology that have provided us with the basic, down-to-earth facts about the land's natural features. Some of our knowledge was first gained through the official reports made by explorers such as Meriwether Lewis and William Clark, and the lively descriptions brought back by intrepid fur-trappers and mountain men who wandered through the unknown wilderness of the West long ago. One of

Above: The towering rock buttes that dramatically pierce the landscape in Monument Valley on the Utah-Arizona state line are instantly recognizable symbols of the American West made famous throughout the world by many early Western movies.

Left: The craggy peaks of Mount Owen and Teewinot Mountain soar into the sky in the magnificent Grand Teton National Park, Wyoming. Into this northwestern corner of Wyoming's Rocky Mountains nature has packed some of her most spectacular scenic treasures.

The Old Trail Town reconstructed at Cody, Wyoming, symbolizes the opening up of the American West by the intrepid pioneer families of the last century. Among the buildings here is the Museum of the Old West, which houses many fascinating relics of those colorful frontier days.

them was John Colter, whose dramatic account of the volcanic oddities of Yellowstone was laughingly referred to by his contemporaries as "Colter's Hell," although we now know the geological reasons for those spurting geysers and bubbling hot springs.

Over the years the map of America has been systematically filled in and what emerges is a land of infinite contrasts, of incredibly beauty, of staggering extremes of climate, and of vast open spaces and bustling, crowded cities. The sheer size of the country, nearly 3,000 miles across the North American continent from the Atlantic to the Pacific, not counting the enormous expanse of Alaska or the islands of Hawaii, makes it difficult to fix an overall view in the mind of the countless scenic treasures on offer, a problem which no single tour or visit can ever overcome. A trip in the mind's eye is perhaps the best way to gain a general impression of the principal features of the land, to be filled in by the details set out in the rest of this book.

Imagine a journey across America in a very high airliner or, better still, a space shuttle, from the east coast around Delaware Bay to the west coast by San Francisco, with panoramic views through cloudless skies of the vast expanses of territory laid out below. Approaching the silver, twisting line of beaches, bays, and inlets of the Atlantic seaboard the vista sweeps down from the craggy coast of Maine and the white sandy hook of Cape Cod southwards beyond Long Island and the great hazy metropolitan areas of New York, Philadelphia, and other large cities as far as the sun-drenched

beaches, swampy Everglades, and island Keys of Florida. Behind the coast appears a multicolored patchwork of farmland, forests, small villages and cities, such as Washington, D.C., divided up by the glittering threads of rivers and streams, the ground gradually rising westward into the high blue-green waves that mark the rounded, forested north–south ridges of the Appalachian chain, with here and there a patch of lighter green or silvery blue to indicate a pastoral valley or a lake. Farther west the land descends into a checkerboard of rolling farming country and forests where the snaking Ohio and Tennessee rivers slither westward into the flat horizon to meet the "Father of Waters," the mighty Mississippi.

Now an immense plain stretches into the haze as far as the eye can see, neatly laid out in rectangular patterns of farm colors and crossed by the broad winding line of the Mississippi. Looking north, the river disappears beyond the flat fields of Illinois, past the sleek skyscrapers of Chicago which tower beside the silver sheet of one of the five Great Lakes, and into the horizon, where the lakes of Minnesota sparkle among the dark forests along the Canadian border. To the south the great river meanders lazily through the flat farming country of Louisiana and Mississippi, pushing out its delta around the old city of New Orleans before merging sleepily with the Gulf of Mexico.

On and on the vast treeless plains march westward, rolling like an ocean beyond the island of high, forested, and lake-strewn hills formed by the Ozark Plateau of Arkansas and Missouri, across the flat cattle ranches of

Since its construction in 1886, the Statue of Liberty in New York Harbor has been a world-famous symbol of freedom and hope, greeting thousands of immigrants from many lands at the end of their long sea journeys. The 152-foot (46.3 m) figure, standing on its 150-foot (45.7 m) base, was presented to the United States by France to commemorate their friendship during the War of Independence.

Texas to the southwest and the immense wheatfields of Iowa, Kansas, and Nebraska farther north. Now the land begins to rise slowly into the High Plains, broken only by the granite knobs of South Dakota's Black Hills, with several large rivers running down the gentle slopes through high cattle country in the west, among them "Big Muddy," the great Missouri, looping in from Montana and North Dakota, the shallow, broad Platte, which someone once called "the sorriest river in all America," the Arkansas, the Red, and several more, the banks of their tributary streams lined with cottonwoods. Once misleadingly labeled the "Great American Desert," the High Plains are now dotted with reservoirs, and the high buildings of cities such as Denver glint in the sunlight, signaling to others farther south in Oklahoma City and Dallas.

Two-thirds of the way across the country, the landscape suddenly changes as the Rocky Mountains rear up high above the plains, a spectacular line of jagged peaks running south into New Mexico and curving northwestward through the broken plateaus of Wyoming and beyond Montana into Canada. Enclosed in this majestic mountain scenery are four of America's great national parks: Glacier National Park, in Montana; Yellowstone National Park, in both Montana and Wyoming; Grand Teton National Park, in Wyoming; and Rocky Mountain National Park, in Colorado. Beyond the mountains, huge areas of New Mexico, Arizona, Colorado, and Utah seem to crumble into a high plateau region of flat-topped mesas and towering

The dazzling signs that illuminate Las Vegas, Nevada, by night make no secret of the fact that this outrageously hedonistic city is the gambling and entertainment capital of America, if not the world.

buttes, where the rivers have carved deep gashes in the multicolored rock layers. The most spectacular is the celebrated Grand Canyon sliced through northern Arizona by the rugged Colorado River, which runs away southwestward through a series of dams and lakes to the distant Gulf of California. Farther north the Great Salt Lake of Utah can be seen, glistening amid the hot, shimmering expanses of salt flats and desert on the edge of the arid Great Basin, which stretches over vast distances across western Utah and Nevada in a series of north–south mountain ridges darkened with patches of pine trees. And beyond, to the north, is the craggy, lava-covered Columbia Plateau extending from Nevada into southern Oregon and Idaho.

Before descending into California, a final mountain barrier looms ahead: to the north, the spectacular forested and snow-capped peaks of the volcanic Cascade Range run from northern California across Oregon and Washington to the Canadian border, while to the south, the rugged Sierra Nevada curves around beautiful Lake Tahoe into southern California, enclosing the natural wonders of Yosemite, Kings Canyon, and Sequoia National Parks. A colorful pattern of fields and orchards now spreads out below in California's immense agricultural Central Valley, echoed by Oregon's green Willamette Valley farther north, and contrasting with the desolate, arid expanses of Death Valley and the Mojave Desert, which lie shimmering in the baking hot sun to the south. Along the western horizon the green humps of the protecting Coast Ranges run right along the western shoreline from

Though the long history of the Indian peoples on the American continent came to a tragic conclusion with the coming of the white man, many Indians are still proud to carry on and preserve their age-old customs. The traditional method of making bread, for example, is followed by this Navajo woman in Arizona.

Washington to the city of Los Angeles, a coastline of superb rugged beauty on the edge of the deep blue waters of the Pacific. Here beautiful San Francisco emerges from its sea fog on its spectacular large bay, flanked in the far north by Seattle, hidden deep in Puget Sound, and in the south by glittering Los Angeles and San Diego, basking by the sandy beaches of southern California. Away to the north beyond the horizon are the snow-covered wildernesses and mountains of Alaska, and halfway across the Pacific to the west, the warm paradise islands of Hawaii.

The Indian peoples who inhabited this beautiful country for thousands of years before the coming of the white man made little impact on the landscape although, here and there, their earliest ancestors left behind curious burial mounds of tremendous size and, in the southwest, constructed simple adobe houses in remote village communities. Their simple lifestyle, in tune with nature, created the myth of the "noble savage" which captured the imagination of late eighteenth-century Europe. Yet the arrival of the Europeans in America from the early sixteenth century set in motion a

In the far southwestern corner of the United States the warm waters of the Pacific Ocean wash the rocks of Sunset Cliffs near San Diego in southern California. California's union with the United States in 1848 represented a glorious culmination of the policy of westward expansion as far as the Pacific pursued by the explorers and pioneers of the nineteenth century.

Boats lie immobile in the frozen harbor at Homer Spit, Alaska, the most northerly of the American states. The territory, the largest in the Union, was purchased from Russia for a little over $7 million in 1867.

relentless train of events that inevitably led to a fundamental clash of cultures and the tragic destruction of the Indian way of life. First came the Spaniards, motivated by thoughts of "God, Gold and Glory," who set up their empire in the arid southwest; then the French, who came down the St. Lawrence River to lay claim to the whole Central Plains region, which they named Louisiana in honor of their king; and later the Dutch and the Swedes, who competed with, and lost to, the British, who founded their thirteen colonies along the eastern shoreline.

The story of the growth of the United States after winning its independence in the Revolution of 1776–81 is a saga of westward expansion by doughty settlers in the face of mounting Indian hostility. As one pioneer woman whimsically noted in her diary:

> *When God made man,*
> *He seemed to think it best*
> *To make him in the East,*
> *And let him travel west.*

The 1840s was the most crucial decade in this epic story. In 1845 a New York newspaper declaimed that it was "our manifest destiny to overspread the continent allotted by Providence for the free development of our yearly multiplying millions," and the call was eagerly taken up. People swarmed into the wide open spaces of the West both by sea and along the fabled overland trails in response to tales of fabulous gold strikes, promises of fertile farming land, or simply their own vague ideas of finding a fortune in the Second Eden. By the end of the decade the northwestern territories of Washington and Oregon, until then disputed with Britain, and California, Texas, and the old Spanish southwest, taken over by Mexico some 20 years earlier, had been incorporated into the United States, due in no small measure to the political skills of President James K. Polk. In 1867 Alaska was bought from the Russians for just over $7 million, and 31 years later the United States annexed Hawaii.

The Indians, of course, had no part in this drama, except as bemused onlookers who saw the old traditional buffalo grazing lands taken over for the cattle and sheep ranches and the homesteads of the white settlers. The idea of land as real estate to be fenced off, bought, and sold was totally alien to their way of life, in which everyone was entitled, as least in theory, to share in the bounty provided by nature. Early friendliness turned to suspicion and then open hostility in the bloody Indian wars that wracked the West in the latter part of the century. But despite fierce resistance by such charismatic leaders as Red Cloud, Sitting Bull, Crazy Horse, and Geronimo, the fate of the Indians was sealed and their removal to reservations the ultimate white man's solution.

Enriching the nation's cultural heritage with their historic traditions and colorful festivals, large numbers of immigrants from Europe – Britons, Irish, Germans, Poles, people of every nationality – swelled the growing population of the now vastly expanded United States during the late nineteenth and the present century. Large numbers of Chinese and Japanese also moved into the states bordering the Pacific, where their presence still gives additional spice to the ethnic mixture that characterizes the American population as a whole. By 1970 people of Asian origin in the United States included some 435,000 Chinese, 591,000 Japanese, and 343,000 Filipinos, the bulk of the population comprising around 178 million whites, 22 million blacks, and 793,000 Indians.

The incredibly beautiful country which is the national birthright of all these Americans contains some of the most spectacular scenery in the world, and over the years great efforts have been made to preserve it unspoiled for future generations. Since 1872, when the volcanic wonders of Yellowstone were designated the country's first national park, many areas of outstanding natural beauty have been placed under the protection of the National Parks Service, as have many other sites of historic interest and recreational appeal. Yet the beauty of America encompasses much more than scenic grandeur; it is found wherever one looks, in the simple everyday sights that meet the eye up and down the country – the springtime cherry blossoms of Washington, D.C.; the exciting skyline of New York City; the shimmering heat of the Great Plains, where the corn grows "as high as an elephant's eye"; a ride on the "El" railroad above Chicago's Loop district; the colonnaded mansions of the old South, in their settings of magnolias and trees trailing Spanish moss – an endless procession of wonderful scenes that transform America into a beautiful experience to savor and cherish.

The people of Hawaii added yet another dimension to the cultural and ethnic diversity of the United States when their islands were annexed in 1898.

The Northeast

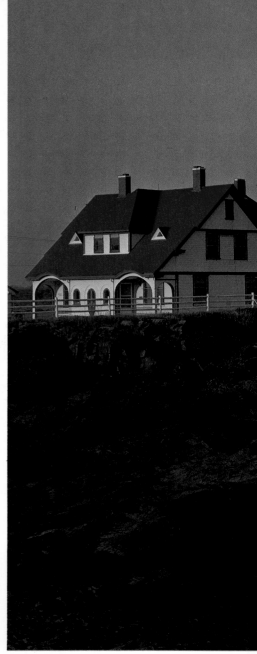

The Northeast, including New York and the six New England states, played a central role in American history. It was the "hotbed of the American Revolution" and the pioneer of economic, cultural, and educational life. Nearly 500 years before Columbus, the bold Vikings sailed down its coasts, and, in the 1490s, John Cabot led English expeditions here to explore what he thought was part of China. But it was not until 1614 that Captain John Smith, hero of Jamestown, charted the coastlands between Cape Cod and Penobscot Bay and christened them New England. His map and enthusiastic report, including the significant statement "Plymouth Bay has an excellent harbour, good land, and needs only industrious people," proved helpful to the Pilgrim Fathers of the *Mayflower*, who landed in 1620. The Pilgrim Fathers and other Puritans, who arrived soon afterwards, survived at first only with help from local Indians, although sadly English–Indian relations quickly soured. But the Puritan work ethic and sense of discipline enabled the early colonists to prosper in this initially hostile environment with its short growing seasons and long winters.

Left: The charming town of Wiscasset, Maine, overlooks the Sheepscot River not far from the sea. It was a major shipbuilding port in the eighteenth century. Today its many elegant homes and other well-preserved buildings are a delight to the eye.

Winters in the Northeast, extending from November through April, are cold and snowy: Maine, New Hampshire, and Vermont in particular have magnificent ski resorts. The short spring, enlivened by the white and pink blossoms of the dogwood, is followed by a warm summer from mid-June through August, which can be so hot that New Englanders and New Yorkers often vacation in cool highland resorts. Fall in September and October is marked by an amazing symphony of color, when woods and forests are a blaze of yellows, golds, scarlets, and pinks, modulated by the green tones of the conifers.

The Northeast is renowned for its natural beauty. Its long, jagged coastline contains fine harbors, beaches, rocky cliffs, and wilderness islands. Inland, the narrow coastal plains are backed by rolling uplands and mountain ranges which are part of the great Appalachian system that runs from Quebec to Alabama. Highlands and lowlands alike show the marks of the last Ice Age. The rugged interior contains thousands of sparkling lakes in ice-worn or moraine-dammed hollows, while much of the lowland as far south as Long Island, Nantucket, and Martha's Vineyard is blanketed by moraine, which contains many stones and boulders, a constant problem to farmers who have used them to build walls. Because of the climate and infertile soils, farming has never dominated the economy and, from early times, many people turned to logging or fishing rather than agriculture. The Northeast was the first American region to industrialize and it is now one of the world's great manufacturing and financial areas. However, away from the urban areas, it remains delightfully rural and tranquil.

South Portland, with its impressive lighthouse, stands on a promontory that projects into the island-strewn Casco Bay. Casco Bay is one of the many inlets that indent the craggy Atlantic seaboard coast of Maine.

The Pine Tree State

Forests cover more than four-fifths of Maine, the most northeasterly state in the Union, and lumber and pulp and paper manufacturing are the leading industries, alongside agriculture and fishing, especially for shellfish – for gourmets, Maine's meaty lobsters and tender clams are sufficient reasons for vacations in the state. Maine makes up almost half of the total area of New England, but its vast areas of uninhabited wilderness give it the lowest average population density of the region. It was settled in the early seventeenth century by English and French colonists and it was disputed between them until 1763 when the English secured it under the terms of the Treaty of Paris. Maine was part of Massachusetts until 1820 when it became the twenty-third state.

Scenically, the state is best known for its craggy coastline with its many islands and deep inlets, long peninsulas, fine beaches often with fantastic surf, and charming villages, such as the unspoiled York Village and York Harbor in the extreme southwest, with their lovely seventeenth- and eighteenth-century buildings. To the north is the pleasant town of Kennebunk, where most visitors make a short detour to see the bizarre Wedding Cake House, built, according to legend, by a sea captain to compensate his bride for his having to return to sea so quickly after their wedding that there was no time for a reception. Continuing up the coast one reaches Prouts Neck, where Winslow Homer lived and painted, and Portland, Maine's largest city, which contains the handsome Wadsworth Longfellow House, the great poet's boyhood home. Near Freeport is the Desert of Maine, an area of high shifting sand dunes, while beyond Freeport, in Brunswick, is Stowe House, where Harriet Beecher Stowe wrote *Uncle Tom's Cabin*.

Many and varied are the attractions of the Maine coast beyond the Kennebec River estuary which drains Moosehead Lake (Maine's largest) in the north. They include the lovingly preserved seafaring town of Wiscasset, the major resort of Boothbay Harbor, the impressive Ocean Point, and Pemaquid Peninsula, with its much photographed lighthouse, the modern city and fishing port of Rockland, and the superb town of Camden, a musical and theatrical center and home port of many windjammers. From Camden there are fine views of Penobscot Bay to the east, across which lies the scenic Nasket Peninsula. But for many, the crowning glory of Maine is Acadia National Park comprising Mount Desert Island, the Isle au Haut, and the mainland Schoodic Point. Mount Desert Island, named by the explorer Samuel de Champlain for the lack of trees on its upper slopes, is one of the world's supreme wilderness areas. It contains the resort of Bar Harbor, the starting point for visitors who can either follow 100 miles of hiking trails or drive around the island's scenic roads. These roads eventually lead to the top of Mount Cadillac which, at 1,532 feet (467 m) above sea level, is the highest point on North America's Atlantic coast; here, travelers are rewarded with magnificent views. The islands' scenery has been molded by ice; there are many steep-walled valleys and one of the loveliest features is a fjord, Somes Sound. Most people visit Acadia between the spring and the fall, but cross-country skiing has become popular on Mount Cadillac in recent years.

Skiing in Maine takes place between mid-December and mid-April and there are more than 30 major ski resorts on the mainland, both in the hilly eastern New England upland behind the coastal plain and in the interior White Mountains which extend into Maine from New Hampshire. In these mountains is Maine's largest ski resort, Sugarloaf Mountain, in the northwest. Maine's highest peak is the isolated Mount Katahdin, reaching 5,268 feet (1,606 m) above sea level, in Baxter State Park where bear, deer, and moose can be seen. Mount Katahdin marks the start of the great Appalachian Trail which is followed by hikers all the way to Georgia. The White Mountains contain much superb country, with glittering lakes, sprawling forests, and rushing rivers. The Allagash Wilderness Waterway to

Northeast Harbor is one of the delightful towns on the coast of Mount Desert Island which provide cruises to other nearby islands. Mount Desert Island forms part of Maine's finest scenic attraction, Acadia National Park, the only national park purchased by private funds.

This serene lake set in a rugged landscape is near Crawford Notch, close to the heart of the White Mountain National Forest. Crawford Notch State Park is one of more than 30 beautiful state parks in New Hampshire.

the northwest of Baxter State Park offers especially fine canoeing, fishing, and camping, although parties must be registered because access to the area is limited. Another great fishing and hiking area in the Sebago–Long Lake region in southwestern Maine. Winter explorations of the wilderness north can now be undertaken with snowmobiles.

High Winds and White Mountains

New Hampshire, the Granite State, was first permanently settled by Europeans in the 1620s and, in 1776, it was the first of the 13 colonies to adopt a constitution and become wholly independent of Britain. Rapid industrial growth began after the Civil War and today manufacturing dominates the economy, with tourism ranking second in importance.

Just like the rest of New England, New Hampshire is a four-season vacationland. In spring and summer, the coastal beaches and exquisite mountain scenery, with plenty of facilities for hunting, fishing, and boating, draw people from urban areas. The fall is marked by one of New England's most splendid displays of foliage; radio and television stations advise on the best places to go at particular times. December through March is the time for winter sports and New Hampshire has more than 30 major ski resorts, including those of Washington Valley, near Jackson and North Conway, and nearby Waterville Valley.

The scenery of New Hampshire is extremely varied. The state has a very short coastline, but it contains several resorts, including Hampton Beach and Great Boar's Head, which attract thousands of summer visitors. The narrow coastal plain contains rustic villages and the historic town of Portsmouth at the mouth of the Piscataqua River. Portsmouth contains the restoration of Strawbery Banke, the name given to the first settlement established on the site of the town in 1630.

Behind the coastal plain are uplands that belong to the Appalachian system. Southern New Hampshire is part of the eastern New England upland that runs from Maine to Connecticut, and here this region consists of a plateau broken by hills and occasional mountains. These isolated mountains, which geologists call monadnocks after Mount Monadnock in the southwestern corner of the state, are remnants of resistant rock left behind after the rocks around them have been worn away. There are six monadnocks in eastern New Hampshire; the northernmost, Mount Moosilauke, is the highest at 4,810 feet (1,466 m) above sea level. About 1,300 lakes are scattered throughout the state; the largest, Lake Winnipesaukee, is a major resort area. The chief rivers are the Connecticut River which forms the border with Vermont and the Merrimack River which eventually reaches the sea via Massachusetts. Several interesting towns are in the fertile Merrimack valley: Franklin was the birthplace of Daniel Boone; Concord, the elegant state capital, contains much fine architecture; and south of Concord is Manchester, an industrial center and New Hampshire's largest city. Its state park has a memorial to General John Stark of that colorful corps of frontiersmen, Roger's Rangers, who coined the phrase "Live free or die," which became the state motto.

Northern New Hampshire contains the spectacular White Mountains, named for the ubiquitous white birch trees. The range includes Mount Washington which, at 6,288 feet (1,917 m) above sea level, is the highest peak in the Northeast. Although energetic hikers can reach the top on foot, many prefer to ride on the cog railway, the nation's first which was completed in 1869. Warm clothes should always be worn on the mountain, for it was here that the world's fastest surface wind, 231 mph, was recorded in 1934. Despite high winds, the trip is worthwhile for the fantastic views. But perhaps the most incredibly scenic place in the White Mountains is an eight-mile-long pass, called the Franconia Notch, north of Lincoln. In the Franconia Notch State Park it is possible to ride on the Cannon Mountain Aerial Tramway and see the Old Man of the Mountains, a profile etched in the side of the mountain that was made famous by Nathaniel Hawthorne's short story "The Great Stone Face." Also not to be missed is the nearby Flume, a deep chasm containing a series of waterfalls. For those who venture to the far northeast, there is much unspoilt wilderness towards the Canadian border.

Portsmouth was founded in 1630 on the northern end of New Hampshire's short coastline at the mouth of the Piscataqua River. Portsmouth is rich in history dating back to colonial days when its ships traded in every part of the world.

The sparkling Kinsman Falls are in the western part of the White Mountain National Park of New Hampshire. Towering mountains, clear streams, colorful fall foliage and winter sports are some of the attractions of this region which is part of the Appalachian system.

Moonlight and Maple Sugar

Vermont, the Great Mountain State, brings to mind several images: moonlight, maple sugar (the sugar maple is the state tree), and awe-inspiring fall foliage (forests cover three-quarters of the state). Today Vermont takes pride in another image which immediately strikes the first-time visitor – the rarity of litter and an absence of billboards – both consequences of strictly enforced conservation laws. Historically, the Green Mountain Boys played an important part in the Revolutionary War and fought in one of its earliest battles when Ethan Allen seized Fort Ticonderoga, now in New York, on the southwestern shore of Lake Champlain in 1775.

Vermont, the only state in the Northeast without an Atlantic coastline, contains several distinctive land regions. In the northeast is an extension of the White Mountains of New Hampshire, but most of eastern Vermont is part of the rolling western New England upland, separated from the eastern New England upland of New Hampshire by the Connecticut River. The state's backbone is provided by the north–south Green Mountains, which include an impressive section of the Appalachian Trail. This range contains Mount Mansfield in the north which is the state's highest peak at 4,393 feet (1,339 m) above sea level. The mountain is one of Vermont's major ski centers, as are nearby Bolton Valley and Stowe, where the Trapp Family Lodge is located – the same family as that portrayed in *The Sound of Music*. Another resort, Killington, in the central Green Mountains, has North America's longest gondola ski lift, with a breathtaking round trip of seven miles. A famous ski area in the southern Green Mountains is the Golden Triangle, formed by the resorts of Bromley, Magic Mountain (near Londonderry), and Stratton.

In the northwest, the Green Mountains descend to the fertile Champlain valley with its picturesque dairy farms, apple orchards, and wheatfields. Farming is relatively more important in Vermont's economy than it is in the rest of the Northeast, although manufacturing and tourism remain the chief

Above: This snow-covered landscape, laced with trails and caves, stretches eastward from Mount Mansfield, the highest peak in Vermont's Green Mountains. This north-south range is a year-round tourist attraction and the Mount Mansfield area contains some of the leading ski resorts in the Northeast.

Top: The attractive town of Brandon, north of Rutland in western Vermont, lies at the foot of the Green Mountains. A short distance to the east is the impressive Brandon Gap in the scenic Green Mountain National Forest.

sources of revenue. Lake Champlain, which straddles the New York border, is New England's largest lake. It contains several islands, including the Grand Isle, where near South Hero the nation's oldest original log cabin can be seen – Hyde Log Cabin, built in 1783. In the southwest is the beautiful Vermont Valley, beyond which the land rises again to the Taconic Mountains, with their scenic lakes and swift-flowing streams, on the New York state line.

Besides the magnificent Green Mountain National Forest in central and southern Vermont, there are 30 state parks, six state forests, and two recreation areas. Vermont also has many lovely villages with tranquil village greens encircled by pretty white houses. The largest city, Burlington on Lake Champlain, contains the burial place of Ethan Allen, and although an industrial center, it is still a handsome city with fine views of the lake. Southeast of Burlington is the capital Montpelier, with its impressive, gold-topped State House and other fine public buildings, and nearby Barre has the world's most extensive granite quarries. In the northeast, the nation's largest maple sugar plant at St. Johnsbury, including the Maple Grove Museum, is a magnet to tourists, as are the thundering McIndoe Falls to the south. Rutland, Vermont's second largest city, contains some fine old houses and is a center of a marble-producing area. East of Rutland is the superbly preserved colonial community of Woodstock, the beautiful Quechee Gorge, and Plymouth Notch, where Calvin Coolidge's Homestead is located. It was here that Coolidge took the oath of office in 1923 on the death of President Harding. In the far south, the road from Bennington to Brattleboro is particularly recommended for stretches of marvelous mountain scenery.

Manchester in southern Vermont is particularly beautiful in the fall. It contains many stately homes and is one of the many picturesque towns and villages of which Vermont is justly proud.

Paul Revere's House at 19 North Square is the oldest wooden home in Boston, Massachusetts. Built in about 1677, it was occupied by the large Revere family from 1770 to 1800. Today it is one of the most popular attractions on Boston's historic Freedom Trail.

The Bay State

The Pilgrim Fathers established the first permanent European settlement in Massachusetts at Plymouth in 1620 and, soon afterwards, other Puritans founded Salem and Boston. In the eighteenth century Massachusetts was in the vanguard of the struggle for independence and, in the nineteenth century, it led the way in American scholarship and culture, with Boston earning the title of the literary "Athens of America."

Boston is now a great manufacturing center, with America's tenth largest metropolitan area population, comprising nearly half of the people of Massachusetts. But it is also a handsome city, a fascinating mixture of old and new, with crowded, narrow cobbled streets in the historic section overlooked by glittering modern skyscrapers. Two of these, the John Hancock Tower and the Prudential Tower with its Skywalk on the fiftieth floor, provide panoramic views of the city. The historic section is best explored on foot. Starting at Boston Common where Puritans used to duck offenders against the Sabbath laws in the old Frog Pond, the Freedom Trail which is signposted and marked by red lines on the sidewalk can be followed as it winds about one and a half miles through the downtown and North End sections of the city. It includes the graceful, gold-domed State House; Park Street Church, dating from 1809 and described by Henry James as "the most interesting mass of bricks and mortar in America;" the Old Granary

Burial Ground, the last resting place for patriots John Hancock and Paul Revere; and Paul Revere's House which was built in the 1670s and is Boston's oldest home. (Devastating fires and property development have eliminated other seventeenth-century wooden structures.) The Freedom Trail also includes King's Chapel, Boston's first Episcopal church; the Old South Meeting House where Bostonians were roused into staging the Boston Tea Party of 1773 at Griffin's Wharf (the spot is now marked at the junction of Atlantic Avenue and Pearl Street); and Benjamin Franklin's birthplace on Milk Street. Outside the Old State House, built in 1713 and the seat of the colonial government, is the spot where the Boston Massacre of 1770 took place. Faneuil Hall, called the "Cradle of Liberty," was a meeting place used by the revolutionaries, and the Old Corner Bookstore was a literary center in the nineteenth century. Other sites on the Freedom Trail are Old North Church, built in 1723; Copps Hill Burial Ground; the site of America's first state school which was opened in 1635; and the statue of Benjamin Franklin near the Old City Hall. Across the Charles River, in Charlestown, is the U.S.S. *Constitution*, or "Old Ironsides," the Navy's oldest commissioned ship, and in Monument Square, the Bunker Hill Monument commemorates the battle of 17 June 1775.

Boston is also famed for its elegant nineteenth-century architecture, some of which was designed by the distinguished architect Charles Bulfinch (1763–1844). The sumptuous, gas-lit Beacon Hill contains several of Bulfinch's buildings, such as the impressive red brick Harrison Gray Otis House. The whole area is characterized by lovely bowfront windows and iron railings

Louisburg Square on the elegant gas-lit Beacon Hill, the center of Bostonian society, is one of the city's most charming areas. In the square's sedate homes, which surround a small park, lived such people as Louisa May Alcott, William Dean Howells, and Jenny Lind.

and balconies. Particularly charming is the central Louisburg Square, where such famous people as Louisa May Alcott and Jenny Lind made their homes. Beacon Hill housed, and still houses, many prominent Bostonian families, whose supposed elitist attitudes inspired the famous lines of John Collins Bossich:

And this is good old Boston,
The home of the bean and the cod,
Where the Lowells talk only to Cabots
And the Cabots talk only to God.

The city has many other attractions, including art galleries, museums, theaters, and the great Boston Symphony Orchestra, one of the world's foremost, many of whose members participate in the famous Boston "Pops" concerts in May and June. And no visit would be complete without a trip to the pretty suburb of Brookline to see John F. Kennedy's boyhood home.

Near Boston is the architecturally distinguished town of Cambridge. This is the home of Harvard University, the nation's oldest college founded in 1636, and the famous Massachusetts Institute of Technology (MIT). West of Boston are historic Lexington and Concord where, in the Minute Man National Historical Park, is North Bridge. Here, as Ralph Waldo Emerson wrote, "once the embattled farmers stood and fired the shot heard 'round the world." Near Concord is also the site of Walden Pond, immortalized by Henry David Thoreau's *Walden*.

The coast north of Boston is rocky with many harbors, such as those at Salem, which is remembered for its seventeenth-century witch trials, and the scenic fishing port of Gloucester, featured in Rudyard Kipling's *Captains Courageous*. North of Gloucester is Ipswich with its charming seventeenth-century colonial houses. South of Boston, the coast changes character and long stretches of shoreline are fringed by low, sandy beaches. The town of Plymouth remains consistently popular with American visitors who want to see for themselves the place where so much of America's heritage began. A special attraction is the accurate recreation of the original Pilgrim colony, called Plimoth Plantation.

The Pilgrims' first landing point was at the tip of the curved Cape Cod peninsula, at which is now Provincetown. Today this pretty resort is known as an artists' colony and cultural center; it was here that many of Eugene O'Neill's early plays were launched. The Cape Cod National Seashore, established in 1961, is a region of glorious beaches, rolling dunes, swamps

Left: The forests and woodlands of the Northeast are magnificent sights when the leaves change color in the mellow days of the fall, as here at Mount Tom, near Easthampton in upstate Massachusetts.

and marshes, and scrub and grassland, with abundant wildlife. The peninsula consists mostly of debris dumped by glaciers in the Ice Age, as do the islands of Martha's Vineyard and Nantucket. Both islands are resort areas, although Nantucket, described by Herman Melville in *Moby Dick* as "a mere hillock, and elbow of sand; all beach, without a background," is the wilder of the two. The town of Nantucket was the home of the fictional Captain Ahab, and its whaling traditions have been preserved in its nineteenth-century mansions built for wealthy sea captains and the popular Whaling Museum. Echoes of *Moby Dick* are also to be found in the old whaling port of New Bedford on the south coast of mainland Massachusetts, notably the Bethel (chapel) described so vividly in the novel.

West of the coastal lowlands, the land rises to the eastern New England upland, part of the region stretching from Maine to Connecticut. This region

Nantucket town, Massachusetts, was once the world's leading whaling port and the fine mansions built along Main Street for wealthy nineteenth-century sea captains testify to its early prosperity. Today Nantucket Island is a major tourist resort and its harbor is often crowded with pleasure craft.

Cape Cod is an ideal vacationland for those who enjoy boating, fishing, or simply lazing on glorious, peaceful beaches, which extend for about 300 miles. The protected northern beaches have warmer water than the southern and eastern shores that are exposed to the restless Atlantic waves.

Below: Clapboard beach houses and well-preserved villages are features of the Cape Cod peninsula in Massachusetts, which curves like a bent finger into the sea. Cape Cod was the first landing point of the Pilgrim Fathers in 1620 before sailing on to Plymouth.

contains many old towns and villages, including Old Sturbridge Village, southwest of Worcester, which contains old buildings brought from all over the state and has a strong atmosphere of pioneer days. The Connecticut River valley separates the eastern and western uplands of Massachusetts. This fertile region contains Springfield, a city famous for its rifles, Amherst, the lifelong home of Emily Dickinson, and Old Deerfield, a frontier village much raided by Indians.

Western Massachusetts contains the western New England upland and the forested Berkshire Hills, an extension of Vermont's Green Mountains, that include the state's highest point, Mount Greylock, which reaches 3,491 feet (1,064 m) above sea level in the north, where it overlooks part of the Mohawk Trail. In the far west is the Berkshire Valley and part of the scenic Taconic Mountain range. The beautiful Berkshires are famous for winter sports, art and music in summer, including the well-known Tanglewood concerts at Lenox given by the Boston Symphony Orchestra, and its fall foliage. Well worth a visit is the Hancock Shaker Village built around 1790, and located near Pittsfield, another town renowned for its music.

Little Rhody

Rhode Island, or Little Rhody, is the smallest state in the Union, settled in 1636 by Nonconformists from Massachusetts who were seeking religious freedom. Their leader Roger Williams, an English scholar and liberal, founded Providence (named for "God's merciful providence") at the head of Narragansett Bay (named for the local Indians). Despite its name, the bulk of Rhode Island is on the mainland. South of Providence in the middle of

A lighthouse overlooks a field of wild grasses which anchor loose sand on Cape Cod. The Cape Cod National Seashore is a pleasure ground for naturalists because of the varied flora and fauna found on its rolling dunes, pine woods, swamps, grassy marshlands, and wetlands.

the bay, Rhode Island itself, the largest of the 36 offshore islands, was called Aquidneck until 1644. The towns on the mainland were known as the Providence Plantations and so the official name of the colony became Rhode Island and Providence Plantations, or Rhode Island for short.

Unlike other states in the Northeast, Rhode Island is mostly low-lying, although part of the hilly eastern New England upland is in the northwest. This area includes the state's highest point, Jerimoth Hill, which is only 812 feet (248 m) above sea level, and contains many sparkling streams, lakes, forests, and state parks, with plenty of scenic trails for hikers. The coast is deeply indented by the beautiful Narragansett Bay, which reaches 28 miles inland. The mainland coast contains superb sandy beaches, salt ponds, and lagoons enclosed by sand spits. Most of the islands, however, are partly bordered by cliffs, such as the impressive 200-foot-high (61 m) Mohegan Bluffs on Block Island, about 15 miles off the south coast. The state offers many opportunities for fishing and birdwatching – the wildfowl migrations on Block Island are truly remarkable – while the Great Swamp in the southwest, the site of a battle between northeast Indian tribes and English settlers in King Philip's War of 1675–76, is a marvelous wildlife reserve.

Although lacking rugged mountain scenery, Rhode Island retains much rural charm and possesses some of America's most beautiful architecture, ranging from the seventeenth century to the present. Providence, the capital, is a major industrial city – manufacturing is again the leading sector of the state's economy – but it contains many splendid buildings, including the late Georgian John Brown House (1786), the stately civic center and the marble State Capitol. Also worth seeing in Providence are the Roger Williams National Memorial, the First Baptist Meeting House (1638, America's oldest) and Brown University (chartered as Rhode Island College in 1764). To the south in northern Rhode Island (Aquidneck) is the interesting town of Portsmouth, the site of the state's only major battle in the Revolutionary War. In the south of the island is prestigious Newport, founded in 1639, which is the state's most famous resort and a veritable museum of architecture. It is best known for its modestly named summer "cottages"

Providence, capital of Rhode Island, was founded in 1636 by the Nonconformist Roger Williams. Although Providence is now a vibrant modern city it contains many fine eighteenth-century buildings, some of which are open to visitors.

which, in reality, are grandiose mansions built for the rich, primarily after the Civil War. They are modeled on European *châteaux* and palaces and they are set in superb grounds. One of the most oustanding is the 70-room "The Breakers" (1895), which overlooks Newport's scenic Cliff Walk. It resembles a sixteenth-century Italian palace and was built for Cornelius Vanderbilt. Other opulent mansions include the ornate "Marble House" (1892), the lavish "Chateau-sur-Mer" (1852), which contains a mirrored ballroom, and "The Elms" (1901), which was modeled on a *château* near Paris and built for the Philadelphian coal magnate Edward J. Berwind. Newport has many other attractions, such as Touro Synagogue (1763), America's oldest synagogue, the Quaker Meeting House (1762), and the Jacobean-style Wanton–Lyman–Hazard House (1675), Newport's oldest building.

The Constitution State

Connecticut, the third smallest state after Delaware and Rhode Island, has a typically prosperous New England economy based on manufacturing and tourism. But it retains a rural character – some three-quarters of its area is forested – and it is famed for its beauty in spring, when apple trees, dogwood, and mountain laurel (the state flower) are in bloom, and in the fall when the foliage dramatically changes color. In summer, the coastal resorts on Long Island Sound are alive with tourist activity, while the state has become increasingly known for its winter skiing.

The Dutch were the first to claim Connecticut but, in the 1630s, dissidents from Massachusetts founded English settlements at Windsor, Hartford, and New Haven. The early settlers drew up a governing document called the "Fundamental Orders," many of the provisions of which were later incorporated into the U.S. Constitution. Connecticut soldiers played an important part in the Revolutionary War, but although British forces made several raids on Connecticut towns, no major battle took place on its soil.

The coastal plain which borders Long Island Sound in the south extends inland for between six and 16 miles. Behind it are the southernmost parts of the eastern and western New England uplands, which are separated by the fertile, 20-mile-wide Connecticut River valley lowland. The western uplands are the most pronounced and they rise to the Taconic Mountains in the far northwest. Here is Connecticut's highest point, 2,380 feet (725 m) above sea level, which is located on the southern slope of Mount Frissell – Mount Frissell's peak is in Massachusetts. The state has 88 state parks and 30 state forests which together provide many hiking, camping, and other recreational facilities.

The coastal plain is fringed by a chain of resort towns, fishing ports, and manufacturing centers. In the southwest, near Bridgeport, is the pleasant

This farm is near Ridgefield in southwestern Connecticut, a prosperous region with great rural charm, although it lies within commuting distance of one of the world's greatest urban areas, New York City.

Yale University, which was founded in 1701, was moved to New Haven, Connecticut, from Old Saybrook in southeastern Connecticut in 1716. The university, one of the nation's oldest and most distinguished, contains ivy-covered, Gothic-style buildings surrounding quiet courtyards, as well as some modern structures.

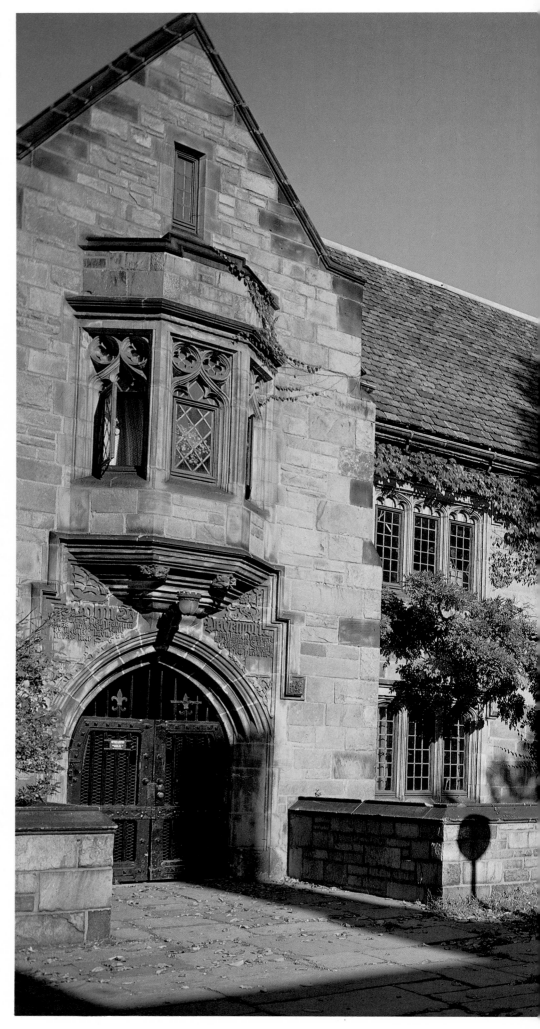

town of Fairfield where, at Greenfield Hill, there is an incredible display of dogwood blossoms every spring. East of Bridgeport is Stratford where there is, like its British counterpart, a Shakespeare Memorial Theater, which has a gorgeous view over the area where the Housatonic River enters the sea. Nearby is New Haven, home of Yale University which was founded in 1701, while to the east is the beautiful town of Guilford, which has some exquisite seventeenth-century houses. Beyond Guilford the visitor comes to the old whaling port of New London, the boyhood home of Eugene O'Neill, whose *Long Day's Journey into Night* and *Ah, Wilderness* were set there. Much of New London was burned in a raid led by Benedict Arnold in the Revolutionary War and little early architecture has survived. Whaling is also recalled in the delightful Mystic Seaport. Covering 17 acres, it recreates a nineteenth-century New England coastal village, while the veteran wooden whaleship *Charles W. Morgan* (1841) and the square-rigged *Joseph Conrad* (1882) rock gently at anchor on the waterfront.

The green interior of the state is graced by fine colonial towns and villages with white-spired churches on their village greens. Exceptional is Litchfield in the northwest where the Congregational Church has a graceful, tall, white tower and a lovely classic portico. The Litchfield area is distinguished for its mountain scenery, and nearby Bantam Lake, Connecticut's largest natural lake, is a popular summer resort. Canaan, Cornwall, Lakeville, Salisbury, Sharon, and Washington are other charming colonial settlements in the

Mystic Seaport, in southeastern Connecticut, extends along the Mystic River waterfront where many historic vessels are moored. Behind the waterfront the Mystic Seaport Museum contains shops, homes, and work buildings that portray life in a nineteenth-century New England maritime community.

northwest, while Mohawk Mountain State Park is Connecticut's chief skiing area. Skiing has recently become important despite the lack of high mountain slopes and the heavier snowfall of the states farther north, although snow-making machines compensate for Nature's deficiencies. The lower eastern New England uplands contain much beautiful forested scenery, narrow river valleys, and small lakes. Jonathan Trumbell's House at Lebanon and Nathan Hale's Homestead at Coventry are popular attractions.

The state capital, Hartford, is a bustling modern city on the Connecticut River, whose elegant skyscrapers contrast with the graceful Old State House, with its white dome; erected in 1796, it was designed by the famous architect Charles Bulfinch. Also in Hartford, on Farmington Avenue, is "Nook Farm," the rambling Victorian home of Mark Twain who lived there for some 20 years, while next door is a house once occupied by Harriet Beecher Stowe. South of Hartford is the lovely Webb House at Wethersfield, where George Washington and the Count de Rochambeau discussed strategy in 1781. North of Hartford is Windsor, which has much attractive architecture, while the pretty town of Farmington to the west contains some well-preserved colonial homes.

Hartford, Connecticut, contains this elegant State Capitol. Settled in 1635–36 and named in 1637 for Hertford, England, Hartford is now the state's largest city.

The Empire State

New York State, the largest in the Northeast, is an area of tremendous contrasts. Here are found vast wildernesses, forests, rugged mountains, sparkling lakes and rivers, cascading waterfalls, fertile farmland, historic sites, and huge urban and industrial centers, notably New York City whose metropolitan area includes more than half of the state's 17½ million people.

Many books have been written, and will continue to be written, about this fascinating metropolis, with its soaring skyscrapers and noisy streets, where the fast, exciting pace of urban life never slackens, even at night. New York City is the financial and cultural capital of the Western Hemisphere, and it is also one of its great manufacturing centers as well as America's fashion

The dramatically lit Metropolitan Opera House is one of the buildings in the immense Lincoln Center for the Performing Arts, which was completed in 1969 in New York City, the nation's cultural capital. The Opera House contains giant murals by the Russian-born artist Marc Chagall.

Left: An early morning view of Park Avenue, a manmade canyon lined by towering skyscrapers with the elegant Pan Am Building in the distance, shows an unfamiliar, tranquil face of the normally hectic borough of Manhattan, in New York City.

capital. Like all great cities, it has a cosmopolitan character and is a fitting home for the United Nations, whose elegant, glittering headquarters overlook the East River.

The city is made up of five boroughs: Queens and Brooklyn which occupy the western end of Long Island; the Bronx, across the Harlem River in the north, where there is a world-famous zoo; the relatively thinly populated Richmond (or Staten Island) in the south; and the island of Manhattan. Manhattan which, as every American schoolchild knows, was bought in 1626 by the Dutchman Peter Minuit from the Indians for trinkets worth 60 guilders or $24, got its name from the Indian *Man-a-hat-ta*, meaning "The Heavenly Land." It was here that the Dutch established Fort Amsterdam, which was later renamed New Amsterdam and then New York when the British took over in 1664. In the late 1780s New York City served as capital of the newly created Union. The first Capitol, where George Washington was sworn in as President in 1789, stood on the site of what is now the Federal Hall National Monument in Wall Street.

This "long, shrill city," as Henry James called it in 1881, may alarm those used to peaceful rural life, and it certainly has its quota of urban dilemmas – air pollution, crime, traffic congestion and slums. But there is also much that is beautiful, particularly in the smallest borough, Manhattan, whose spectacular skyline is known throughout the world. Although a modern city, around 100 buildings erected before 1800 still survive, testifying to the early days. They include the lovely St. Paul's Chapel (1776) and the Morris–Jumel Mansion (1765) which once served as Washington's headquarters. Nineteenth-century architects used a mixture of styles: Greek revivals include the Federal Hall National Monument (1842) and Grant's Tomb (dedicated in 1897), while among the Gothic revivals is St. Patrick's Cathedral (opened in 1879). The Cathedral Church of St. John the Divine, begun in 1892, will be the "largest Gothic cathedral in the world" when it is eventually finished. Other characteristic buildings are the brownstones with their cast- or wrought-iron railings, although their numbers have been much reduced in recent years.

Today skyscrapers are the city's most familiar architectural feature. One of the earliest was the Flatiron Building (1902), a 20-story structure decorated in Florentine Renaissance style, on Madison Square. In 1913 the Woolworth Building in downtown Manhattan – "a Gothic cathedral of commerce" –

An aerial view of Manhattan looking north shows Central Park, a verdant oasis in a great metropolis, and, in the distance, the George Washington Bridge which spans the Hudson River, linking New York City to New Jersey.

became the world's tallest building, until it was superseded successively by the Chrysler Building in 1920, the Empire State Building in 1931 and, ultimately, by the twin-towered World Trade Center in 1972. However, in 1973, the title passed from New York City to the Sears Roebuck Building in Chicago. Changes in materials and techniques have caused changes in architectural styles. In recent years, ornamentation has given way to pure straight lines, as in the Seagram Building, designed by Philip Johnson and Mies van der Rohe, the CBS Building, designed by Eero Saarinen, and the Pan Am Building, designed by, among others, Walter Gropius. New York City has many other beautiful structures, such as Frank Lloyd Wright's controversial Guggenheim Museum, Marcel Breuer and Hamilton Smith's Whitney Museum of American Art, the Lincoln Center, the Museum of Modern Art, and so on. And one must not forget the bridges, including the Verrazano Narrows Bridge, connecting Brooklyn to Staten Island, which is one of the world's longest suspension bridges.

Many statues and sculptures adorn the city, including Paul Manship's *Prometheus* in the Plaza of the Rockefeller Center and the *Atlas* in front of the International Building. But the city's most famous statue by far is the *Statue of Liberty*, on Liberty Island in New York Harbor. This work by the Alsatian sculptor Frédéric-Auguste Bartholdi was a gift from France.

New York City has a plethora of things to offer. There are the parks – notably Central Park, a delightful verdant oasis in the heart of Manhattan – the great museums, art galleries, music, opera and ballet, theaters, and sporting facilities for spectators and participants alike. And each neighborhood seems to have its own distinctive character, from the bohemian SoHo and Greenwich Village, with its graceful Washington Square, to the "Great White Way" around Times Square, which looks tawdry by day but is brilliantly lit by night. There may be people who find it hard to love this extraordinary city, but there must be few who do not admire it. As O. Henry wrote: "Beneath the hard crust of the lobster is found a delectable and luscious food."

The coastal plain of New York State is confined to Staten Island and Long Island. The latter consists mainly of moraine dumped by glaciers in the Ice Age and geologists estimate that three-quarters of Long Island would vanish if all the glacial rocks were removed. While western Long Island is highly urbanized, there is also much charming countryside, including farmland, lovely resorts, and some magnificent secluded places. The northwest contains several places of interest, including Theodore Roosevelt's summer home at Sagamore Hill, and Huntington, the township where Walt Whitman was born. At Riverhead in the east, the island splits into two forks. The narrow

Central Park is a place to exercise man's best friend, one of the many activities pursued by New Yorkers in this popular area of greenery. Although more than fifty blocks long the park is only three blocks wide.

North Fork has some marvelous beaches and, at Orient Beach State Park, a desolate region ideal for birdwatchers, while the South Fork includes the lovely Montauk peninsula, with its wooded hills, cliffs, sand dunes, and clean sandy shores. The south coast of Long Island is fringed by long, narrow sand bars, including Fire Island National Seashore, which is reached by ferry from Long Island.

The lowest part of the Hudson River valley and the island of Manhattan form parts of the New England uplands, which continue along the borders with the New England states. This region includes part of the Taconic Mountains and the prosperous, forested Westchester County.

A journey up the Hudson River valley takes one through some spectacular countryside and places full of interest, including Mount Vernon, Tarrytown (the site of Washington Irving's Gothic-style mansion, Sunnyside), the U.S. Military Academy at West Point, Vassar College at Poughkeepsie, and Franklin D. Roosevelt's home at Hyde Park. To the north are the old town of Kingston, Catskill, the gateway to the mountain resort area, and Albany, the state capital, which was founded in 1614 as Fort Nassau, a Dutch fur trading post. Today the city is distinguished by its beautiful public buildings. In the northern Hudson valley are Saratoga Springs and the Saratoga National Historical Park, which commemorates the American victory in 1777, one of the turning points in the Revolutionary War. West of Albany, the Mohawk Valley, a major route for early pioneers, remains an important highway linking the east to the Great Lakes region.

The Adirondacks, an extension of the extremely old rocks of the Canadian Shield, are a roughly circular upland with many rugged peaks, including Mount Marcy, the state's highest at 5,344 feet (1,629 m) above sea level. The Adirondacks contain about 200 lakes, several of which are famous resorts. Lake George and Blue Mountain Lake are breathtakingly beautiful; Saranac Lake is a health resort; and Lake Placid, the site of the 1980 Winter Olympics, is near to the marvelous skiing slopes of Whiteface Mountain. The vast Adirondack Park, with an area greater than Massachusetts, contains much wild country for hikers, and the fishing in the clean streams and lakes is outstanding. Not to be missed in the northeast is Ausable Chasm with its thundering waterfalls and surging rapids. This spectacular gorge is not far from Lake Champlain, which straddles the border with Vermont. North of the Adirondacks is the St. Lawrence lowland, a farming area containing the beautiful Thousand Island region in the St. Lawrence River.

The Catskill Mountains, part of the Appalachian Plateau in New York, is a famous resort area. A year-round vacationland, it contains nature trails that enable hikers, such as this group on Slide Mountain, to enjoy all the glories of its superbly forested landscapes.

The Erie–Ontario lowlands border the two Great Lakes, and have a rolling surface composed of moraine. Buffalo, the state's second largest city, is a mainly industrial port on Lake Erie, but it is a well-planned city with many parks and is also a major cultural center, with an excellent Philharmonic Symphony Orchestra and the superb Albright–Knox Art Gallery. Northwest of Buffalo are the awe-inspiring Niagara Falls, one of the most fantastic of America's natural wonders. The Falls are divided into the 182-foot-high (56 m) American Falls and the 176-foot-high (54 m) Canadian Falls by Goat Island. They can be viewed from a helicopter, a river boat or an observation tower, the base of the Falls can be approached via wooden catwalks or sightseers can travel in viewmobiles to a series of overlooks. The Falls should definitely be seen at night, when they are lighted in various colors.

The Appalachian Plateau south of Lake Ontario is the state's largest natural region. It is a highly glaciated upland and includes the tranquil Finger Lakes, southeast of Rochester, which are enclosed in a beautiful wooded region. Ithaca, on Cayuga Lake, is the home of Cornell University. North of Ithaca is the 215-foot-high (66 m) Taughannock Falls, while west of the Finger Lakes is a lovely gorge cut by the Genesee River. The rolling Catskill Mountains in the eastern Appalachian Plateau are an extremely popular tourist area, known for its splendid forest landscapes cut by wild rivers and ravines and, increasingly, for its winter sports facilities.

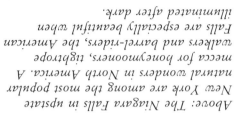

Left: Luxury summer homes have sprung up around the Lower Saranac Lake, a health resort area in the Adirondack Park in northern New York. The Adirondack Park is a vast and ruggedly beautiful region, littered with lakes that fill hollows gouged out by glaciers during the Pleistocene ice ages.

Above: The Niagara Falls in upstate New York are among the most popular natural wonders in North America. A mecca for honeymooners, tightrope walkers and barrel-riders, the American Falls are especially beautiful when illuminated after dark.

The Middle Atlantic States

Grouped together to the south of New England and New York, the Middle Atlantic, or Mid-Atlantic, states are geographically a continuation of the Appalachian mountain system and coastal plain that border the Atlantic shoreline of America. Nature has endowed this highly populated region with superb beaches and an array of scenic wonders whose beauty is enhanced by the changing seasons. The rounded, tree-clad hills emerge from snow-covered winter bedecked with spring-flowering redbud, dogwood, and laurel, a colorful display surpassed only in the fall, when the leaves burst into a glorious blaze of red and gold.

History, too has contributed to the beauty of the region, for this is the heartland of America, ''George Washington Country'', which witnessed the resolute fight for independence from Britain and the tragic horror of civil war. The evidence is everywhere – historic buildings, elegant mansions, and awesome battle sites, which together make up the rich and beautiful heritage of the Middle Atlantic states.

The Garden State

Spanning the Hudson River with its elegant sweep, the George Washington Suspension Bridge links the West Side of New York City with the neighboring state of New Jersey and its network of fast highways. The most densely populated state, with nearly 7½ million inhabitants, New Jersey is also one of the smallest, with a wide range of activities condensed into its

The old red-painted mill at Clinton blends with the beautiful wooded country of Hunterdon County in northwestern New Jersey. The mill, now housing the Clinton Historical Museum, is one of the town's many attractions, which also include the Hunterdon Art Center and Spruce Run reservoir as well as fine restaurants and quaint shops.

The Delaware Memorial Bridge strides across the Delaware River near Pennsville in southeastern New Jersey, carrying traffic on the New Jersey Turnpike into neighboring Delaware just south of Wilmington. The bridge is a major link in the highway system along America's eastern seaboard.

restricted space. Its proximity to such large conurbations as New York and Philadelphia has helped to mold New Jersey not only into a major industrial zone but also an important food-producing region and relaxation area for enormous numbers of people. Known as the Garden State, New Jersey grows vast quantities of vegetables and fruit, including its famous blueberries and strawberries, for consumption across the whole nation.

Lying on the eastern side of the Appalachian chain, New Jersey has all the principal land features of an eastern shoreline state. From the low hills of the northwestern region, the land descends across the gently rolling country of the center to the flat expanses bordering Delaware Bay and the Atlantic coast, and each area has its own special attractions.

After leaving New York and entering the vast industrial belt outside Newark, however, it is difficult to believe New Jersey has much to please the eye. Yet scenic beauty there is, and all over the state are fine old houses and historic monuments that bear witness to its eventful past. As elsewhere on the eastern seaboard, many of these are the relics of the first Dutch and Swedish settlers, while others commemorate the campaigns fought on New Jersey territory by George Washington during the War of Independence.

Some of the best of the state's scenery is to be found in Sussex and Warren counties in the far northwest, where, among the ridges and valleys of the Kittatinny Mountains, there are extensive dense forests, rushing streams and beautiful lakes. Among them are the Worthington and the Stokes State Forests and the delightful Lake Wawayanda with its dark pine-clad shores. Here too the Appalachian Trail cuts a path for hikers through summer-flowering rhododendrons and laurels. An obelisk in High Point State Park marks the highest altitude in the state at 1,803 feet (550 m) above sea level, from where a distant view can be gained of the Catskills in New York State and, across the Delaware River, the Pocono Mountains in Pennsylvania.

Along the edge of the Hudson River, to the east, the Henry Hudson Drive follows an attractive winding route along the foot of the Palisades cliffs north of George Washington Bridge, an area which is enchanting in May when the dogwoods are in bloom. Farther south, in the central part of the state, are the university towns of New Brunswick, with the Rutgers University campus, and about 20 miles away, Princeton, where the Treaty of Peace ending the Revolution was signed in the old Nassau Hall and where Albert Einstein lived and worked. On the Delaware River stands Trenton, the state capital, with its white marble public buildings and lovely colonial homes, and downriver is the industrial and shipbuilding town of Camden, which offered a home to Walt Whitman in his last years.

Inland from Camden, a vast, flat, and occasionally swampy stretch of scrubland, pine forest, and oak trees has appropriately come to be known as the Pine Barrens. Behind it, to the east, the Atlantic coastline runs for about 125 miles from Sandy Hook in the north to the charming Victorian-style resort of Cape May at the southern end. Scattered along the sandy beaches, inlets and bays, and low offshore islands is a string of holiday resorts, some with gambling casinos, that are so important to New Jersey's tourist industry. Each has its own character, but the queen of them all is Atlantic City, or "Las Vegas with a Seashore," where every fall the pick of the nation's most beautiful girls parade in the hope of being chosen "Miss America."

The Keystone State

The vast tract of territory that makes up the state of Pennsylvania is crossed diagonally from northeast to southwest by the mountains and valleys of the Appalachian range, flanked on either side by more gently rolling country. The mountains, here called the Alleghenies, are intersected by a network of sparkling streams and rushing torrents that criss-cross the hills, often in deep

A preference for traditional methods of agriculture is shown by the Amish farmers of Lancaster County, in southeastern Pennsylvania. A seven-mule hitch is more likely to be seen than a modern tractor for pulling machinery to cultivate the fields.

ravines, to form the state's three main river systems: the Ohio–Allegheny–Monongahela rivers in the west, and the Susquehanna and Delaware rivers in the east, the latter providing the state's eastern boundary.

"Virtue, Liberty, and Independence," the motto on the state coat-of-arms, have been the proud ideals of Pennsylvania since the territory was first granted to the Quaker William Penn by King Charles II of England in 1681. Those ideals, together with the tolerance and human understanding that made Penn's land of "Sylvania" a haven for European religious refugees, were to provide the moral foundation for the American colonists' Declaration of Independence from British rule which they signed in Philadelphia in 1776. They were also the underlying principles of Abraham Lincoln's historic address at the site of the Civil War battle of Gettysburg some "Four score and seven years" later. Pennsylvania, the Keystone State, played a crucial role in the birth of the United States and created a heritage of liberty and tolerance that has proudly survived to this day.

Philadelphia, the largest city in the original 13 colonies, was at the hub of the new nation's early history and hosted the two Continental Congresses that met prior to the Declaration of Independence. Still to be seen among the many historic buildings in the city are the red-bricked Independence Hall, where the famous document was signed; Congress Hall and Carpenters' Hall; and the house of Betsy Ross, who, according to legend, stitched together the first "Stars and Stripes" flag of the new republic. Also preserved is the beloved Liberty Bell, which rang out defiantly when the independence document was signed. The beauty of old Philadelphia is also represented by delightful Head House Square, in Society Hill, and Elfreth's Alley, one of the oldest streets in the whole North. But as well as the charm afforded by its long history, the city has grown up with all the problems of a large urban metropolis, although in recent years, redevelopment has removed some of its crumbling eye-sores and created, for example, such traffic-free shopping malls as Chestnut Street.

Beyond the city's boundaries, the beautiful, undulating country of the southeastern part of the state, with its rich farmland and abundant crops, gives Pennsylvania considerable agricultural wealth. Early in the state's history, the area around Lancaster was settled and farmed by German Protestant refugees, mostly Amish and Mennonite, who were attracted to America by Penn's benevolent regime. But, as is often the case where language is a problem, the newcomers soon came to be known, erroneously, as the Pennsylvania "Dutch" by the rough local farmers who simply misinterpreted the word "*Deutsch*". The simple way of life of the "Plain People," as they are sometimes known, has remained unchanged over the

An old covered bridge over a rippling creek adds to the scenic charm of the Appalachian Mountains in Junata County, central Pennsylvania.

Below left: The majestic Grand Canyon of Pennsylvania has been carved by Pine Creek through the green forested hills of Tioga County in the northern part of the state.

centuries and is reflected in their somber appearance and dress and their preference for old-fashioned tools to the gadgets of modern American life. But although they ride around in the horse and buggy rather than the automobile, their cooking attains a mouth-watering appeal that can satisfy the most fastidious of gourmets. Even their farms, cultivated by the horse-drawn plough, are cheerfully enlivened with barns decorated with curious "hex" signs to keep away evil.

Not far northwest of Lancaster is another unique phenomenon, a child's wonderland in the form of the town of Hershey, the chocolate capital of America, where even the streetlights may take the shape of a "candy kiss." Farther east, towards the Delaware valley, the religious atmosphere of the Dutch country finds an echo in the biblical names of such places at Bethlehem, Nazareth, and Emmaus, the first growing to become a large industrial city noted for its steel furnaces and its annual Bach festival.

To the north, near Stroudsburg, the Delaware River emerges from its struggle through the Appalachian barrier in a spectacular deep gorge known as the Delaware Water Gap, where the steep hillsides are renowned for their spring-flowering mountain laurels. From here the Appalachian Trail offers lovely walks through the superb scenery of the Pocono Mountains, whose name in the Indian language – "a stream between the mountains" – aptly epitomizes the area's character. A favorite spot for hikers, horse-riders, and

The red blush of sunset illuminates the tall buildings of the "Golden Triangle" district of Pittsburgh, Pennsylvania, the one-half square mile downtown business area behind the historic Point, where the Allegheny and Monongahela rivers meet and the great Ohio begins.

skiiers alike, the Poconos are also a popular refuge for honeymoon couples, while the rushing torrents of the Delaware River provide excitement for both fishermen and canoeists.

Spectacular mountain, forest, and river scenery are a feature of the entire Allegheny mountain area, but among the most impressive sights is Pine Creek Gorge, a gash 50 miles long and 1,000 feet (305 m) deep in the north of the state that justifiably merits its title of "The Grand Canyon of the East." Not far away an expanse of unspoiled forest can be seen in the Allegheny National Forest, which stretches for some 45 miles south of the New York state line around Warren and is filled by wildlife of all kinds. The southwest, too, has its scenic beauty, much of it in the Laurel Highlands, where Mount Davis, Pennsylvania's highest peak, rises to 3,213 feet (979 m) above sea level. And beneath the ground the Laurel Caverns offer a fascinating display of beautifully lighted rock formations. The whole area abounds in fine scenery, and it was in the beautiful natural setting provided by the hills and streams that the architect Frank Lloyd Wright placed one of his best-known houses, Fallingwater at Bear Run, a superb example of his unique skill in blending manmade structures with natural forms.

From the mountains of southwestern Pennsylvania the Monongahela River follows a northerly course to a point where it meets the Allegheny River flowing from the opposite direction. It is here that the majestic Ohio River begins and the great city of Pittsburgh stands. A French fort in its early days, the site was captured by the British and renamed for their Prime Minister, William Pitt. Over the years the town became a thriving manufacturing center based on steel and glass and fueled by locally mined coal, earning for itself the unenviable nickname of the "Smoky City." A successful campaign against industrial pollution, however, has transformed the city's gray, grimy image, and Pittsburgh now has beautiful parks and imposingly glossy new skyscrapers, most of the old steel mills having moved out of town. The revitalization of the downtown district, poetically labeled the "Golden Triangle," has produced fine new buildings in the modern idiom.

The First State in the Union

Southeast of its giant neighbor Pennsylvania, the tiny state of Delaware, the nation's smallest next to Rhode Island, extends southwards in a long narrow triangle for 96 miles along the western shore of Delaware Bay. Lying as it does on the edge of the Atlantic Ocean, the terrain is gentle, descending from the rolling hills flanking the Delaware River in the north, across the undulating fields and forests of the center to the cypress swamps and sandy beaches and inlets of Sussex County in the south.

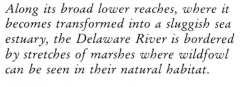

Along its broad lower reaches, where it becomes transformed into a sluggish sea estuary, the Delaware River is bordered by stretches of marshes where wildfowl can be seen in their natural habitat.

The industrialized area around Wilmington apart, Delaware is essentially rural in atmosphere. Its farms produce beans, asparagus, and tomatoes and raise the chickens for which the state is renowned. Wheatfields and peach trees cover much of central Kent County, with acres of forests north of Smyrna and near Georgetown farther south. The peace and charm of the small country towns scattered around the state add to the appeal of Delaware as a delightful vacation area for East Coast city dwellers.

Beginning with Henry Hudson's exploration of Delaware Bay for the Dutch in 1609, the early history of European settlement in the area is one of fierce rivalry, even conflict, between the Dutch, Swedes, and British. Ultimately it was the British who gained control, until Delaware finally shook off their rule to declare itself proudly for independence and become the "First State" to ratify the new Constitution.

In the north of the state, where the Delaware River enters its huge bay, the Swedes established their first stockade and log cabins in 1638. It was a good site, and on the same ground today stands Delaware's largest city, Wilmington. Its Swedish heritage is still much in evidence as a result of the preservation of such buildings as the log-built Hendrickson House and the Old Swedes Church on Seventh Street, built in 1698 and still in use today. The eighteenth-century houses of Willingtown Square, the Old Town Hall, and the Mall, with its restored Grand Opera House, are other reminders of the city's long history. Nevertheless, Wilmington is essentially a modern industrial city, centered on the giant Du Pont chemical company which started as a gunpowder factory on the Brandywine River back in 1802. Just outside the city, at Winterthur on the northwestern side, the home of Henry Francis Du Pont has become a world-famous museum packed with fine early American furnishings.

Among Delaware's other delightful old towns must be mentioned the small community of New Castle, just outside Wilmington, one of the prettiest and best-preserved of the state's early settlements, with its large central green, the cobblestone street called the Strand, the Old Dutch House, and many other charming old houses. In the center of the state is the lovely capital city of Dover, with buildings laid out in 1717 around the original green, among them the splendid Old State House. Lewes, farther south on the Bay shore, is the site of Delaware's first European settlement, established by the Dutch in 1631 and commemorated by the Dutch-style Zwaanendael Museum.

Not far from Lewes are Silver Lake, a haven for wild geese and ducks, and the superb Rehoboth Beach, an ideal spot for pleasant seaside relaxation, while farther south is a maze of saltwater inlets and bays where, particularly at Indian River, surfboarders find a more exhilarating form of enjoyment.

"Maryland, My Maryland"

Lying to the west of Delaware, the oddly-shaped state of Maryland is almost completely cut into two parts by the 196-mile-long Chesapeake Bay. On the western side of the bay the rolling country abruptly gives way to the first ridges of the Appalachians, among which, in the far west, is Backbone Mountain, at 3,360 feet (1,024 m) above sea level the state's highest peak. Maryland's southern boundary follows the course of the Potomac River, while the famous Mason–Dixon Line separates the state from Pennsylvania and Delaware in the north and east.

The British, led by the second Lord Baltimore, were the first Europeans to settle in the territory, which they named for Queen Henrietta Maria, consort of King Charles I. The colony thrived from the start and subsequently played a major role in the nation's affairs during the Revolution, the War of 1812 against the British, and the Civil War.

A paradise for both fishermen and boating enthusiasts, Chesapeake Bay provides a rich harvest of oysters, crabs, clams, and terrapins that are relished across the entire nation, and from jetties and harbors all round the bay, boats of all types and sizes put out to take their share. On the east side of the bay is a mosaic of short, pretty rivers and creeks (known as "gunkholes" to the locals), prosperous farms, imposing private homes standing in extensive grounds, and delightful old fishing villages and country towns such as Wye Mills, Easton, Chestertown, and St. Michaels. Facing the open sea on the Atlantic seaboard, the resort of Ocean City welcomes vacationers with miles of white sandy beaches, and offshore Assateague Island provides a bracing, remote home for wild ponies of the famous Chincoteague breed.

On the western shore of Chesapeake Bay, wide river estuaries, including that of the Potomac, reach far inland into rich farming country and forested areas where, on one of the peninsulas, is the city of Annapolis, which has been the colonial and then state capital since its foundation in 1649. Beautiful old buildings, including America's oldest State Capitol, still grace the Colonial-period downtown area, where the fine eighteenth-century waterfront is also preserved. The city of Baltimore, the capital's large neighbor to the north, is one of the country's major ports. In recent years it has undergone an exciting program of redevelopment involving the restoration of its old ethnic neighborhoods, the renovation of the old Inner Harbor, and the construction of many fine modern buildings by some of the world's leading architects. At the same time the city authorities have successfully preserved Baltimore's many historic attractions. One of these is

Egrets and gulls rest in the peaceful seclusion of the Blackwater National Wildlife Refuge some 20 miles south of Easton in the Tidewater region of Maryland. The largest number and greatest variety of wildfowl in the entire United States can be seen here.

Fort McHenry, at the entrance to the harbor, which heroically defended the city from a British attack in 1814 and, in so doing, inspired Francis Scott Key to compose the immortal words that became the National Anthem.

Inland across the rolling country west of Baltimore, the lovely old town of Frederick grew up at the foot of the first green hills of the Appalachians. Magnificent vistas over the town and beyond can be enjoyed from overlooks amid the beautiful scenery of the Catoctin Mountains to the northwest. Hidden in this peaceful spot is Camp David, the Presidential retreat.

The lovely valley cut through the Appalachian ridges by the Potomac River has long provided travelers with a convenient route to the interior of the continent – it was also followed by the engineers who dug the renowned Chesapeake & Ohio Canal – and it gives western Maryland its long panhandle shape. Upstream from Harpers Ferry, a small town across the border in West Virginia that is impressively cradled in an encircling bowl of mountains, the site of the bloody Civil War battle at Antietam is commemorated near Sharpsburg. Farther on, in the far western reaches of the state beyond Cumberland, the high forested Allegheny Mountains around Deep Creek Lake have become a popular resort area.

The Nation's Capital

Appropriately, the siting of the nation's federal government was itself the result of a political compromise between Northern and Southern states in the early years after independence from the British. In 1791 George Washington commissioned the French engineer Pierre Charles L'Enfant to plan a brand-

The elegantly tapering shaft of the Washington Monument in Washington D.C. creates a double image in the long Reflecting Pool stretching west to the Lincoln Memorial. Behind it, to the east, the immense dome surmounting the Capitol can be glimpsed in the distance at the other end of the Mall.

The White House, the official residence of the American President, stands in beautiful grounds on the north side of the Mall in Washington D.C. Under President Monroe the south portico was added in 1824 to the original design created by the Irish-American architect James Hoban.

new capital city for the nation on a ten-mile-square piece of land – the District of Columbia – which lay astride the Potomac River and had been acquired from both Maryland and Virginia. L'Enfant set about his monumental task with great energy and created a grandiose scheme that would be unsurpassed anywhere. Unfortunately, his brusque impatience caused a few problems, resulting in his dismissal, and thereafter the work proceeded only slowly and with some changes to his plan. Yet L'Enfant's vision has transcended nearly two centuries of additional building and development and, although Washington has outgrown the confines of the original ten square miles, the city must today rank as one of the most beautiful and impressive capitals in the world. Not essentially a bustling hive of commercial activity and nightlife excitement, Washington has the quiet elegance and dignified charm which might be thought fitting for a seat of government and diplomacy at the center of world affairs.

The focal point of the city is the spacious sweep of grass laid out in the form of a cross centering on the Washington Monument. The staff of the cross is the wide Mall, at the head of which, towards the Potomac River, is the Lincoln Memorial, and at the foot the Capitol building; the limbs of the cross contain the Jefferson Memorial to the south and, balancing it on the north side, the White House.

The Washington Monument, constructed between 1848 and 1884, is a towering marble obelisk 555 feet (169 m) high, a beautiful, sleek landmark visible for miles around. The panoramic views of the city from the top are breathtaking. However, for its ability to evoke a deeply emotional response in the visitor, the Lincoln Memorial is unequaled, especially if seen illuminated at night. Inside this huge, austere classical temple, completed in 1922, the immense, brooding statue of the seated sixteenth President has an aura of majestic dignity.

Looking east along the Mall, the Washington Monument is marvelously mirrored in the frame of the long Reflecting Pool, and on a low hill a mile and a half beyond stands the imposingly domed Capitol building, the home of the Congress, which was finished according to the original design in 1827. Flanking the impressive central Rotunda, the wings housing the Senate and the House of Representatives create a pleasing architectural balance.

The White House, the official residence of the President, was built between 1792 and 1800 to a classical design that won $500 in a national contest. After being burned down by the British in 1814, the house was restored and painted in the gleaming white which has given it its name. Among the many fine rooms inside the building, the stately, elegantly proportioned East Room is regarded by many to be the most beautiful.

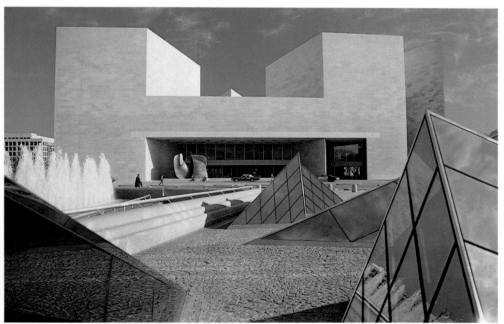

Above right: The magnificent East Building of the National Gallery of Art in Washington D.C. is a recent addition to the outstanding architectural heritage of the nation's capital. The exciting modern design, created by I. M. Pei, is based on interlocking triangular shapes.

Turning one's eye beyond the Washington Monument, the circular Jefferson Memorial stands like an exquisite Greek temple beside the reflecting waters of the Tidal Basin in East Potomac Park. One of the most beautiful settings in the whole of Washington, the whole area becomes a blaze of pink every spring when the Japanese cherry trees lining the basin burst into flower.

But as well as a showplace of government buildings and national shrines, Washington is also a vigorous, modern cultural center whose international standing is sustained by a wide range of institutions, all housed in buildings of architectural interest. Among the most important are the Library of Congress; the Smithsonian Institution and its various museums: the National Gallery of Art, a treasury of some of the world's greatest masterpieces, now enlarged by the addition of the magnificent East Building; and the John F. Kennedy Center for the Performing Arts, in its lovely setting by the Potomac River.

Although Washington's many other splendid buildings and monuments are too numerous to describe here, no appreciation of the city's beauty would be complete without mentioning the picturesque old riverport quarter of

One of the world's most impressive buildings, the Capitol in Washington D.C. was constructed according to the winning design submitted in a contest by Dr William Thornton of the West Indies. George Washington laid the cornerstone in 1793.

A quiet street in Georgetown typifies the quaint charm of this old quarter in the hilly northwestern part of Washington D.C. In colonial times a prosperous port on the Potomac River, Georgetown has now become a fashionable residential area.

Georgetown, now a desirable residential district with elegant brick houses and tree-lined streets; lovely Rock Creek Park lining the steep, wooded banks of the stream whose name it bears; and, across the Potomac, in that part of the District of Columbia given back to Virginia in 1846, Arlington Cemetery, the last resting place of many great national figures including John F. and Robert Kennedy, and Arlington House (also known as the Custis-Lee Mansion), the home of the Confederate General Robert E. Lee, with its fine views of the city he failed to conquer.

The Mountain State

With its average height of 1,500 feet (457 m) above sea level, the Mountain State of West Virginia is the highest state east of the Mississippi. Crossing it from southwest to northeast and continuing through neighboring Pennsylvania, the ridges and valleys of the Allegheny Mountains are a natural paradise for lovers of hiking, climbing, whitewater rafting, and many other outdoor activities that bring thousands of visitors to the state every year. Long used by Indians as a hunting ground, this land of high rounded mountains, spectacular underground caverns, lush forests, and sparkling streams crossed by picturesque covered bridges is the home of independent, hard-working, yet friendly folk. Adopting the motto "Mountaineers always free," these proud people broke away from Virginia, of which they were part, to create their own state during the Civil War. Their prosperity has since been built not only on the tourist attractions of the landscape but also on industry and mining, for West Virginia sits on top of vast natural gas resources and one of the largest coal deposits in the world. Scattered throughout the state, amid the superb scenery, are down-to-earth coal-mining towns, industrial centers manufacturing such products as glassware, and small rural communities that keep alive all kinds of traditional crafts.

The eastern part of West Virginia curves in a long panhandle along the southern bank of the Potomac River as far east as the point where it joins up with the Shenandoah to force a way through the last remaining hill barrier

The delightful Glade Creek Grist Mill, reconstructed from parts of old mills throughout West Virginia, is used to provide fresh cornmeal and buckwheat flour for visitors to the popular Babcock State Park. Located in rugged country along the New River northeast of Beckley, the park offers a wide range of facilities and activities in its 4,127 acres.

The quiet old hillside town of Harpers Ferry in West Virginia nestles below the wooded bluffs overlooking the confluence of the Potomac and Shenandoah rivers. John Brown's ill-fated raid on the federal arsenal here in 1859 ended in his execution by hanging on the orders of Colonel Robert E. Lee. The Harpers Ferry National Historical Park, comprising several buildings along Shenandoah Street, includes the engine house where Brown was captured.

on the journey to the sea. At this beautiful spot, encircled by high bluffs, is Harpers Ferry, a town of narrow streets and old stone and brick houses where John Brown launched his famous antislavery raid on the federal arsenal in 1859. Northwest of here, the main industrial town of the area, Martinsburg, nestles among apple and peach orchards, and farther on, Berkeley Springs proudly lays claim to be the oldest spa town in all America.

From here the Allegheny ridges roll away southwestward into the blue haze. Close to the Virginia state line is a curious natural freak known as Ice Mountain, whose foot remains permanently frozen, even in high summer, and in the aptly named Lost River State Park, the river in question vanishes underground before emerging some miles away as the Cacapon River. To the west, in the beautiful broad Potomac valley, the town of Petersburg, noted for its golden trout hatchery, marks the edge of the Monongahela National Forest. This vast area of wooded hills, largely replanted since 1920 to repair long destruction through mining activities and fire, encompasses the headwaters of the Ohio, Potomac, and James rivers and some of the most captivating scenery in all West Virginia.

Musicians taking part in the West Virginia State Folk Festival held every June at Glenville concentrate on old-time melodies that originally came from such faraway lands as Scotland, Ireland, and Germany, though now well seasoned with the musical traditions of generations of Mountain Folk.

Below: The rugged face of the Seneca Rocks, a challenge to rock climbers from far and wide, towers 1,000 feet (305 m) above the South Fork of the Potomac River in the Monongahela National Forest of West Virginia. This beautiful backcountry region of forested, round-topped hills is also a popular area for hikers and campers.

Upstream from Petersburg are the fascinating Smoke Hole Caverns, used in the past by Seneca Indians for smoking meat, and some miles farther on, the towering, rugged Seneca Rocks, popular with climbers as well as sightseers. Nearby, Spruce Knob, the state's highest peak, rises to 4,862 feet (1,482 m) above sea level and affords marvelous views of the surrounding national recreation area from its observation tower. Farther south, modern technology has intruded into the landscape in the form of the curved 300-foot (91 m) dish of the radio telescope at the National Radio Astronomy Observatory, Green Bank, and the delightful Cass Scenic Railroad, which offers breathtaking vistas as the old steam engine puffs up Bald Knob mountain with its flatcars loaded with excited visitors. This southern end of the Monongahela National Forest also encloses a wonderland of rare plants known as the Cranberry Glades, and beautiful Watoga State Park, West Virginia's largest.

In the fashionable old spa town of White Sulphur Springs, near the border with Virginia, many of the nation's most famous citizens have relaxed at the renowned "Old White," later renamed the Greenbrier Hotel, well sited for exploring West Virginia's mountain scenery. Not too far away to the west, for example, is one of the state's most spectacular scenic wonders, the huge canyon known as New River Gorge in the coal-mining area around Beckley. From here the West Virginia Turnpike winds its way northward to Charleston, the state capital and a major industrial center on the Kanawha River, the Renaissance-style Capitol building of which is considered one of the most beautiful in all America.

Flowing north, the Kanawha eventually runs into the majestic Ohio River, the Indians' "river of the whitecaps," which demarcates West Virginia's border with the state of Ohio, from the industrial city of Huntington upriver to the northern panhandle, its banks lined with rich farmland, green pastures, orchards, and industrial towns such as Wheeling. On the west bank of this great river, the vast rolling country of the Midwest begins.

The majestically beautiful Capitol of West Virginia stands amid gigantic oak trees and fresh green lawns in the city of Charleston. Designed by Cass Gilbert and completed in 1932, the Renaissance-style structure incorporates a classical portico, and a colonnaded dome rising 300 feet (91 m) above the ground.

The South

In 1865 the South was in ruins. Its pre-war economy, when cotton was the undoubted king, had collapsed, although gracious mansions set in decaying plantations with empty slave quarters were constant evocations of the past. Recovery was slow and painful at first, but for the last 50 years the South has been one of the nation's fastest changing regions. Manufacturing is now the most valuable sector of the economy, the urban population has steadily expanded, and agriculture has become more diversified and efficient. With these changes have come new attitudes and patterns of life.

The South's special identity is not just a function of its history, but also of its pleasant climate. Outside the highest mountain areas, average January temperatures are above freezing point, while the Deep South of Alabama, Florida, Georgia, Louisiana, Mississippi, and South Carolina, together with parts of Arkansas and Tennessee have short, mild winters. In *The Heart Is a Lonely Hunter*, Carson McCullers, a native of Georgia, recalled that "summers were long and the months of winter cold were few. Nearly always the sky was a glassy, brilliant azure and the sun burned down riotously bright... The winters were changeable, but the summers were burning hot."

Southern landscapes are extremely varied, although low plains cover a much higher proportion of the land than in the Middle Atlantic and North-eastern states. But there are also magnificent, forested mountains, including Mount Mitchell in North Carolina – the highest peak east of the Mississippi River – sandy coastal beaches, wilderness swamps and lagoons with fascinating plant and animal life, mighty rivers, and huge lakes. Many of the most beautiful lakes are manmade. They were created to provide cheap electricity to the new, emerging industries and to control flood waters, but they have also played a vital role in soil conservation and reafforestation programs that have transformed damaged and derelict land into superb recreation areas.

The South's main highlands are in the Appalachian system which reaches into Georgia and Alabama. This system includes the lofty Blue Ridge Mountains, lower wooded ridges and valleys, and gently sloping plateaus, notably the Piedmont in the east and the Appalachian, or Cumberland, Plateau to the west. The only other uplands in the South are the Ozark Plateau and the Ouachita Mountains in Arkansas.

Bluegrass Country

Kentucky, which Daniel Boone opened up in the late 1760s and 1770s, is essentially a border state. This was exemplified by the fact that two of its most famous sons were the Civil War protagonists, Abraham Lincoln and Jefferson Davis, and even though the state stayed in the Union, three out of every ten Kentuckyans who fought in the Civil War served in the Confederate Army. After the war, the state was gripped by the severe depression that afflicted the entire South. Today, however, Kentucky is again prosperous, with an economy based on manufacturing although farming still makes an important contribution. Its best-known products are probably thoroughbred horses and whiskey.

The greatest concentration of people is in the gently rolling Bluegrass region, so named for the bluish hue of its lush pasture. Louisville, a colorful city in the northwest of the state on the Ohio River, is Kentucky's largest urban area. Founded in 1778, it is a major industrial city of the Bluegrass country and produces much of the nation's bourbon. But it also contains lovely parks, and Churchill Downs is the home of the annual Kentucky Derby, run on the first Saturday in May. East of Louisville are the state capital Frankfort, where Daniel Boone is buried, and Lexington, the center of the horse-breeding region. More than 350 horse farms are located around Lexington and many are open to the public. This delightful Bluegrass country is embellished by white fences, mortarless stone walls, colorful horse barns, and elegant mansions. Lexington itself contains several beautiful old houses, and the White Hall State Shrine, the opulent, Italianate home of the diplomat Cassius Marcellus Clay, lies nearby to the south. Southwest of Lexington, the Bluegrass region also takes in Harrodsburg, site of Fort Harrod, the first permanent white settlement in Kentucky (1774), while just to the south is Perryville Battlefield State Shrine, where Kentucky's bloodiest Civil War battle occurred in October 1862. Southwest of Harrodsburg, near Springfield, is the Lincoln Homestead State Park, where Lincoln's father grew up, and farther west, near Hodgenville, is the Abraham Lincoln Birthplace National Historic Site. Here an imposing granite memorial, bearing the inscription "With malice toward none, with charity for all," encloses the log cabin in which Lincoln was born.

Some of Kentucky's finest scenery is located in the eastern Appalachian, or Cumberland, Plateau which includes, east of Lexington, the Daniel Boone National Forest. This extends from the state's southern border almost to the Ohio River in the north. Not far from Lexington is a particularly spectacular beauty spot – the rugged Red River gorge and a rock arch called Natural Bridge. The Appalachian Plateau contains some grimy coal-mining towns, but even they have scenic backdrops. In the southeast, near Middlesboro, is

*Louisville, which stands on the mighty Ohio River, is Kentucky's largest city. In summer visitors to this colorful but busy industrial city can enjoy a river cruise on the **Belle of Louisville**, one of the few surviving river sternwheelers.*

The Bluegrass Region around Lexington, Kentucky, is known for its many horse farms where prized thoroughbreds are born and raised. Some of these farms are open to the public.

Below: Bardstown, Kentucky, which is about 25 miles south of Louisville, contains the Federal Hill estate, popularly called "My Old Kentucky Home," for it was here in the charming mansion that was built on the estate in 1795 that Stephen Foster supposedly wrote his much-loved ballad. The estate became a state park in 1922.

the historic Cumberland Gap National Historic Park, the old gateway to the West, located at the point where Kentucky, Tennessee, and Virginia meet. Another scenic attraction is the Cumberland Falls State Park to the west, which includes a 68-foot-high (21 m) 150-foot-wide (46 m) waterfall.

Most of southern Kentucky is in the rolling Pennyroyal region, named for a common perennial herb of the mint family. This region stretches westwards to the flat and rather swampy East Gulf Coastal Plain bordering the Mississippi River. The Pennyroyal region contains some superb lakes, but south-central Kentucky's best-known feature is the Mammoth Cave National Park, where there is one of the world's largest cave networks. Visitors can undertake tours lasting from one hour to a whole day (private exploration is not permitted), and see many subterranean marvels, including colorful and fantastic rock formations and blindfish, which have no need for sight in their pitch black environment.

While open-cast coal-mining has disfigured parts of western Kentucky, there is also much natural beauty to enjoy. Prominent in the southwest are the vast manmade Kentucky and Barkley lakes, created by the damming of the Tennessee and Cumberland rivers. These lakes and a huge conservation area called "The Land between the Lakes" now form a marvelous recreation area that is shared with Tennessee.

The Volunteer State

The Appalachian system continues from Kentucky into eastern Tennessee, but Tennessee is fortunate in possessing even more varied scenery than its northern neighbor. In addition to a section of the Appalachian plateau, it also contains a beautiful ridge and valley zone, while part of the majestic

Left: Tennessee contains much attractive rural scenery. In spring the blossoms of the dogwood make a special contribution to the charm of the Tennessee River valley.

Above: Cherokee Lake, on the Holston River near Jefferson City, is in the Appalachian Ridge and Valley region of eastern Tennessee. It is one of several beautiful lakes that have formed behind dams built by the Tennessee Valley Authority.

Left: The dams and hydroelectric plants built by the Tennessee Valley Authority have brought prosperity to the region. The lakes behind the dams are now major recreation areas, while the reafforestation of eroded valley slopes has created new habitats for birds and other wildlife.

Appalachian Mountains skirts the eastern border with North Carolina. This mountain range, here called the Great Smoky Mountains, contains Clingmans Dome, Tennessee's highest point at 6,643 feet (2,025 m) above sea level, and 15 other peaks that top 6,000 feet (1,830 m) Clingmans Dome, which lies on the famous Appalachian Trail which runs from Georgia to Maine, is in the heart of the Great Smoky Mountains National Park which Tennessee shares with North Carolina. Some eight million visitors every year testify to the supremacy of this glorious park in the public's affection. For those who love nature, there is a substantial area of virgin forest, more than 150 species of trees, and a blazing array of wildflowers. There are superb trails for hikers and riders, who must watch out for the park's 350 or so black bears, and there are many sparkling streams for fishermen. This natural wonderland was named for the blue, smoky mist that often bathes the mountains; scientists tell us that it is a mixture of water vapor and plant oils. To the southwest of the Great Smokies and also shared with North Carolina is the Cherokee National Forest, a scenic wilderness of forests, swift-flowing streams, waterfalls and rapids, and exquisite gorges. This National Forest is divided into two sections, one to the north and the other to the south of the Great Smoky National Park. Thanks to the Tennessee Valley Authority (TVA), the Appalachian region is also a major lakeland. In fact, the state's manmade lakes now have a combined shoreline of about 10,000 miles which, surprisingly, exceeds that of the Great Lakes.

In the Civil War, Tennessee – called the Volunteer State for its military traditions – was divided in its allegiances, the east being generally loyal to the Union and the west to the South. Knoxville, now the largest city in the east, was besieged by Confederate forces in 1863. Southwest of Knoxville, near the Georgia state line, is Chattanooga, a name which evokes many Civil War associations, for it was near this strategically placed city that three major battles were fought. One especially fierce clash occurred at Chickamauga, another at Missionary Ridge and a third at Lookout Mountain. Lookout Mountain rises about 1,700 feet (520 m) above the city and is now a tourist haunt because of its dizzying views of seven states. Signal Mountain, a few miles to the north, affords travelers another splendid view, particularly of the winding Tennessee River. The Appalachian plateau slopes gently towards the central plains in east-central Tennessee, but it also contains much rugged scenery, such as the region in the north associated with the World War I hero, Sergeant Alvin C. York, who grew up at Pall Mall, north of Jamestown.

Central Tennessee consists largely of a raised plain enclosing the rich farming area of the Nashville basin. Nashville, the state's capital and second largest city, stands on the Cumberland River and is a mecca for country music fans who come in their hundreds of thousands to attend performances at the Grand Ole Opry. This graceful southern city contains beautiful parks, such as the Tennessee Botanical Gardens, and so many fine buildings that it has been given the title of "Athens of the South."

For those interested in historic houses, the Hermitage, the imposing and well-maintained home of President Andrew Jackson, is only 13 miles east of Nashville. Running south from Nashville is the Natchez Trace Parkway, an historic route on which the explorer Meriwether Lewis was mysteriously killed in 1809. South of the Meriwether Lewis Monument at Lawrenceburg, is the David Crockett State Park, a recreation area on a site where this folk hero lived and worked. West of Lawrenceburg, just across the Tennessee River, is the Shiloh National Military Park, which commemorates a battle of terrible carnage, even by Civil War standards, in April 1862.

West of the Tennessee River is the Gulf Coastal Plain which slopes down to the Mississippi Bottoms, a flat alluvial plain alongside the Mississippi River. In the southwest, on high bluffs overlooking the river, stands the proud modern city of Memphis, the largest in the state. Founded in 1819, it retains its Southern character, despite its skyscrapers, with haunting reminders of the past in its Confederate Park. There are also associations

Memphis overlooks the great Mississippi River in southwestern Tennessee. A river port and a major commercial and industrial city, it was named in 1819 for the ancient city of Memphis, which also stood on one of the world's most important rivers, the Nile in Egypt.

with the birth of the blues in Beale Street, and with rock and roll particularly at Graceland, the mansion home of the late Elvis Presley.

In the far northwestern corner of Tennessee, the Reelfoot Lake area was created, not by TVA engineers, but by earthquakes in the early nineteenth century. It now contains a wide range of flora and fauna for the naturalist, including partly submerged and rather eerie forests. East of Reelfoot is the resort area around the Kentucky and Barkley lakes, which has already been mentioned in the section on Kentucky. Near Lake Barkley is the Fort Donelson National Military Park, another grim reminder that more Civil War battles took place on Tennessee soil than in any other state except Virginia, its neighbor to the northeast.

*Jamestown·Festival Park, near Jamestown, contains full-size reconstructions of the three small ships, **Susan Constant**, **Godspeed**, and **Discovery**, which were involved in the epic voyage in 1607 that brought the settlers to Virginia 13 years before the Pilgrim Fathers landed on Plymouth Rock.*

The Old Dominion

Like its northern neighbor Maryland, the state of Virginia stretches, like a flattened triangle, from the heights of the Allegheny Mountains in the west, through the Piedmont foothills, down to the Tidewater lowlands, and the beaches of the Chesapeake Bay area and the Atlantic shoreline. Here, in this heartland, the story of America had its beginning, for it was in the southeast of the state near the mouth of the James River, at Jamestown, that the first permanent European settlement was shakily established in 1607. Modern reconstructions of the simple homes the colonists built here and of the three ships they sailed in from Europe eloquently honor their epic adventure. Prosperity came to the community only after 1612, when John Rolfe realized the commercial value of the tobacco leaves smoked by local Indians, and plantations were created all over the region to grow the new crop. With the burgeoning wealth of the colony, beautiful and elegant mansions sprang up, such as the Carter's Grove and Shirley Plantations along the James River, and they stand today as monument's to the pioneering energy and determination of those early Americans.

Not far from Jamestown, the superbly restored town of Williamsburg, the second capital of the "Old Dominion,' provides a living record of life in Colonial America during the eighteenth century. Among the finest of its architectural treasures are the Governor's Palace, the Colonial Capitol, and the famous College of William and Mary, reputedly designed by England's Sir Christopher Wren. Not far away is Yorktown, the third old town in Virginia's "Historic Triangle," which saw the British surrender in 1781, marking the end of the Revolutionary War and the beginning of America's independence.

At the mouth of the James River the great naval base of Norfolk in the port area of Hampton Roads provides forceful reminders of life in the present century, with its parade of modern warships, the adventurous design of the Scope Convention and Cultural Center, and the impressive engineering of the Chesapeake Bay Bridge Tunnel that strides boldly out across the bay to the southern tip of the Eastern Shore area. About ten miles from the southern end of the Bridge–Tunnel at the lively seaside resort of Virginia Beach on the Atlantic, the pressures of modern life can be eased in a wide variety of vacation activities or in the peace and quiet at Seashore State Park. Across the water, on the Eastern Shore, quiet towns, sandy beaches and islands offer excellent sea fishing, mouth-watering seafood restaurants, and a glimpse of wild ponies, deer, and sea birds.

Away from the coast, the green landscape of Virginia's Piedmont interior is dotted with old country towns, fine houses, and battle sites that remain as silent witnesses of the momentous events that shaped not only Virginia's but the entire nation's destiny. For this is the land of George Washington and Robert E. Lee, a whole region packed with historic associations. On the Potomac River, not far from Washington, D.C., is Mount Vernon, the beloved home of the nation's first President, and downriver, close to his birthplace at Pope's Creek Plantation, stands historic Stratford Hall, where Lee was born. The great Civil War clashes between Lee's Confederate armies and Union forces on Virginian soil are commemorated today at such battlefield sites as Manassas, Fredericksburg, and Petersburg, and Lee's final surrender is vividly recorded at Appomattox Court House, about 70 miles west of Richmond. Although largely destroyed by fire in the last days of the war, the Confederate capital, Richmond, is today a fine modern city which has managed to preserve many of its old buildings. Its most revered treasures include the Capitol designed by Thomas Jefferson and the lovely St. John's Church, where Patrick Henry spurred his fellow countrymen on to revolution against British rule with those impassioned words: "Give me liberty or give me death."

At Charlottesville, northwest of Richmond, Jefferson spent years building his home, Monticello, a magnificent Palladian-style villa beautifully sited on

Mount Vernon, which lies 15 miles from Washington D.C. via the George Washington Memorial Parkway, was the President's beautiful plantation home from 1754 until his death in 1799. The tomb of George and Martha Washington is on the estate.

Colonial Williamsburg, Virginia, is a wonderful reconstruction of an eighteenth-century town where the daily life of colonial days is lovingly re-enacted, and in Market Square visitors can watch the militia drill. Work began on this highly accurate and world-famous restoration in 1926.

Rural Virginia retains an old-world charm that recalls the early days of colonization when European culture was transplanted and nurtured in the New World.

a hillside to afford fine views of the Blue Ridge Mountains to the west. Here too is the elegant Rotunda he designed for the University of Virginia, which he founded in his last years.

West of Charlottesville, in the forested ridges and valleys of the Appalachians, Virginia offers its most beautiful natural scenery. From the Skyline Drive and the Appalachian Trail that wind along the crest of the wooded Blue Ridge through lovely Shenandoah National Park, there are magnificent vistas of the colorful patchwork of forests, farmland, and orchards that make up the fertile and beautiful Shenandoah Valley. And beneath the valley's rich soil is a honeycomb of awesome caves filled with amazing rock formations, among which the Luray Caverns are the most famous. Another natural wonder of the valley is the cluster of seven limestone pillars near Harrisonburg known as the Natural Chimneys, which suggest the towers of some old, ruined castle and have inspired twentieth-century "knights" to revive the ancient sport of jousting. Farther south, the Lexington area has the breathtaking Goshen Pass river gorge and the 215-foot-high (66 m) rock arch known as Natural Bridge, which Jefferson considered the "most sublime of Nature's works."

Southwest beyond Waynesboro, the Skyline Drive continues as the Blue Ridge Parkway and provides a superb scenic route to Virginia's mountainous far west, a remote pioneer country of rolling pastures, bubbling streams, still lakes, and high peaks clothed in the thick cloak of the Jefferson National Forest. In this region is Virginia's highest peak. Mount Rogers, which rises to 5,729 (1,746 m) above sea level, east of Bristol on the North Carolina border. Of the southwest's natural curiosities, the most spectacular are the colossal gorge, five miles long and 1,600 feet (488 m) deep, in Breaks Interstate Park on the Kentucky state line and, farther southwest, the huge Natural Tunnel and its accompanying chasm in Clinch Mountain.

The extreme western corner of Virginia – "on the trail of the lonesome pine" – funnels into the famed Cumberland Gap, that historic gateway to the great central plains of America opened up by Daniel Boone and followed by thousands of courageous pioneer families in search of a new life in the wilderness beyond.

The Land of the Sky and the Outer Banks

North Carolina's varied landscapes can be grouped into three main regions: the largely wooded mountains bordering Tennessee in the west; the undulating central Piedmont with its busy industrial centers; and the Atlantic coastal plain which is fringed by the Outer Banks – long, narrow sand bars and spits that enclose brackish lagoons.

The western mountains are part of the Appalachian system and are an extension of the mountains of Tennessee. Various local names are used, including the Bald, Balsam, Great Smoky, Nantahala, Snowbird as well as Blue Ridge mountains. North Carolina shares with Tennessee the spectacular and ever-popular Great Smoky Mountains National Park and the Cherokee National Forest. Also shared are the glories of the natural world, with vivid displays of white dogwood and silver bell in early spring, followed by mountain laurel, flame azalea, purple rhododendron and then white rhododendron. And in the fall, the deciduous oaks, chestnuts, hickories, and other species change color, creating splashes of yellows, golds, and crimsons against the greens of the conifers. The "Land of the Sky," as this region was named by the author Christian Reid in 1876, contains much impressive mountain scenery, including Mount Mitchell which, at 6,684 feet (2,037 m) above sea level, is the highest peak east of the Mississippi River, and 44 other peaks that rise above the 6,000-foot (1,830 m) mark.

A special pleasure for motorists is the Blue Ridge Parkway, which winds along the mountain crests from North Carolina's entrance to the Great Smoky National Park northwards to the Shenandoah National Park in Virginia. Along this protected parkway, there are dozens of overlooks that simply take the breath away. Adjoining the Great Smoky Mountains National Park is a Cherokee reservation, one of the largest Indian areas in the east. The 5,000 Cherokees here are descendants of those left behind when the Cherokee nation was driven west along the "Trail of Tears" in the late 1830s.

Not far from the reservation is Fontana Lake, created by the Tennessee Valley Authority and impounded behind the highest dam east of the Rockies. It is now a major resort area, as is Boone, the center of a fast-developing skiing region in the far northwest.

The gateway and oldest resort in the western mountains is Asheville, boyhood home of the writer Thomas Wolfe. Within easy reach of Asheville are Mount Mitchell and the scenic wilderness of the Pisgah National Forest, including the lovely Linville Falls, while southeast of Asheville is the tall

The Great Smoky Mountains rise in western North Carolina along the Tennessee state line. This beautiful region, once Cherokee Indian territory, is often called the "Land of the Sky."

The charming rural Oconaluftee Settlement, with its old split log fencing, is in the Great Smoky Mountains region of western North Carolina.

Chimney Rock, the summit of which, reached by elevator, provides a great view of the Blue Ridge Mountains. South of Asheville is Hendersonville, near to which is Flat Rock, home of the late poet Carl Sandburg. And just outside Asheville is the extraordinary French Renaissance-style Biltmore House, completed in 1895 by George Vanderbilt. This 250-room house is elegantly furnished and is surrounded by well-planned gardens, with particularly fine rose beds.

North Carolina's Piedmont is the region where most North Carolinians live. It is bordered to the east by the Fall Line where, as in Virginia, rivers and streams tumble off the plateau through narrow channels, interrupted by falls and rapids, down to the coastal plain. North Carolina's largest cities are in the Piedmont, notably Charlotte, a bustling industrial center in the south, and Greensboro in the north; both major textile centers. Northwest of Greensboro is the Guilford Courthouse National Military Park, site of the Revolutionary War battle in 1781. West of Greensboro is Winston-Salem, which combines the industrial, tobacco-producing town of Winston with the Old World charm of Salem, which was founded by the Moravians in 1766. The state capital since 1792, Raleigh is the center of a tobacco region near the Fall Line. It is distinguished by its historic granite Capitol (1840) and the Andrew Johnson House. Johnson was one of three American presidents from North Carolina; the others were Andrew Jackson and James K. Polk.

The Atlantic coastal plain contains rich farmland behind the Tidewater region. Swamps, shallow lakes and rivers fringed by Spanish moss-hung cypresses become increasingly common towards the coast. These areas, like Dismal Swamp in the northeast, are rich in wildlife.

The northeastern coast is indented by deep estuaries around the Albemarle and Pamlico Sounds. These large lagoons are bordered by a series of island sand bars, including the gently curving Cape Hatteras National Seashore, which consists of part of Bodie, Hatteras and Ocracoke islands and includes 70 miles of glorious beaches. This seashore includes several small fishing villages, but all commercial activity is forbidden. Nag's Head on Bodie is a major tourist center. North of Nag's Head is Jockey's Ridge, the highest sand dune on the east coast of America, and beyond it is the Wright Brothers National Memorial near Kitty Hawk. West of Nag's Head is the small Roanoke Island where attempts were made in 1585 and 1587 to found an English colony; the first party returned to England and the second vanished. The story of this "Lost Colony" is re-enacted every summer at the Waterside Theater in the Fort Raleigh National Historical Site. Hatteras Island includes the Pea Island National Wildlife Refuge, a major attraction for birdwatchers. At Cape Hatteras, the island makes a sharp turn to the southwest, this spot marked by the towering 208-foot-high (63 m) lighthouse reminding us that this region is called the "Graveyard of the Atlantic" because of the hundreds of ships that have foundered on treacherous, ever-shifting sandy shallows.

South of Ocracoke Island is the Cape Lookout National Seashore, the home of wild horses and fascinating plant life. This largely wilderness area has no roads, and extends southwards to include Shackleford Banks beyond Cape Lookout. To the south is a lagoon-lined coast alive with pretty fishing villages, lively resorts and several historic sites, including three coastal forts. The largest city in the southeast is the historic port of Wilmington.

The Cape Hatteras National Seashore in North Carolina is a protected stretch of sandy islands called the "outer banks." This view was taken from Cape Hatteras Lighthouse. Wrecked vessels and lighthouses along the shore testify to the dangers of this coast to shipping.

Above: The superb beaches of North Carolina are fine places to fish and to relax.

Right: The Elizabethan Garden is a memorial on Roanoke Island, North Carolina, to the "lost colonists" of 1587, whose disappearance still baffles historians. This peaceful spot includes sculpted lawns and fragrant herb gardens.

The Single Brothers House in Old Salem, in the heart of Winston-Salem, North Carolina, is one of the graceful, late eighteenth- and early nineteenth-century buildings that bring to mind Salem's Moravian heritage.

Memories of the Old South

The flavor of the Old South lingers on in South Carolina's graceful historic cities, beautifully maintained mansions enclosed by moss-strewn live oaks and boxwood hedges, plantations, and gardens. The gardens are nothing less than magnificent and South Carolinians proudly proclaim them to be the nation's finest. And yet South Carolina, like the rest of the South, has moved with the times and manufacturing is now its principal activity. Farming remains important, however, and the state is known for its tobacco, cotton, peaches, and soybeans. And its mountains, historic sites, and excellent beaches make tourism a thriving industry.

The "Low Country," or the Atlantic coastal plain, covers two-thirds of the state. It contains pine forests, two large lakes, Marion and Moultrie, which are celebrated for their fish, and there are swamps near the coast. The coastline itself contains a series of bays, but they are generally less pronounced than those in North Carolina. South Carolina also lacks the extensive sand bars and lagoons that typify the coasts to the north. Instead there is a chain of offshore "Sea Islands," some of which are resorts.

The chief coastal resort area is the 55-mile-long Grand Strand around Myrtle Beach in the north. Nearby Georgetown is known for its impressive historic buildings, plantations, and gardens, some of which occupy old ricefields. Rice and sea-island cotton were two of the crops introduced by wealthy English planters from the West Indies who settled here and made their fortunes. South of Georgetown, beyond the Santee River estuary, is the Cape Romain National Wildlife Refuge, a haven for migratory birds and giant sea turtles, while the inland Francis Marion National Forest is a sanctuary for the endangered American alligator and other species.

Charleston, the state's second largest city, boasts many lovely homes, gardens, and historical sites that conjure up the days when it was the commercial and political hub of the South. Perhaps its most famous site is Fort Sumter, on an island in the harbor, where the first shots of the Civil War were fired. Also preserved is the original Charles Towne Landing, where the first settlers arrived in April 1670. Other highlights include the Charleston Museum, America's oldest municipal museum, the Hayward–Washington House (1770), the Old Slave Mart Museum, the grim Provost Museum, and so on – space precludes mention of all of Charleston's delights. But it is impossible not to include some of the places in and around the city that are magical to any lover of flowers. Outstanding is Middleton Place, built in 1755, and its fine landscaped gardens. Begun in 1741 these gardens feature a 1,000-year-old oak and what are claimed to be the oldest camellias in America. The Magnolia Plantation and Gardens, called "the most beautiful in the world" by the British novelist John Galsworthy, contains some 900 varieties of camellias and 250 varieties of azaleas, besides many other species. And for those who visit the South inspired by Margaret Mitchell's *Gone with the Wind*, there is the restored Boone Hall Plantation, seven miles north of the city, which appeared in the famous movie. Charleston has only recently begun to realize its huge tourist potential, one of the more recent innovations being the establishment of the American counterpart of Gian Carlo Menotti's Spoleto Arts Festival, which takes place every year in late May to early June.

South of Charleston are other attractions, including the vacation resort of Kiawah Island, large parts of which are totally unspoiled and rich in wildlife, the lovely town of Beaufort, with more marvelous gardens, and the nearby Port Royal with its Civil War associations.

West of the Fall Line is the Piedmont, a plateau rising gradually from about 400 to 1,500 feet (122–457 m) above sea level. This, the state's most

White rhododendrons bloom in a forest glade near Charleston, South Carolina. Charleston is a wonderland for anyone who likes flowers and the gardens in and around the city are among the most dazzling and colorful in the world.

industrialized region, contains the state capital and largest city of Columbia, with its outstanding three-story granite State House, set in a beautiful park. The Piedmont includes many historic sites. There is Abbeville in the west, where citizens gathered in 1860 on Secession Hill to select delegates to a state convention and where President Jefferson Davis and his cabinet met on 2 May 1865 and decided that continued resistance to the Union army was useless. North of Columbia is Camden, founded in 1732, which has beautifully restored eighteenth- and nineteenth-century buildings and Civil War memorabilia. And in the far north are two important Revolutionary War sites: Kings Mountain National Military Park and Cowpens National Battlefield.

Beyond the Piedmont, the land rises sharply to a narrow mountain zone, consisting of an extension of the Appalachian mountains. This region is less rugged than its counterpart in North Carolina, reaching a highest point at Sassafras Mountain, which is 3,560 feet (1,085 m) above sea level. This scenic area is largely covered by pine and hemlock forests.

Dock Street Theater is one of the many interesting old buildings that adorn the graceful city of Charleston. Opened in 1736, it was twice burned down and rebuilt. It is now used by a community theater group.

The old but intact slave cabins of Boone Hall Plantation, not far from Charleston, are surrounded by Spanish moss-festooned trees. This former cotton plantation with its restored mansion was featured in that archetypal movie about the Old South, **Gone With the Wind**.

"Georgia on My Mind"

"Tennessee has the mountains and Georgia has the hills," remarks a character in a novel by the Georgian Flannery O'Connor, and it is true that the state's share of the Appalachian Mountains is confined to a comparatively small area in the northeast. But this encompasses large tracts of beautiful mountain scenery, including the magnificent Chattahoochee National Forest, glittering lakes, and sparkling, unpolluted streams, as well as Brasstown Bald mountain, the state's highest at 4,784 feet (1,458 m) above sea level. Northwestern Georgia, which was Cherokee country until the Indian nation was expelled in 1838, includes extensions of the Appalachian plateau and of the ridge and valley regions of Tennessee. This attractive but scenically less dramatic corner of the state includes part of the Chickamauga and Chattanooga National Military Park, which commemorates the brave men who died on both sides in the Civil War battles.

South of these regions is the Piedmont, which occupies north-central Georgia, sloping down from around 1,500 feet (457 m) to less than 400 feet (122 m) at the Fall Line, which runs through or near the cities of Augusta, Milledgeville, Macon, and Columbus. The northwestern Piedmont is dominated by the state capital and largest city, Atlanta. Although largely destroyed in 1864 during Sherman's March to the Sea, the fine, modern city of Atlanta has risen phoenixlike in recent years to become the leading economic center of the Southeast and a symbol of the New South. Its dazzling skyline contains several skyscrapers, such as the cylindrical, mirrored Peachtree Center Plaza, which provides an impressive view from its seventieth floor. There is the splendid Atlanta Memorial Arts Center on Peachtree Street, the "Fifth Avenue" of the South, and the Omni Center, a gigantic complex containing a contemporary hotel, office buildings, boutiques, an ice skating rink, and many sports and entertainment facilities. Older buildings include the gold-domed State Capitol, the antebellum Tullie Smith House maintained by the Atlanta Historical Society, and Wren's Nest, the nineteenth-century home of the writer Joel Chandler Harris. An outstanding feature of the city is the pleasant, wooded northern residential area, which is lit up in spring by the blooms of dogwoods and azaleas. Grant Park contains the famous, three-dimensional panoramic painting of the Battle of Atlanta, with special lighting and sound effects.

North of Atlanta is the Kennesaw Mountain National Battlefield Park, while Stone Mountain to the east comprises a 1½-mile-long granite monolith, formed deep underground from molten rock about 300 million years ago and subsequently uncovered by erosion. On its north face is a relief carving of Jefferson Davis, Robert E. Lee and Stonewall Jackson, executed by Gutzon Borglum, who also did the famous carving at Mount Rushmore in South Dakota. The Piedmont contains several other major manufacturing centers, including Georgia's second largest city of Columbus, the picturesque Macon and the textile center of Augusta – Georgia has recently become one of the South's foremost manufacturing states. There are also many graceful smaller towns, with preserved antebellum houses, including Washington, Athens, and Madison. Southwest of Atlanta, near Pine Mountain, is Callaway Gardens, which has superb displays of azaleas, magnolias, and the wildflowers of the southern Appalachians. Nearby is the tranquil Warm Springs where President Franklin D. Roosevelt died.

Beyond the Fall Line are the plains that cover half of the state. Generally the southwestern plains are more fertile than those in the southeast. In the southwest there are many attractive towns that act as centers for the farming regions around them – Tifton, Cairo, and Thomasville, which is famed for its April Rose Festival. To the north near Americus is Andersonville National Historical Site, commemorating the Confederate prison, and Plains, home of President Jimmy Carter. The most famous feature in the southeast is the Okefenokee Swamp, a great wilderness area with fascinating wildlife, including alligators, snakes (some extremely poisonous), round-tailed muskrats, giant turtles, and many other species, including a large number of birds. The plant life in this mysterious area is extremely varied, with cypress trees festooned with moss, hollies, live oaks, long-leaf pines, magnolias, orchids, and sweet gums.

Although most of Georgia is flat or gently rolling hill country, the far north is an extension of the Appalachian mountain system and the northeast contains some splendid and largely unspoiled mountain scenery in the Chattahoochee National Forest.

The coast contains many indentations, the chief ports being Savannah and Brunswick, and a string of offshore islands, some of which are excellent resorts. Savannah seems to personify the Old South. Founded in 1733 by General James Oglethorpe, the handsome downtown area still follows his original plan. Local preservationists have made Savannah a joy to see and a large area is now designated as a national landmark. In the vicinity of Savannah there are five forts, the most important being the Fort Pulaski National Monument, which was built between 1829 and 1847 and taken by Union forces in 1862. Near the busy port of Brunswick is St. Simons Island, one of Georgia's Golden Isles. Here is located the Fort Frederica National Monument on the site of the settlement established by General Oglethorpe in 1736. Bordering the mainland near Brunswick are the largest salt marshes on the American east coast, made famous by the Georgian poet Sidney Lanier, whose atmospheric "Marshes of Glynn" begins:

Glooms of the live-oaks, beautiful-braided and woven
With intricate shades of the vines that myriad-cloven
Clamber the forks of the multiform boughs...

Wren's Nest in Atlanta, Georgia, is the former home of Joel Chandler Harris (1848–1908), creator of the famous character "Uncle Remus" who told stories about how the ingenious "Br'er Rabbit" managed to outwit his adversary "Br'er Fox." This house contrasts with the dazzling skyscrapers that form the soaring skyline of downtown Atlanta.

Beaches and Wetlands

St. Augustine in northeastern Florida is the oldest continuously inhabited white settlement in the United States, founded by the Spaniard Don Pedro Menéndez de Avilés in 1565 after he had massacred the inhabitants of a French Huguenot settlement, established the previous year at Fort Caroline to the north. Many buildings in St. Augustine betray their Spanish roots, including the Mission Nombre de Dios, the St. Augustine Cathedral, completed in 1797 and now the only surviving Spanish church in Florida, and the Castillo de San Marcos National Monument, which was begun in 1672 to replace a wooden fort.

Spanish contacts with Florida date back to 1513 when the 63-year-old Juan Ponce de León discovered the peninsula while seeking a mythical island where the old were made young again. In 1539 came the *conquistador* Hernando de Soto, who used Florida as his starting point in his search for the Seven Cities of Cibola, legendary places supposedly rich in treasure. De Soto never achieved his aim, but he did explore Florida, Georgia, the Carolinas, Tennessee, Alabama, and part of the Mississippi valley before his death in 1542. Spain ruled Florida from 1565, apart from a short period of British rule in 1763–83. In 1821, however, Spain sold Florida to the United States for $5 million and, in 1845, it became the twenty-seventh state.

Modern Florida is prosperous without being industrialized. It generally lacks power and minerals, apart from phosphates, but it has capitalized on its sunshine – the average annual temperature at Tallahassee in the north is 68°F and at Key West in the south it is 77°F. Florida is now one of the nation's greatest year-round resorts. In winter it welcomes visitors from the cold Northeast and it provides retirement homes for many older citizens. Southern Florida is also a producer of early vegetables, citrus fruits flourish in the center, and the northern pine forests are an important source of pulpwood.

Florida is part of a vast plain that covers much of the Southeast. The highest land, with an average elevation of only 200 to 300 feet (61–91 m) above sea level, is in the northwestern hinterland and in the northern part of the peninsula. But flatness does not mean that Florida lacks its share of natural beauty; there are some magnificent shorelines and seascapes and truly extraordinary wetlands.

Eastern Florida contains 580 miles of Atlantic shoreline and is largely fringed by sand bars, lagoons, and bays. Behind the coast is a broad, flat plain between 30 and 100 miles wide. In the northeast, not far from the Georgia state line, is the port of Jacksonville, a good base for exploring this historic region where Spain struggled to maintain its supremacy against

A snow-white egret poses for the camera in Okefenokee Swamp, a vast, beautiful and mysterious wilderness in southeastern Georgia. The swamp is drained by the St. Marys and Suwannee rivers.

Overleaf: Palm trees, dazzling beaches, modern hotels, and tourist facilities of every kind have made Miami Beach one of the world's most celebrated resorts, especially in winter when the "snowbirds" arrive. "Snowbirds" is the name used in Miami for human, not feathered, migrants who flock to Miami to escape the cold winters of the Northeast.

threats from the English-speaking north. South of Jacksonville, the coast is dotted with small resorts and towns, including historic St. Augustine. The first major tourist complex on the Atlantic coast is Ormond Beach–Daytona, from which the charming inland resort town Orlando can be reached. About 20 miles south of Orlando is the world's largest amusement park, Walt Disney World, where the whole family can surrender to its fun and fantasy. East of Orlando, on the coast, is the famed Cape Canaveral and the John F. Kennedy Space Center, where the fantasy of science fiction was translated into fact. To the south lies Florida's Gold Coast, including the millionaires' playground of Palm Beach, Fort Lauderdale, and Miami. It is now hard to imagine that the booming metropolis of Miami was mainly mangrove and sawgrass swamp only 50 years ago. Today swaying palms and elegant modern hotels line its beautiful beaches, while in and around the city are recreational facilities of every kind, including a spirited nightlife.

The bulk of southern Florida, however, consists of wetlands, notably the Big Cypress Swamp and the fascinating Everglades, where some Seminoles found refuge in 1841 when the majority of these Indians were moved to Oklahoma after the Seminole Wars. The Everglades National Park, the nation's third largest, is a complex network of varying habitats, ranging from mangrove swamps in brackish coastal regions, to small islands with palmettos, and hammocks (small, jungle-like forests), surrounded by a maze of channels and ponds between the ubiquitous sawgrass. The Everglades supports a wide range of animals, including alligators, whitetail deer, turtles, otters, black bears, bobcats, the threatened Florida panthers, snakes, and hundreds of bird species, many of them rare. The water in the Everglades comes from the Lake Okeechobee region to the north, but it flows extremely slowly across this broad, shallow trough which is mostly under 20 feet (6 m) above sea level. In effect, therefore, the Everglades is a huge, shallow, and extremely sluggish river which eventually reaches the sea.

Boating and fishing are the leading pastimes at Matecumbe Key, in Florida Keys, a chain of coral islands that extends in a broad curve from Key Biscayne, just south of Miami, to Key West in the Gulf of Mexico.

Inland, away from the crowded beaches, Florida has some superb uninhabited wetlands which contain a considerable variety of habitats for plants and animals. The Everglades National Park is the most famous of these wetlands.

Another attraction in the south is Florida Keys, a chain of coral islands set in the emerald-green waters of the Gulf and the deep blue sea of the Atlantic. The islands curve southwestwards for about 150 miles, linked by 42 bridges. Off Key Largo, glass-bottomed boats provide views of the whites, pinks, and oranges of the amazing living coral and its resplendent tropical fish, turtles, barracudas, and sharks. At the end of the island chain is the unusual old town of Key West, haven of fishermen and authors such as Ernest Hemingway who wrote many of his finest works here.

The beaches of Florida Keys are not the best for bathing because the coral is often sharp, but the mainland Gulf coast has more long sandy bars, ideal for visitors. The leading resort area is around St. Petersburg and Tampa, not far east from which are the splendid Cypress Gardens, a magnet for plant lovers, and the tranquil Mountain Lake Sanctuary, a refuge for birds. The peninsula is dotted with lakes, about 30,000 in all, and many of them occupy sinkholes – that is, hollows dissolved in the limestone that underlies most of the peninsula. Limestone areas are associated with caves and some do occur in the higher regions, but most of Florida is so flat that the limestone caverns are completely flooded. Beyond the winding Suwannee River (from which Stephen Foster got his song title "Swanee") in the north is the inland state capital of Tallahassee, known for its lovely gardens. The northwestern coast is lined by mile upon mile of dazzling white beaches between Apalachicola and Pensacola, making this a major summer resort area.

The Heart of Dixie

The first European contacts with Alabama, as in Florida, were made not by the British but by Spaniards and, later, Frenchmen, although Alabama finally became the twenty-second state in 1819. In 1865, after the Civil War, the cotton-based economy of this, the "Heart of Dixie" was shattered. However, recovery was underway by the end of the nineteenth century when a great industrial center was arising at Birmingham, the "Pittsburgh of the South" in the middle of the state. And in the twentieth century the economy continued to expand with the diversification of agriculture (corn is now the main crop) and more industrial development utilizing electricity from the Tennessee Valley Authority (TVA).

The southern two-thirds of Alabama consist mostly of flat plains. In the far south, the main feature of the 53-mile-long Gulf coastline is the large Mobile Bay, with excellent beaches of white sand along the eastern shore as far as Perdido Bay. Mobile, the second largest city after Birmingham, was founded by French Canadians in the early 1700s. Today it is a busy port with shipbuilding and fishing industries, but it has many lovely homes and gardens. The best known is Bellingrath south of Mobile which boasts more than 200 varieties of azaleas. The southwest contains some swamp and bayou country, whereas the southeast is rich farmland. In west-central Alabama the gently undulating Black Belt, or Prairie, which extends from the Mississippi state line to just beyond Montgomery, is another fertile region. Montgomery contains many graceful antebellum homes and it was here that Jefferson Davis was sworn in as President of the Confederacy on the steps of the beautiful State Capitol. West of Montgomery is Selma, which also has many fine buildings despite heavy Union bombardment, while Tuscaloosa to the northwest is the charming home of the University of Alabama. These northern plains are known for their expanses of pine, such as the scenic Talladega National Forest between Selma and Tuscaloosa.

The main uplands are in the north and northeast. A low plateau in the northwest is drained by the Tennessee River and its manmade Wilson and Wheeler lakes are major recreation areas. The TVA has also helped to develop the north industrially, major centers being Decatur, which was almost totally destroyed in the Civil War, and the Tri-Cities of Florence, Sheffield, and Tuscumbia, where the typically Southern birthplace of Helen Keller still stands. East of Decatur is the important city of Huntsville, site of the Alabama Space and Rocket Center.

Protruding diagonally across northeastern Alabama are three distinctive Appalachian regions. The northernmost Appalachian, or Cumberland, Plateau contains much fine scenery, forests, and glittering manmade lakes. Near Fort Payne in the northeast is the De Soto State Park, which contains the Little River Canyon, claimed to be the deepest east of the Mississippi, and a 110-foot-high (34 m) waterfall. This park is close to the border with the second Appalachian ridge and valley region. This beautiful area contains reserves of coal, iron ore, and limestone, all of which made possible the growth of mighty Birmingham whose symbol is the 55-foot-high (17 m) iron statue of Vulcan. The third Appalachian region, the largely forested Piedmont, extends as far south as the Fall Line, approximately marked by

Alabama, like Georgia, is often thought to be flat, but it also has its share of scenic grandeur, notably in the northeast where wooded gorges cut through the plateaus and the ridge and valley region of the Appalachian system.

Phenix City. On the northwestern edge of the Piedmont is Alabama's highest point, Cheaha Mountain, at 2,407 feet (734 m) above sea level. The Piedmont also contains much rugged country, another large section of the Talladega National Forest, and a scenic, manmade lakeland near Alexander City.

Magnolias and Stately Homes

Mississippi, the Magnolia State, contains plains, pine forests, and gently rolling hills, including the scenic Tennessee River Hills in the far northeast where the state's highest point is located – Woodfall Mountain, 806 feet (246 m) above sea level. Also in the northeast is part of the Black Belt, or Black Prairie, a fertile region which extends into Alabama. In the west is the mighty Mississippi River the alluvial plains of which are rich cotton and soybean country. Agriculture still plays a significant part in the economy, although here, as elsewhere in the South, things are changing as oil production and expanding manufacturing industries become increasingly important. And yet many urban areas are adorned with stately antebellum houses, most rural areas still retain the unhurried character of the Old South, and everywhere, you are conscious of the past.

Nowhere is this more true than in the Mississippi valley, that meandering highway followed by, among others, explorers, trail-blazing frontiersmen, traders, bandits, and riverboat gamblers. It was somewhere between the present Tennessee state line and Clarksdale that Hernando de Soto caught his first glimpse of the Mississippi River in 1641, while Natchez in the south was once the roughest river port on the American frontier. The Mississippi valley assumed great strategic importance in the Civil War, because Union control of the river would split the South geographically and so damage its economy. The 47-day siege of Vicksburg, which overlooks the river from lofty bluffs, was, therefore, one of the war's most crucial struggles. Today the tranquil, crescent-shaped Vicksburg National Military Park provides 16 miles of historical markers, memorials, trenches, and cannons that help visitors to imagine the sound and fury of the battles. Also in Vicksburg is the Old Courthouse, built in 1858, where General Grant raised the Union flag on 4 July 1863, as well as several elegant antebellum houses with exquisite gardens filled with venerable live oaks and lovely magnolias. To the south of Vicksburg is Grand Gulf which was razed to the ground in the

*Far right: The historic Mississippi River is a major highway. Today a few riverboats, such as the **Mississippi Queen** and the **Delta Queen**, recall the tough but romantic days when frontiersmen, gamblers, and an assortment of other colorful characters, savory and unsavory, made journeys up and down this great river.*

Civil War, Port Gibson, which Grant spared because of its beauty, and historic Natchez.

Natchez was founded in 1716 and is now a manufacturing town, but at its heart is one of the finest concentrations of antebellum houses in the country. Natchez was also the starting point for the Natchez Trace, which wound northeastwards to Nashville, Tennessee. This trail, once used by migrating buffalo, Choctaw and Chickasaw Indians, and frontiersmen, was later the main line of communication between Mississippi Territory and Washington, D.C. The Natchez Trace Parkway now approximately follows the trail and its markers (there are no billboards) indicate historic sites and sections of the trail that have hardly changed for hundreds of years. The parkway leads through Jackson, the busy state capital and largest city, and continues to Tupelo in the northeast. Within 26 miles of Tupelo are three battlefields, one dating back to 1736 and two to the Civil War.

West of Tupelo is Oxford, home of the late Nobel prize winner William Faulkner, a reminder of Mississippi's substantial literary tradition; Oxford is the "Jefferson" of Faulkner's novels, while Lafayette County became "Yoknapatawpha," home of the irresistible Snopes family. South of Tupelo is Columbus, birthplace of Tennessee Williams, whose dramas have focused on the influence of Old South values on contemporary life.

The 44-mile-long southern coastline is the state's chief vacationland. It was here that Mississippi's first permanent European settlement was founded in 1699 at Ocean Springs, the original site of Biloxi, by the Frenchman, Pierre Lemoyne, Sieur d'Iberville. Biloxi, which contains Beauvoir, last home of Jefferson Davis, is now one of several attractive coastal resorts. Ship Island to the south contains the ruins of Fort Massachusetts, a Civil War prison and yet another reminder that you cannot escape history in Mississippi.

Bayou Country

Louisiana's colorful and highly individual lifestyle is attributable to its history. Its distinctive heritage derives in part from the Creoles – the descendants of French and Spanish settlers – from the Acadians (or Cajuns) whose forbears were French Canadians expelled by the British from Acadia (Nova Scotia) in 1755, and from the blacks who contributed much, not least their music, to the fascinating cultural mix. The Mississippi valley was first claimed for France in 1682 by the explorer Robert Cavalier, Sieur de la Salle, and the French colony of Louisiana was founded in 1699. It was held by

Below: A statue of a Confederate soldier in the peace of Vicksburg National Military Park stirs the imagination. The long siege of the city in 1863 was of great strategic significance in the Civil War.

France, except for a period of Spanish rule in 1763–1800, until Napoleon sold it to the United States in 1803.

The land is low-lying with flat plains, semitropical, eerie swamps, and oil-rich bayou country in the south. The north is rolling hill country and Driskill Mountain, the state's highest point, reaches 535 feet (163 m) above sea level in the north-center. The main land feature is the fertile Mississippi alluvial plain, with its many oxbow lakes, which are stagnant remnants of former river bends. The lower part of the valley is the delta, including the Atchafalaya basin, which was the site of the delta hundreds of years ago. The present bird's-foot-shaped delta, a giant cone of riverborne sediment, is constantly growing, an estimated 400 million tons of silt being added to the delta every year, pushing the shoreline forward by about six miles every 100 years.

The land of the southern bayous contains vast tracts of alligator-infested swamp grass, broken by clusters or forests of Spanish moss-hung cypresses and live oaks. Another feature of the coastlands is the incidence of large lakes and lagoons. Lake Pontchartrain, the largest, contains brackish water, and is so big that, for about eight miles in the center of the 23.9-mile-long Second Lake Pontchartrain Causeway, travelers cannot see land in any direction. Opened in 1969, this causeway is the world's longest.

The causeway leads into the great city and port of New Orleans, which was founded by Jean Baptiste Lemoyne, Sieur de Bienville and brother of Pierre, founder of Old Biloxi, Mississippi. In its heart is the French Quarter, or *Vieux Carré*, an enchanting blend of French and Spanish architecture. Its narrow streets and passageways should be explored on foot. You will be impressed by the ornate cast-ironwork on the balconies and the cool, flower-filled courtyards inside Creole mansions, where you might catch a whiff of one of the city's favorite seafood dishes, such as jambalaya or gumbo. And outside such buildings as the handsome Spanish St. Louis Cathedral (1794), the former Spanish headquarters called the Cabildo, or the French-style Pontalba apartments, you might be forgiven for thinking yourself outside the United States. New Orleans offers the visitor many delights. Festivity, one of its characteristics, reaches a frenzied climax on *Mardi Gras* (Shrove Tuesday) when the streets are thronged with noisy, colorful parades. Music is another feature, for this is the "cradle of jazz." The original joyful jazz, often played by veterans whose memories go back to the early days, can still be heard in such places as Preservation Hall on St. Peter Street. And while in New Orleans, visit the bayou country of the delta and the Chalmette National Historical Park, site of the Battle of New Orleans when General Andrew Jackson defeated the British and secured the Mississippi valley for

St. Louis Cathedral, built between 1789 and 1794, overlooks Jackson Square, an elegant green park in the heart of New Orleans. Jackson Square, laid out in 1721 as a drill field, was called the Place d'Armes by the French and the Plaza de Armas by the Spaniards.

the United States. If you are interested in modern architecture, the Louisiana Superdome should not be missed; completed in 1975, it houses the world's largest indoor stadium.

Northwest of New Orleans is the state's handsome capital of Baton Rouge, which today has many manufacturing industries. West of the city is Henderson where there are boat trips into the unspoiled Atchafalaya basin, while beyond Henderson is Lafayette, with its strong Cajun atmosphere. Northwest of Alexandria, in the geographical center of the state, is Louisiana's first permanent European settlement, Natchitoches, which was founded in 1714 as a French trading post. This attractive town with its many old buildings lies close to some splendid fishing country and sections of the Kisatchie National Forest, which are lovely wildlife preserves. The north has a generally rural character, though discoveries of large reserves of oil and natural gas have enabled Monroe and Shreveport to develop into lively industrial cities.

The French Quarter of New Orleans constitutes the original town which was laid out by the French. The old buildings, which are a blend of French and Spanish colonial styles, have been lovingly restored and conserved, such that the atmosphere of the French Quarter often seems more European than American.

Spacious, cool, green courtyards shaded from the sun and cut off from raucous street noises are among New Orleans's special delights. Here in the Court of the Seven Sisters, visitors can relax and enjoy a cool drink.

Land of Opportunity

Arkansas, like Louisiana, was claimed for France by Robert Cavalier, Sieur de la Salle in 1682, becoming part of the United States only after the Louisiana Purchase of 1803. Arkansas supported the Confederacy in the Civil War and antebellum homes and battlefields testify to its Southern heritage, although Fort Smith in west-central Arkansas near the Oklahoma state line still retains the atmosphere of a Western frontier town.

The scenery is varied with rugged highlands in the north and west and plains in the south and east. The economy of Arkansas, which is nicknamed the "Land of Opportunity," is mainly agricultural, although manufacturing and mining (notably bauxite, bromine, and oil) are making an increasing contribution. Farmland covers about two-fifths of the state, with forests blanketing most of the rest. The chief farming region is the largely flat Mississippi alluvial plain in the east. The Mississippi's chief tributary is the Arkansas River. Near the confluence of the two is the Arkansas Post National Memorial on the site of a trading and military post established by Henri de Tonty, lieutenant to La Salle, in 1686.

The state's highlands consist of the Ozark Plateau and the Ouachita Mountains, two regions that are separated by the Arkansas River valley which extends from Fort Smith to Little Rock, below which the river flows over the Mississippi alluvial plain.

The Ozark Plateau, which extends into neighboring Oklahoma and Missouri, brings to mind the plateaus of the southern Appalachians in that it is highly dissected by gorges, rushing rivers, and serene, manmade lakes. Three particularly magnificent manmade lakes, Beaver, Bull Shoals (the state's largest) and Norfork, offer splendid recreational facilities in the north. There are many other beautiful and interesting places in the Ozarks. West of Beaver Lake is the Pea Ridge National Military Park, commemorating the most important Civil War battle west of the Mississippi. And east of the lake is the picturesque Victorian Eureka Springs – there are actually 63 natural springs within its boundaries. It also boasts the impressive 65-foot-high (20 m) statue of Christ of the Ozarks which overlooks an amphitheater where a Passion Play is performed throughout the summer. East of Eureka Springs is Harrison, "the hub of the Ozarks," and Dogpatch USA, a theme park filled with Al Capp characters from the comic strip, *L'il Abner*. Southeast of Harrison is the scenic, canyon-lined Buffalo River National Park, the white rapids of which provide terrific sport for canoeists. Farther east, Mountain View is the home of the Ozark Folk Center, where the region's crafts,

The Buffalo National River in the Ozarks of Arkansas offers many opportunities in spring to white water enthusiasts, while hikers can follow self-guided trails and bask in the superb, unspoiled, forested river scenery.

Left: King cotton still reigns in the fertile alluvial plains of the Mississippi valley in eastern Arkansas and agriculture is still the state's most important activity. But here, as elsewhere in the New South, industry is making an ever-increasing contribution to the economy.

The uninhabited Ozark National Forest in northeastern Arkansas contains majestic highland trails that wind past caverns, unusual rock formations, and thundering waterfalls.

customs, and music are preserved, while north of the town is the eerie Blanchard Springs Caverns. Southwest of here, the Ozarks rise to heights of more than 2,300 feet (700 m) above sea level in the Boston Mountains in the mostly uninhabited Ozark National Forest. These mountains contain some particularly spectacular gorges.

South of the Ozarks, the Arkansas River valley contains a series of ridges which include Magazine Mountain, the highest point in Arkansas at 2,753 feet (839 m) above sea level. Nearby is the beautiful Lake Dardanelle State Park, a major recreational area. But the main attraction of this region is probably Fort Smith. Here one can see the Fort Smith National Historical Site, including the foundations of the first fort begun in 1817, reconstructed frontier buildings, antebellum homes, and, in late May or early June, there is a rodeo week when all the pageantry of the Old West is revived.

In the southeastern corner of the Arkansas River valley region, close to the center of the state, is the capital Little Rock, an elegant, modern city and the state's chief industrial, financial, and transportation center. Southwest of Little Rock is Hot Springs National Park, the state's leading tourist attraction. Probably visited by De Soto in 1541, it boasts 47 mineral-rich thermal springs. Hot Springs itself is a major resort, nestling in some charming wooded country near the edge of the Ouachita Mountains. This region consists of wooded ridges alternating with narrow, cultivated valleys that run from west to east, and it bears a strong resemblance to the ridge and valley zone of the Appalachians, with its beautiful, manmade lakes and peaceful pine and hardwood forests.

The Midwest

North of the Ozark Plateau of Arkansas, the Midwestern states stretch across America from the Appalachians to the Rocky Mountains, a vast expanse of territory drained by the "Father of Waters", the mighty Mississippi, the Missouri, and rivers such as the lovely Ohio and the Platte. When the immense ice sheets that covered most of this region during the Ice Ages of long ago finally retreated, they left behind a varied landscape of worn-down forested hills, flat prairies of rich soils, and thousands of hollows filled with freshwater lakes, including the Great Lakes themselves.

The Indians who moved into this beautiful country, with its rich diversity of wild animals, followed ways of life that were perfectly suited to their natural surroundings, but then came the white man and, as the saying goes, the rest is history. Every school student knows the main outline of events in the saga: how, after exploration by the French, the whole northern region from the Appalachians to the Rockies was won by the newly independent United States in a mere 20 years between 1783 and 1803; how settlers from the original 13 colonies and other countries courageously moved into the new territories, among them the family of young Abraham Lincoln; how treaty after treaty protecting Indian rights was tragically broken, resulting in much bloodshed, ending only when the dispossessed tribes were enclosed in reservations; and how, as the railroads pushed across the wide open spaces from the east, cattle and cowboys came to the great high plains of the West, and lawlessness etched the names of such characters as Wild Bill Hickok, Wyatt Earp, and Jesse James onto the pages of folklore and history.

Out of the epic struggle of the early pioneers to settle this land, prosperity finally came, and today the Midwest is the nation's main source of food and a major manufacturing region centered on such great cities as Chicago, Cleveland, and Detroit. Vast cattle ranches and sheep farms sprawl over the grasslands of the West, and from Nebraska to Ohio an abundance of farm produce is harvested from the rich patchwork of fields known as the Corn Belt, a changing kaleidoscope of color where, in the fall, the eye rests on enchanting landscapes of "low rolling hills, fold after fold, smooth brown and autumnal, some plowed to soft earth-color, some set with corn stalks of pale tarnished gold." Peace, stillness, and silence reign over this beautiful land where, "at night, when the wind is down, you can hear a scream for miles, and conversation is audible from a wagon coming over the horizon."

The Mother of Presidents

Named the Buckeye State because of the large number of buckeye trees that once grew all over its territory, Ohio, the most easterly of the Midwestern states, is now one of America's major industrial regions, with manufacturing centers scattered throughout its rich farmlands. Having sent eight of her sons (one of them – William Henry Harrison – adopted from Virginia) to the White House, the state also claims the title of "Mother of Presidents," although Virginia (also boasting eight chief executives) might reasonably dispute the matter. History has left many memories throughout Ohio, from the beautiful effigy mounds built by Indians centuries ago, such as the Great

Serpent Mound near Hillsboro, to the names of its towns, many of which reflect the origins of its many immigrants from the Northeast and Europe, places like Toledo, Dublin, and New Philadelphia.

With its excellent network of rail, road, and water routes, Ohio is well placed in the heartland of America to be the "Gateway State" linking the populous Atlantic coastlands with the great farming plains of the interior. The vast fertile Corn Belt reaches into the western counties of Ohio, where farms grow huge quantities of grain and raise large numbers of livestock. Much of this agricultural wealth finds its way into the processing plants of Cincinatti, which stands amid tree-covered hills on the Ohio River in the southwestern corner of the state. Having survived the slur bestowed on it by President-to-be William Henry Harrison as "the most debauched place I ever saw," the city was liked by Charles Dickens and, more recently, was awarded an accolade as "one of the most livable cities in the United States." Certainly the city has a pleasant cosmopolitan atmosphere, with fine international restaurants and a flourishing cultural life, and – a blessing in the age of the automobile – comparatively traffic-free streets in the downtown area centered on attractive Fountain Square. From time to time a reminder that the "Queen City of the West" is also the "Gateway to the South" bursts on the ear when the mournful whistle of one of the steamboats plying the Ohio River echoes around the surrounding hillsides.

Running west to east across the farming country of central Ohio, a region of low hills containing the state's highest point, 1,550-foot (472 m) Campbell Hill, encloses the beautiful Hocking Hills State Park, with its sandstone cliffs, gorges, waterfalls, and caves. Here too is the state capital, Columbus, which boasts the finest Doric-style Capitol building in the whole country. But the most scenically attractive part of Ohio is to be found among the steep hills, valleys, and lakes of the Allegheny Plateau region in the east, where the thinner soils support extensive tracts of the Wayne National Forest and grazing lands for large numbers of sheep and dairy cattle. This area also contains rich deposits of coal, natural gas, oil, and clay, and enough salt to keep the entire nation supplied for thousands of years, and here several major industrial centers have grown up: the steel cities of Canton and Youngstown, and Akron, the "rubber capital of the world."

A farm near the little town of Somerset in southeastern Ohio typifies the quiet rural charm of the Midwest. On the thinner soils of this part of Ohio, much of it covered by tracts of the Wayne National Forest, intensive crop farming gives way to dairying and the raising of hogs.

By night the twinkling lights of downtown Cleveland, Ohio, give this tough industrial city a certain magic and charm. The mixture of various nationalities in the city's patchwork of ethnic neighborhoods is a legacy of the days when immigrant labor flocked in to build the prosperity of their new home by the sweat of their brow.

These rugged industrial towns are an echo of the vast manufacturing belt that extends along the Lake Erie shore for nearly 50 miles around Cleveland. Once called "Forest City," Cleveland is now indeed a jungle of heavy industry and commerce concerned with steel, shipping, machine tools for the automobile industry, and many other activities, although it is not without its attractions. Burgeoning prosperity led also to the growth of the city's affluent suburbs, among which Shaker Heights became the most desirable.

Inland from Lake Erie's shoreline, as far west as the glassmaking city of Toledo, the flat fertile plain is intensively cultivated for truck farms, orchards, and vineyards, a beautiful rural landscape in which the blossoming peach trees of the Marblehead Peninsula create a particularly enchanting spectacle in the spring.

The Beautiful Peninsula

Across the waters of Lake Erie northwest of Ohio, the shoreline of Michigan winds away into the distance for 3,288 miles around the inlets, bays, and islands of four of the five Great Lakes. This "Water Wonderland," as the state is sometimes called, glistens with sparkling rivers, rushing creeks, and thousands of mirror-still inland lakes left behind by retreating glaciers. As the state motto urges, "If you seek a beautiful peninsula, look about you," yet even this is perhaps too modest, since Michigan's territory occupies not one peninsula but two, separated by the five-mile-wide Straits of Mackinac. Once roamed by French trappers, whose pelts gave the state its nickname – the "Wolverine State" – Michigan's economy grew out of the exploitation of its vast resources of timber, copper, and iron, its prosperity developing through its huge car-making industry centered on Detroit, its agricultural wealth, particularly the growing of enormous quantities of cherries, blueberries, and navy beans, and its tourist appeal.

Surrounded on three sides by the waters of Lakes Huron, Michigan and Erie, the Lower Peninsula is mostly a flat checkerboard of farming country interspersed with orchards and vineyards. Here and there, low hills rise above the general level of the land, particularly in the north, where the lovely Au Sable River, famous for its trout, winds through the Huron National Forest on its way to the eastern shore. On the other side of the peninsula, Indian legend tells us, the 480-foot-high (146 m) Sleeping Bear Sand Dune lies grieving for her two cubs, the North and South Manitou Islands, lost while swimming in Lake Michigan.

Tradition and history abound in the Lower Peninsula, where a flavor of the past can be tasted at such interesting places as the Dutch village recreated at Holland in the west, the Bavarian village of Frankenmuth, near Flint, or the Greenfield Village and Henry Ford Museum at Dearborn, outside Detroit, set up by the car magnate with the clear objective that "When we are through, we shall have reproduced American life as lived." Ford's genius helped to make Detroit the car-making capital of the world, its prosperity reflecting the fluctuating fortunes of the industry in which it specialized. The decay that afflicted the city's downtown district after World War II, however, is now being repaired with such ambitious redevelopment schemes as the aptly named Renaissance Center, a complex of four tall steel and glass towers dominated by a 73-story hotel.

At the northern end of the Lower Peninsula, just west of historic Mackinac Island, the elegant Mackinac suspension bridge leaps across the water separating Michigan's two parts. From here the Upper Peninsula sweeps away westward between Lakes Superior and Michigan, a beautiful land of thick forests, scenic shorelines, rushing streams, waterfalls, and swamps, and, in the west, several mountain ranges including the remote forested wilderness of the Porcupine Mountains and 1,980-foot-high (604 m) Mount Curwood, the highest point in the state. Places of special scenic interest here include the colorful eroded Pictured Rocks, the spectacular Tahquamenon Falls and, across the waters of Lake Superior, the cluster of islands in the wildlife wilderness of Isle Royale National Park. The colorful Indian names of some of these lovely places are also beautiful, even poetic, when rendered into English – Lake of the Clouds, Laughing Whitefish Falls, and Mirror of Heaven Springs, for example. The enchantment of this part of Michigan was wonderfully captured by Henry Wadsworth Longfellow in his long poem *The Song of Hiawatha* about an Indian brave who lived:

> In the solitary forest,
> By the rushing Taquamenaw.

The Crossroads of America

While it seems obvious that Indiana was named for the Indians, no one knows for sure how it got its nickname of the "Hoosier State," although some say the Hoosiers were workmen from the state employed by canal

May brings out the tulips and the visitors to Windmill Island Park at Holland, West Michigan, a bit of Old Holland transported to America. One of the attractions here is the reconstructed windmill known as "De Zwaan" (The Swan), a working mill that once operated near Amsterdam in the Netherlands.

contractor Samuel Hoosier in 1826. The state motto is much more informative about Indiana, pointing out its strategic position in the Midwest as "The Crossroads of America," its precise location "On the banks of the Wabash" being indicated by the state song. In fact, the Wabash flows right across Indiana from Ohio before turning south to form the western border and then joining the great Ohio River, the state's southern line.

Indiana's terrain rises gradually from the Lake Michigan shoreline in the north, across the farming plains of the center to the hills and valleys of the south. The lakeshore presents a contrasting scene between the vast industrial belt of oil refineries and steel mills around Gary and the peaceful beaches, sand dunes, and bogs of the Indiana Dunes National Lakeshore farther east. Inland, the fertile glacial soils of the Corn Belt extend across the state eastward, supporting a multicolored checkerboard of waving cornfields, green truck farms, and woods as far as the lakes district of the northeast, with its popular recreation areas.

Guarding this rich country is the former military post of Fort Wayne, now a big manufacturing city of 172,000 people. Farther south the industrial towns of Muncie, Anderson, Kokomo, and Lafayette stand in the encircling farmland like a ring of satellites north of the state capital of Indianapolis, a recently revitalized Midwestern city inhabited by more than 700,000 people. This number, however, swells dramatically around Memorial Day each year when crowds flock in to see the thrilling Indianapolis 500 car race at the Motor Speedway west of the downtown area. Centered on attractive Monument Circle, the city has many places of interest, such as the state's highest structure, the 504-foot-high (154 m) Indiana National Bank Tower, the elegant domed Capitol, the Convention Center, the old city market, the Children's Museum and the shopping center of Keystone at the Crossing, as well as prosperous suburbs, especially on the North Side. But to see buildings by some of the world's leading architects – Eliel and Eero Saarinen and Frank Lloyd Wright among them – a trip to the pleasant city of Columbus is necessary.

The limestone hills around Columbus, with their cliffs, caves, underground rivers and springs, contain Indiana's most beautiful countryside. Especially appealing are McCormick's Creek and Brown County State Parks and, farther south, the immense Wyandotte Cave, which encloses a huge underground hillock known as Rothrock Cathedral. Over much of this lovely part of Indiana the Hoosier National Forest wraps a thick cloak of trees, and it was in this wooded wilderness that Abraham Lincoln grew up, the spot now commemorated in the Lincoln Boyhood National Memorial north of Lincoln City.

Every year the Lilac Festival delights visitors to historic Mackinac Island in the narrow strait between Lakes Michigan and Huron. No automobiles are allowed on the island, a famous Michigan resort.

Farther west, along the lower part of the Wabash valley, there are many other reminders of the past. At historic Vincennes, for example, the state's oldest city dating from French fur-trapper days, the George Rogers Clark National Historical Park recalls the winning of the Northwestern territories from the British in the Revolutionary War. And around the little town of Rockville, in Parke County, there are many of the old covered bridges that give the Midwest so much of its charm.

Like a piece of modern sculpture, the adventurous design of the Science Center at Detroit goes hand in hand with the twentieth-century technology of the "Motor City."

The Land of Lincoln

Once covered with vast grassy plains extending into the distance, Illinois was aptly named the "Prairie State" in its early days. Since then, however, the fertile black soils left behind by the glaciers of past ages have been plowed and sown to create one of the richest farmland regions in the whole country.

The Miner's Castle is a fascinating section of the eroded multicolored sandstone cliffs that run along the Lake Superior shoreline of Michigan's Upper Peninsula. Rising abruptly in places as high as 200 feet (60 m) above the water, the cliffs form part of the beautiful Pictured Rocks National Lakeshore and are best seen from a boat.

Right: The exciting interior of the magnificent Renaissance Center, on downtown Detroit's riverfront, makes ingenious use of space for sophisticated shops, pleasant restaurants and covered walkways. Dominating the entire complex, the tubular 73-story Detroit Plaza Hotel rises inside a group of four 38-story steel and glass rectangular buildings.

Rich farming country stretches across the lowlands of northern Indiana from the Lake Michigan shoreline, in the northwest, to the lakes district around Angola, in the northeast. Many of the farms are operated by the large Amish community in this part of the state.

Sometimes called the "Garden State of the Nation," Illinois now disputes Iowa's claim to be the leading state in the production of corn and hogs, while at the same time producing huge quantities of soybeans, alfalfa, peaches, apples, and melons.

It comes as something of a surprise to those who think that Illinois is just one great patchwork of flat fields to discover that there is dramatic and beautiful hill country, too. Located at extreme ends of the state are the two major highland areas. In the far northwest are the Dubuque Hills, which contain the state's highest point, Charles Mound (1,235 feet/376 m), and the winding Apple River Canyon, with its dramatic ravines and limestone bluffs. And in the south there are the spectacularly beautiful and rugged Illinois Ozarks, clothed in the Shawnee National Forest, a stretch of wooded ridges, valleys, canyons, and river bluffs about 70 miles long rising to 1,065 feet (325 m). Walks through this delightful scenic country reveal fascinating geological wonders such as the Garden of the Gods with its imaginatively named Camel Rock and Anvil Rock and other curious features.

But although Illinois has these lovely hills, magnificent vistas along the Mississippi and other rivers, and many other places of scenic and historic interest, it is above all the "Land of Lincoln," where the memory of the sixteenth President is revered at the many sites along the Lincoln Heritage Trail associated with him. Special among them are the reconstructed New Salem village in Petersburg, northwest of Springfield, where "Honest Abe" ran a store and post office, and Springfield itself, where he rose from poverty to become a respected lawyer and Congressman and finally a beloved President. Springfield, the gracious state capital where Abe now lies buried, is the fourth largest city in the state behind Chicago, Rockford, and Peoria.

Outstripping the others by far, Chicago has a population of over three million and ranks as the nation's second city after New York. From its inauspicious beginnings as a French fur-trading post in 1779, the city grew rapidly in the early 1800s through repeated transfusions of Yankee and European immigrant blood to become the thriving cosmopolitan, business, manufacturing, and cultural center it is today. Now a vibrant, self-confident community with its own identity and personality, Chicago has outgrown its sense of inferiority in the shadow of its bigger sister, its confusion in not

The Chicago River flows modestly through the impressive business heart of Chicago into Lake Michigan, passing on its left bank the imposing twin towers of Marina City, a 60-story living and working complex.

The magnificent skyline of Chicago, America's exciting second city, rises above the green parks and boat marinas bordering Lake Michigan, where craft of all sizes create a constant bustle of activity. The birthplace of the world's first skyscrapers, Chicago now boasts the world's tallest building, the 110-story Sears Tower, whose skydeck on the 103rd floor offers a superb panorama of the great city below.

A colorful patchwork of cropfields and pastures covers much of Wisconsin's rolling country, earning top place for the state in the production of dairy goods and crops such as green peas, corn, and cranberries.

knowing whether its Indian-derived name means "great and powerful" or just "wild garlic," and its long-held, unflattering image as the playground of Prohibition-days gangsters such as Al Capone. The city now holds its head high as a beautiful metropolis offering a wide range of attractions.

Approaching Chicago from Lake Michigan, its best profile, the visitor is immediately thrilled by the exciting skyline of modern skyscrapers, rising on either side of the little Chicago River behind the beautifully ordered lakeshore parks, the harbors bobbing with yachts and launches, and the flat runways of Meigs Field airport lined with impressive executive jets. It was out of the ashes of the Great Fire of 1871, which destroyed much of the downtown area, that this superb cityscape was born, the rebuilding begun by the so-called Chicago School of architects who devised the quick, steel-frame method of construction for tall commercial buildings, such as the Rookery on South LaSalle and the renowned Carson, Pirie, Scott building. Since then the city's architectural heritage has been magnificently augmented with superb buildings designed by architects of international repute, such as Frank Lloyd Wright's Unity Temple and his lovely houses at Oak Park and Mies van der Rohe's elegant apartment blocks lining Lakeshore Drive to the affluent Gold Coast. In recent years the skyline has been pierced by such imposing landmarks as the 110-story Sears Tower, at 1,454 feet (443 m) the world's tallest building, the John Hancock Center with 100 stories, and the towering First National Bank of Chicago at Dearborn and Madison, the world's highest bank. The plaza at its foot enclosing the "Four Seasons" mosaic by Marc Chagall is one of several such open spaces decorated with works of art by world-famous names, including Pablo Picasso and Alexander Calder.

Many of these architectural sights are in the downtown business district known as the Loop, the vibrant heart of the city encircled by the old "El," the elevated railroad. Here, too, is that shopper's paradise, State Street, a car-free mall of department stores, shops, restaurants, outdoor cafés, and theaters. A short distance away, on North Side, are the elegant, sophisticated shops of the "Magnificent Mile" stretch of Michigan Avenue and the eight-level vertical shopping mall of Water Tower Place. Nearby the booming bars and clubs of Rush Street offer nightlife excitement, as do the nightclubs of Old Town farther north along Wells Street. Everywhere there are excellent speciality restaurants providing an astonishing variety of international cuisines reflecting the city's ethnic pot-pourri. Refreshment for the mind is supplied by Chicago's many cultural institutions – its libraries, museums, art galleries, theaters, and historic sites – crowned by the world-famous Art Institute of Chicago, the Lyric Opera, and the Chicago Symphony Orchestra.

With so many attractions, it is easy to agree with Sinatra when he sings: "It's my kind of town, Chicago..."

America's Dairyland

Although someone with a mind for figures has meticulously calculated that in the state of Wisconsin there are 14,949 inland lakes (not counting the unnamed ones), 7,446 streams, and 860 miles of shoreline along Lakes Michigan and Superior, it could be argued that the local Chippewa Indians had a much more delightful way of saying the same thing: they called Wisconsin "The Gathering of the Waters." Either way, there is certainly a lot of water in this beautiful state, much of it in hollows left behind long ago by retreating glaciers, and now vacationers flock to Wisconsin to enjoy the many leisure activities it affords, whether fishing, water-skiing, canoeing, or swimming. Tourism is the state's major source of income after its manufacturing industry, but after a drive through the rolling pastureland of the eastern plains, it is easy to see why Wisconsin is called "America's Dairyland" and leads the nation in the production of milk, butter, and cheese.

The cold winters of northern Wisconsin bring excellent snow for skiing and other winter sports to the forested hills.

The success story began around 150 years ago when, after the defeat of the Indians in the Black Hawk War of 1832, thousands of white settlers flooded in to exploit the territory's rich resources of timber and minerals and to farm its rich soils. The Scandinavian look of the lakes and forests attracted many Finns, Swedes, and Norwegians, as well as other Europeans, their respective national cultures surviving to enrich the life of Wisconsin today in colorful festivals all over the state.

But despite its economic development, the "Badger State" still teems with wildlife and boasts magnificent natural scenery. Behind the bluffs and sandy beaches along Lake Michigan, a quiet landscape of dairy farms and orchards extends into the plains that run across the center of the state. Here, the southward-flowing Wisconsin River passes through several big reservoirs before plunging through a beautiful deep gorge seven miles long called the Wisconsin Dells, on its way to join the Mississippi. South of this scenic area is the attractive state capital of Madison with its impressive Capitol building, and to the east, on Lake Michigan, the port of Milwaukee. A cosmopolitan city with a varied ethnic mix, Milwaukee was once strongly German, perhaps explaining why beer-making became its prime industry. Among its architectural landmarks are the old City Hall, with its high tower and its entrance porch, designed so that honest taxpayers would not get wet, and the beautiful residential district along the lakeshore.

In the southwestern corner of the state the land climbs into more rugged and wooded hill country, where there are many places of scenic interest. Beyond this area, magnificent views can be enjoyed from the high bluffs along the Mississippi, which forms much of Wisconsin's western border. Many vacationers, however, make for the thinly populated, unspoiled northern part of the state where there are extensive tracts of thick forest, large lakes, and high hills, among which the state's highest point, Tim's Hill, rises to 1,953 feet (595 m). Other people prefer the exciting trip down the beautiful St. Croix River through birch and pine forests in the far northwest, an area which also contains many other beautiful places to visit. Among these are the Big Manitou Falls, the highest in the state, which drop 165 feet

Known to the Indians as "The Gathering of the Waters," Wisconsin has thousands of beautiful small lakes dotted throughout its forested country. In the fall these take on a special enchantment as the reddish tints of the trees are mirrored in the tranquil waters.

(50 m) in Pattison State Park south of the city of Superior, and, farther east along the lakeside plain, the remote, wooded Apostle Islands, a National Lakeshore area in Lake Superior off the forested Bayfield Peninsula.

The Star of the North

If there is one place in America where the folklore created by white settlers outshines for its sheer inventiveness even the myths of the Indians, then it must be Minnesota, out of whose deep forests came that legendary lumberman Paul Bunyan and his blue ox Babe. With a delightful confusion of fiction and reality, Minnesota towns such as Bemidji and Brainerd record significant events in the "lives" of these two colorful heroes and their

Deer and other forms of wildlife abound in the unspoiled countryside of Wisconsin, where the local people have a deep respect for nature conservation.

prodigious exploits. But strange tales are not new to Minnesota. It is said, for instance, that the Vikings were the first white men to visit the territory long before the French explorers and fur-traders, and a "runestone" was found by a farmer to prove it – we now know, of course, that it was all an elaborate tall story.

What is certain is that after the French had been wandering through the area for over a century, the United States acquired the territory through the Louisiana Purchase of 1803, and from then on New Englanders, Scandinavians, Germans, and other European immigrants flocked in to exploit its vast timber resources, mineral deposits, especially iron ore, and its fertile soils. Today agriculture is the state's major economic activity, with nearly 30 percent of working people employed in farming or related industries. And tourism has grown, too, with vacationers taking full advantage of the state's scenic atractions and historic sites and, during the cold, snowy winters, a wide range of sports.

Despite Minnesota's involvement with farming, over 40 percent of its land is forested, most of it in the remote wildernesses of the northeast bordering Canada. This is a beautiful region of thickly wooded hills, streams teeming with fish, thundering cascades, and tranquil lakes, where the howl of the timber wolf chills the blood in the silence of night. Here the Boundary Waters Canoe Area Wilderness and the Voyageurs National Park have been created to preserve the region's wild natural beauty. Farther south are the now worked-out iron-ore mines of the Mesabi Range, once among the world's richest and now revitalized through the extraction of lower-grade taconite from open pits. Harbors and taconite-processing plants linked with the mines are scattered along the ruggedly beautiful north shore of Lake Superior between Duluth, a major lake port with that fantastic Aerial Lift Bridge guarding its harbor, and Grand Portage, a National Monument

Opposite: From Lake Itasca, one of the thousands of small lakes that glisten amid northern Minnesota's forests, the mighty Mississippi River begins its 2,552-mile journey south to the Gulf of Mexico as a trickling stream less than two feet deep.

preserving a reconstructed old fur-trading village on the Canadian border. Along this shoreline, with its high bluffs and crashing cascades, is the famous Split Rock Lighthouse, dramatically poised on the edge of a plunging cliff.

In northwestern Minnesota, once covered by ancient Lake Agassiz, the landscape is less rugged, with expanses of flat prairies and rich farmland, marshes and thousands of glistening lakes. From one of these lakes, Lake Itasca, the mighty Mississippi begins its long journey as a pebbly trickle. One of its tributaries, the Minnesota River, crosses the southwestern region, where the rolling farming country is dotted with processing plants and historic sites, including the Jeffers Petroglyphs, ancient Indian rock carvings by the Little Cottonwood River; old Fort Ridgely, which played a crucial part in the Dakota (Sioux) War of 1862; Pipestone National Monument near the South Dakota border, where the Indians quarried the soft red stone for their ceremonial pipes. Here, too, live the gophers which gave the state its nickname. Farther east, behind the wooded bluffs lining the Mississippi, is a beautiful region of low hills and deep valleys covered with thick hardwood forests and drained by sparkling trout streams.

Where the Minnesota River meets the Mississippi, the Twin Cities of Minneapolis and St. Paul have grown up by historic Fort Snelling, established in 1819 and now restored. Nearly half the state's population, around two million people, live in the combined metropolitan area enjoying its flourishing cultural life, exemplified by the world-famous Tyrone Guthrie Theater, its exceptional number of parks and lakes, its varied sporting activities, and its fine shopping centers linked by weather-proof pedestrian skyways. Dominated by the 57-story IDS Center, Minneapolis stands on the west bank of the Mississippi, its downtown shopping area centered on pleasant, tree-lined Nicollet Mall, its evening entertainment provided by the nightspots, bars, restaurants, and theaters of Hennepin Avenue. Its older but smaller twin, St. Paul, sits comfortably on its hills across the river. As the state capital, it boasts a superb statehouse designed by Cass Gilbert, as well as many other attractions, among which Town Square and Grand Avenue are especially popular with downtown shoppers.

With all the interesting places and varied activities that Minnesota has to offer, it is not surprising to find it shining as the "Star of the North" at the top of quality-of-life surveys in recent years.

The Beautiful Land

Shimmering in the hot stillness of summer, the ripening cornfields of Iowa stretch for over 300 miles across the great rolling prairies between the Mississippi and Missouri rivers. Blessed with rich topsoil bequeathed by long-vanished glaciers, the farms of the "Corn State" earn more money from their produce than do those of any other state except California, leading all others in the rearing and processing of hogs, disputing first place in corn production with Illinois, and ranking second in the raising of cattle. This they manage to achieve even though many farmers have left the land in recent years to work in Iowa's developing manufacturing industries, the products of which are now valued at three times the state's income from agriculture. Now more than half of the population of nearly three million lives in the towns.

Despite these figures, over 90 percent of Iowa's land is still used for farming. Everywhere the patterns of fields create a beautiful gentle landscape so wonderfully recorded in the paintings of Grant Wood. The scenic tapestry is woven with colorful patches of green woodland and fruit orchards, quiet villages and towns, all divided up by trickling streams, rivers, and cool lakes, their tree-lined banks occasionally broken by rocky cliffs and bluffs. All over the state, places of special scenic beauty have been reserved as state parks, and in the northwest a number of lakes and reservoirs have been developed to provide facilities for vacationers and sports enthusiasts. In marked contrast to this rolling farmland, the northeastern part of the state

Overleaf: The imposing Minnesota State Capitol, sited on a hill just north of the downtown district of St. Paul, is an outstanding landmark designed by the celebrated architect Cass Gilbert and completed in 1902. A magnificent structure with lavish interior decorations, the building is topped with the largest self-supporting marble dome in the world. At the base of the dome, above the facade, is a gold equestrian monument representing the progress of the state of Minnesota.

Right: The rolling farmlands of Iowa, the "Corn State," stretch for mile after mile across the rich soils of the Midwest between the Mississippi and Missouri rivers. Second only to California in the value of its farm produce, Iowa produces a tenth of the nation's entire food supply.

In this simple two-room cottage just off the main street of West Branch, Iowa, President Herbert Hoover was born, the first American President to be born west of the Mississippi River. Together with his father's blacksmith shop and the library housing his Presidential papers, the cottage now forms the Herbert Hoover Historical Site occupying a 33-acre park in West Branch.

rises into pine-covered hill country, where sparkling trout streams rush down between high bluffs to join the Mississippi. On a 1,300-acre site in this beautiful area across the river from Prairie du Chien, Wisconsin, a favorite spot for hikers, Indians who lived some 2,500 years ago built the huge, imaginative Effigy Mounds in the shapes of animals and birds, some of them 300 feet (91 m) long.

All over Iowa there are places of special interest, whether linked with the Mormons who passed through in 1846, the Amish and Amana religious settlements in the southeast, or the many pioneers from many lands who made their homes on the prairies here. The customs and ways of life of this rich diversity of peoples provide a colorful pageant of festivals throughout the state every year, reaching its peak in the great annual State Fair held in Des Moines, the state capital. This attractive city, with its impressively beautiful statehouse capped by a gold dome, has undergone a revitalization program in recent years, resulting in the construction of the magnificent

Civic Center for the arts. But, of all the many lovely places in their state, Iowans are especially fond of the Little Brown Church in Nashua in the northeast, built on the spot which inspired the hymn:

There's a church in the valley by the wildwood,
No lovelier place in the dale.
No spot is so dear to my childhood
As the little brown church in the vale.

The Indians were right when they called this golden country "Iowa," for the name means "The Beautiful Land."

The celebrated Little Brown Church in Nashua, northeastern Iowa, is a popular choice for weddings. It was built in 1864 by Reverend J. K. Nutting to commemorate the beautiful hymn "The Church in the Wildwood" composed some time before by Dr. William S. Pitts.

Gateway to the West

Visible for miles around, the immense stainless steel Gateway Arch, curving elegantly skywards like a silver rainbow beside the Mississippi at St. Louis, is a brilliant symbol of Missouri's continuing role as the "Gateway to the West." Standing at the point where the "Father of Waters" is joined by "Big Muddy" – the mighty Missouri River – the city grew from its lowly origins as a French fur-trading post to become a vigorous, modern industrial metropolis, communications hub, and cultural center. In recent years the adventurous, thrusting "Spirit of St. Louis" which created its prosperity has been re-enlisted to bring about the revitalization of the downtown district. Behind the Goldenrod Showboat and other sternwheelers moored along the riverfront by the Gateway Arch are the Old Cathedral, the Greek-style Old Courthouse where the notorious Dred Scott case was heard, and the pleasant nineteenth-century district of Laclede's Landing, where the air has been scented for years by the local licorice factory. Scattered throughout the city are the new downtown Convention Center; beautiful Forest Park, with its planetarium and the "Muny," or Municipal Opera; "Shaw's Garden," the city's botanical showpiece complete with the impressive Climatron glasshouse; the gold-domed St. Louis Cathedral, decorated inside with superb mosaics; Maryland Plaza, one of many fine shopping centers; and sumptuous Powell Hall, once a movie house and now the home of the celebrated St. Louis Symphony Orchestra.

North of St. Louis, memories of Mark Twain abound in the Mississippi riverside town of Hannibal, now an industrial center where a delightful sternwheeler bearing the author's name plies sedately carrying sightseers

Moored alongside the riverfront at St. Louis, Missouri, the riverboat **Huck Finn** is dwarfed by one of the Midwest's most famous landmarks, the soaring stainless steel Gateway Arch designed by the world-renowned architect Eero Saarinen in 1948. Two specially designed capsule-trains, one inside each leg of the arch, carry visitors to a breathtaking observation room 630 feet (192 m) above the ground. At the foot of the left leg is the Old Cathedral and, framed in the center, the beautiful Old Courthouse.

along the river. West of here, great rolling plains colored with oceans of golden grain sweep right across the state north of the Missouri River as far as Kansas City, the state's second city on the border with Kansas. Having grown as a distribution and processing center for the rich farmlands of the region, Kansas City is a dynamic but gracious city offering a pleasant lifestyle enriched with a wide range of cultural attractions, highlighted by the famous Nelson Gallery of Art and the open-air Starlight Theater in lovely Swope Park, also the home of the city's splendid zoo. Dominated by its downtown skyscrapers, the "City of Fountains" also has pleasant redeveloped areas, including many fine shopping centers, such as old Westport Square, the Crown Center complex, and lavish Country Club Plaza, where the buildings are outlined after dark with glittering colored lights. And to speed the impressed traveler on his way, there is the magnificent modern airport northwest of the city.

Up the Missouri River north of Kansas City is the city of St. Joseph, where Jesse James fell victim to young Bob Ford's bullet, and one of several starting points for westbound pioneer wagon trains, as well as for the Pony Express. The most important one, however, was the city of Independence, the home of President Harry S. Truman just east of Kansas City. From here the Missouri flows eastward across the state to join the Mississippi at St. Louis, passing on its way the state capital, Jefferson City, whose huge marble statehouse has become a well-known landmark on its bluff overlooking the river. Farther southwest the attractive city of Springfield stands on the edge of the vast highland region of the Ozark Plateau. Fringed by manmade recreational lakes, among which the Lake of the Ozarks is the largest, this beautiful scenic region of forested hills and valleys abounds in gushing springs, dashing torrents, and fascinating deep caves, such as the renowned Meramac Caverns and the romantic Bridal Cave, a mecca for young lovers.

East of the Ozarks the Mississippi emerges from St. Louis on its way south, flowing by the delightful old town of Sainte Genevieve, which preserves its French traditions as well as many lovely early buildings. Downriver the valley widens into the rich farming country, cotton fields, and oak forests of the Boot Heel region bordering Arkansas, where the atmosphere is reminiscent of America's South.

The Breadbasket of the Nation

Abilene, Ellsworth, Newton, Wichita, Dodge City – a rollcall of raucous, dusty cowtowns whose names were indelibly stamped, one after the other, upon the rugged history of Kansas as the railroads pushed boldly westward across its great prairies over a century ago. For these, with the exception of

127

Wichita, were the railheads from which cattle, brought in from Texas along the fabled Chisholm and Western Trails, were shipped out to feed the growing populations of the east. And trying to keep some semblance of order during trail-end roistering in the saloons and dance halls were legendary lawmen such as Wild Bill Hickok, Wyatt Earp, and Bat Masterson. Those rip-roaring boom days are now gone, but the towns are still there, some with reconstructions of the way they once looked, although they have now turned to other pursuits – Wichita, for example, to aircraft production.

Cattle were also raised in Kansas itself from the earliest days, and still are in large numbers, for the land, particularly in the east, was recognized early on as prime grazing country. In the words of the first governor, the prairies of Kansas seemed to be "an endless succession of rolls, with a smooth green surface, dotted all over with the most beautiful flowers. The soil is of the most rich and fertile character, with no waste land." Cultivation and irrigation converted that soil into a sea of grain and crops, so that, despite occasional droughts and grasshopper plagues, Kansas has become the "Breadbasket of the Nation," harvesting more wheat than any other state as well as producing great quantities of sorghum, corn, and many other crops. And everywhere there are wild prairie animals and, among the carpets of wildflowers, the sunflowers which bestowed the nickname "Sunflower State" on this lovely land.

Dodge City, Kansas, has been a cattle center since the 1870s when the little settlement suddenly grew into the "Cowboy Capital of the World", shipping cattle from Texas out of its stockyards along the new railroad to the East. Today Kansas ranks third in the nation's beef-producing states.

From the bluffs along the Missouri River, into which its east-flowing rivers drain, Kansas extends westward for over 400 miles, its rolling country gradually rising from 700 feet (213 m) in the green fields bordering the great river to over 4,000 feet (1,219 m) in the drier, treeless grasslands of the far west, where Mount Sunflower rises to 4,039 feet (1,231 m) above sea level, the state's highest point. Here and there more hilly terrain and manmade lakes break the monotony of the plains, offering more varied landscapes, as in the low grassy limestone ridges of the Flint Hills in the east, the wooded bluffs and valleys of the northeast, including the deep canyons of the Smoky Hills, and the buttes and mesas of the Gypsum Hills around Medicine Lodge. Standing out dramatically in the flat country surrounding them, there are also fascinating rock features, such as the imposing Castle Rock and Monument Rocks sculptured from chalk in the northwest, and the giant Mushroom Rocks and the round boulders of Rock City carved out of sandstone farther east.

Once crossed by the westward routes of the celebrated Pony Express and the Santa Fe, Smoky Hill and Oregon Trails, Kansas has many places of historic interest, including Forts Larned, Scott, and Leavenworth, and the liberal-minded university town of Lawrence, twice burned down by pro-

Above: The old Bollinger Mill which stands by the covered wooden bridge at Burfordville, Missouri, retains the rural charm of a bygone age.

Left: Once disparagingly referred to as part of the so-called "Great American Desert," Kansas is now one of the leading agricultural states in the nation, producing more wheat than any other. As one over-enthusiastic newspaper reporter wrote in 1889, "Kansas is a slice from the juiciest side of the earth ... mellow with the bloom of an almost perennial harvest."

129

The Homestead National Monument, near Beatrice, Nebraska, marks the site of one of the first claims of free land made in the territory under the terms of the government's Homestead Act of 1862. Here Daniel Freeman set up his simple cabin on a 160-acre plot of virgin land, determined to build a new life for his family on the open plains of the Midwest.

slavery raiders in those bitter struggles over slavery in the 1850s and 1860s when the territory was sadly referred to as "Bleeding Kansas." Happily those days have passed and the people's rivalries are now channeled into sporting contests and more lighthearted pursuits, among which the annual International Pancake Race held at Liberal must be one of the most delightful. Kansans are now proud to declare:

> *We have made the state of Kansas*
> *And today she stands complete –*
> *First in freedom, first in wheat.*

Cornhusker Country

North of Kansas, the Great Plains extend for mile after mile through neighboring Nebraska, the "Cornhusker State," where vast cattle ranches, wheatfields and croplands combine to make this one of America's major farming states. From the high, wooded bluffs lining the Missouri, Nebraska's eastern boundary, the land gradually climbs from an altitude of around 800 feet (245 m) to over 5,000 feet (1,524 m) in the drier hill country and badlands of the far west bordering Wyoming. Countless small streams and creeks, lined with cottonwoods and teeming with fish, trickle down the slopes of this rolling country into the three main rivers, which wind their way eastward to join the Missouri.

In the north, the swift, narrow Niobrara surges down its lovely valley from the beautiful Pine Ridge area, where the Agate Fossil Beds yield up the bones of strange ancient mammals. In the south, the slow Republican River loops briefly into Nebraska from Kansas, its waters now slowed by reservoirs and dams. And between them, stealing the limelight, is the historic Platte River, formed by the union of its two branches. Flowing into Nebraska's high western grasslands from neighboring Wyoming, the North Platte winds lazily by colossal Scotts Bluff and the pine-clad Wildcat Hills before merging with manmade Lake McConaughy, its broad, flat valley providing a natural route to the West for the Union Pacific Railroad, blazed in the 1840s by those brave pioneer families who followed its famous natural landmarks along the old Oregon and Mormon Trails. As one of the poets among them put it:

> *The next we came to was Platte River.*
> *Great sights were there to see.*
> *There was Courthouse Block and Chimney Rock*
> *And, next, Fort Laramie.*

North of here, in the center of the state, is that curious geological phenomenon known as the Sand Hills, a region of rolling grasslands supporting huge herds of cattle and interrupted only by two tracts of pine forest, beneath which the ground acts like a gigantic sponge continuously supplying water to the surface streams and manmade wells.

Downriver from the confluence of its two branches, the Platte wanders eastward along its wide valley, a broad, shallow sheet of rippling water flowing, as one early visitor colorfully described it, "near the top of the ground." The Indians called this flat water the "Nibrathka," from which came the name of the entire territory. Passing through the town of North Platte, where Buffalo Bill Cody established his Scout's Rest Ranch, and on by old Fort Kearney, the river runs on to the city of Grand Island, the location of the superb Stuhr Museum, one of several in this part of Nebraska commemorating pioneer life, for after the 1862 Homestead Act was passed giving grants of free land to settlers in the West, thousands of hardy pioneer folk moved into Nebraska's prairies to stake their claim. Near Beatrice, amid the rich farmlands of the southeast, is the Homestead National Monument, a memorial park to their rugged endeavors.

North of here, the soaring 400-foot (122 m) tower of the ornately decorated State Capitol rises above the pleasant city of Lincoln, a majestic landmark visible for miles over the surrounding farmland. And along the Missouri, some 15 miles north of its meeting-place with the Platte, the state's largest city, Omaha, has grown up, its huge stockyards advertising its importance as a major livestock market. With an atmosphere more like a friendly small town, Omaha is nevertheless big enough to be the most

A towering elevator and mountain of grain outside the state capital, Pierre, are a visible reminder of South Dakota's importance as an agricultural state.

important industrial center of the Great Plains region, culturally sophisticated enough to boast a fine art museum, the Joslyn, as well as productions of opera, ballet, and plays at the Orpheum Theater and other playhouses, and progressive enough to have such fine new shopping centers as Westroads and the delightfully renovated Old Market area, as well as permitting the young residents to run that world-famous institution, Father Flanagan's Boys' Town.

On their way north up the Missouri in 1804, the explorers Lewis and Clark paused awhile in Nebraska's northeastern prairies for talks with the Indians. "Rich, pleasing, and beautiful" was Lewis's verdict on this land – and it still is.

The Land of Infinite Variety

Although more than half its area lies on the rolling Great Plains, South Dakota boasts landscapes of such surprising contrasts that it is often called the "Land of Infinite Variety." The appeal of its natural scenery and wildlife, its heritage of historic sites and its countless places of interest,

The Badlands of South Dakota are a desolate, eerie world of steep ravines, pointed pinnacles, and flat-topped buttes carved by the forces of erosion over millions of years into the pink-layered rocks of the Great Plains. The fossilized bones of all kinds of prehistoric animals are found here in great numbers.

leisure, and entertainment have all combined to make tourism the state's second major industry. Farming is, of course, first, for South Dakota raises great numbers of beef cattle and sheep on its vast ranches and grows huge quantities of corn and other crops on its rich farmlands. The development of the state, although suffering periodic crises, has continued unabated since the Government's 1862 Homestead Act encouraged white farmers to fan out over the virgin prairies and, 12 years later, Colonel George Custer's report that "Gold has been found" set off a rush of prospectors to the Black Hills.

Flowing right across South Dakota's territory from the north to the southeastern corner, the mighty Missouri River has been slowed along its course by the construction of huge dams that have created a series of four long, broad lakes now exploited for recreational purposes. To the west, the rolling grasslands extend into the distance, shared among vast sheep and cattle ranches, tranquil wildlife refuges, and the immense, lonely stretches of territory set aside as reservations for the original Indian inhabitants. Here and there, rugged escarpments, isolated buttes, and steep canyons provide scenic relief in this desolate country, and in the far northwest several tracts of the Custer National Forest stand out like oases of deep green.

Opposite: The colossal heads of four of America's great Presidents have been carved out of the towering granite pinnacles of Mount Rushmore in the Black Hills of South Dakota. This tremendous technical feat was the work of Gutzon Borglum, who began his "Shrine to Democracy" in 1927 at the age of 60.

But the most dramatic scenery of all is condensed into the southwest. Here the wind and rain have sculpted a weird, barren landscape of pink and brown rock formations in the Badlands National Park, a fascinating treasure trove for fossil hunters which Custer called "a part of hell with the fires burned out." And farther west, encircled by lonely Bear Butte and a ring of interesting towns – Spearfish, Sturgis, Rapid City, and Hot Springs – is the gem of all South Dakota's scenic wonders: the beautiful Black Hills, the long-cherished "Paha Sapa" still claimed by the Dakota Indians, better known as the Sioux, who gave North and South Dakota their names. These rugged hills, with their granite spires, green meadows and bubbling streams clothed in the pines and spruce trees of the Black Hills National Forest, contain the most enchanting scenery. Here are lovely Custer State Park, in the shadow of 7,242-foot (2,207 m) Harney Peak; the Black Elk Wilderness Area; and the thrilling underground labyrinths and formations of Wind Cave and Jewel Cave, above which is a paradise grazed by buffalo and teeming with wildlife.

But the best-known and most popular sight in this scenic wonderland is manmade: that tremendous feat of imagination and technical skill known as the Shrine of Democracy, consisting of the colossal sculptured heads of four Presidents – George Washington, Thomas Jefferson, Theodore Roosevelt, and Abraham Lincoln – hewn out of the towering crags of Mount Rushmore. And 17 miles away, at Thunderhead Mountain, there is an equally huge and awesome monument to Crazy Horse, the charismatic Sioux leader who defeated Custer at the Little Bighorn.

Trailriding through the grasslands of the Badlands National Park in South Dakota is an invigorating experience, affording magnificent vistas of some of the wildest country in the Midwest.

Of the many raw gold-mining camps that sprang up in the Black Hills after 1874, the best-known is undoubtedly Deadwood, that rough haunt of fortune-hunters, gamblers, and thieves where Wild Bill Hickok and Calamity Jane lie buried in the town's "Boot Hill." Still working is the renowned Homestake mine in Lead, pronounced "Leed," the biggest gold producer of the entire Western Hemisphere.

In the opposite corner of the state, the rolling glaciated country of the northeastern Coteau des Prairies, or Prairie Hills, is sprinkled with beautiful, forest-fringed lakes used for recreation and sport. And farther south the famous candylike Corn Palace in Mitchell, redecorated each year with corn stalks and grasses, is a constant source of delight and just one of the many fascinating places in this part of the state.

Roughrider Country

"Old Four Eyes" they called him when the bookish young city dude came to shoot buffalo on North Dakota's plains in 1883. He may have been a poor shot, but even when the old Roughrider soldier became President Theodore Roosevelt, he always retained his love for the wide-open country, fresh air, and freedom of the Flickertail State. During the last 100 years, despite the searing hot summers and freezing winters, North Dakota's prairies have been turned into great cattle spreads and oceans of grain, putting the state at the top of the league in the production of rye, barley, flaxseed, the hard red spring wheat used to make bread, and the durum wheat needed for pasta. And beneath its patchwork of fields, the earth has also endowed North Dakota with huge reserves of oil and lignite coal, which are now being exploited at the "Magic City" of Minot in the north-central part of the state, and in the Williston region in the west.

Everywhere there are memories of the old frontier days, with old military forts, Indian reservations, and pioneer relics competing for the visitor's attention with western rodeos and lively ethnic festivals. One of the state's early sites is the frontier village of Bonanzaville at West Fargo, which recalls

The incredible Corn Palace at Mitchell, South Dakota, is the latest in a line of colorful oriental-style structures built by the townsfolk since the 1890s to house their annual harvest exposition. The huge mosaics of corn and grasses that adorn the exterior are changed every year.

the boomtime "bonanza farms" established in the 1870s in the flat, fertile Red River valley along the state's eastern boundary, protected by military posts such as the renowned Fort Abercrombie. Still a rich farming region patterned with lush dairy farms and cropfields, the valley is North Dakota's most heavily populated area, with over 60,000 people living in Fargo, the state's largest city.

West of the valley the rolling plains begin their gradual rise towards the distant southwest, the colorful tapestry of fields dotted with countless small lakes left behind by ancient glaciers. Among them is the mysterious, salty Devils Lake, about which many a strange tale has been told by the Indians

A reconstructed blockhouse at Fort Lincoln, in North Dakota, overlooks the meeting point of the Heart and Missouri rivers just south of the city of Mandan. From here Colonel George Armstrong Custer rode out with the Seventh Cavalry in 1876 to meet his fate at the hands of the Sioux at the battle of the Little Bighorn in neighboring Montana territory.

of the nearby Fort Totten reservation. In the far north, the beautiful and colorful International Peace Garden sits astride the U.S.–Canadian border, a symbol and pledge of peace and harmony between the two nations.

Across the center of the state, the Missouri River sweeps in a great arc from the western boundary with Montana down into South Dakota, its broad, glistening waters now captured in the vast expanse of Lake Sakakawea by the immense Garrison Dam. Downriver the startling white "Skyscraper of the Plains," North Dakota's Capitol, rises like an outsize grain elevator above the rooftops of Bismarck, the state's second largest city. Across the river the city of Mandan has grown beside historic Fort Lincoln, Custer's base before the ill-fated Bighorn campaign, and is now the gateway to the higher "Slope" country of the southwest.

Above the flat plains of the southwestern region, isolated buttes stand out in welcome relief, and meandering streams run along rugged courses. The most spectacular of the valleys is the awesome Badlands area along the Little Missouri River, where steep canyons and gulleys have been carved into the multicolored rock layers to create a bare, rough landscape of buttes, mounds, and cliffs in which, here and there, underground fires burning in the layers of lignite have tinged surrounding rocks with bright red hues. It was into the grasslands among this rugged country that that colorful French nobleman the Marquis de Mores swept with his wife Medora to build up a beef-producing business, and his young neighbor Teddy Roosevelt came to set up two ranches. Of this wild, remote spot, a paradise of wildlife now commemorated in the Theodore Roosevelt National Park, the future conservation-minded twenty-sixth President wrote: "There are few sensations I prefer to that of galloping over these rolling limitless prairies," a sentiment echoed by all who have thrilled to the wide-open spaces of the golden Midwest.

Overleaf: An overlook above the Little Missouri River in North Dakota affords spectacular views of the rugged terrain in the North Unit of the Theodore Roosevelt National Park. It was in this wild country that the future President of the United States established his two ranches in the 1880s.

The Southwest

The Southwest is a region of contrasts. Although essentially a sunny land of wide open spaces, with huge cattle ranches, vast tracts of irrigated farmland, forests and empty deserts, it also contains four of the nation's largest cities: Houston, Dallas, San Antonio, and Phoenix. And while it has a prosperous, modern economy based on massive oil and other mineral deposits, there are a few Indians whose ways of life are much the same as their ancestors' thousands of years ago.

The terrain, which has been carved and molded by rivers, winds, and chemical action, is also varied. Featureless coastal plains in the east contrast with the majestic Rocky Mountains in northern New Mexico, whose peaks soar to more than 13,000 feet (4,000 m) above sea level. And while lush forests and sparkling lakes bring enchantment to some areas, there is much parched, barren territory with shifting sand dunes, scattered cacti and yuccas, and bleak rocky outcrops. The Southwest's dramatic landscapes attract millions of tourists who are rewarded with some of the world's most unforgettable scenic wonders, such as the remarkable subterranean sculptures of the Carlsbad Caverns of New Mexico and the Grand Canyon of Arizona, which the American explorer John Wesley Powell dubbed "the most sublime spectacle on the earth."

The human landscape is also diverse, because the Southwest is a blend of three main elements: the varied cultures of the American Indians; the Spanish-American, including the Mexican, element; and, most recently, the culture of the Anglo-Americans.

Home of the Red Man

Oklahoma, a word meaning "home of the red man" in the Choctaw language, first became part of the United States in 1803 as a result of the Louisiana Purchase. At first it was thought to be valueless, development

The rolling prairies of Oklahoma are important for food production and farmland covers 77 percent of the state. But wind erosion of the soil remains a problem in some areas. This farm is near Bartlesville, in northeastern Oklahoma.

The stockyards and meat-packing plants in Oklahoma City are the largest in the state. They testify to Oklahoma's Western heritage and, even today, cattle ranching is a cornerstone of the economy. In 1980 Oklahoma had 5.5 million cattle.

only beginning when the Government resettled Indians from other areas in Oklahoma. Many tribes were involved in this compulsory transfer of population, but the most significant groups in the 1830s and 1840s were the Five Civilized Tribes from the Southeast, namely the Cherokees, Creeks, Chickasaws, Choctaws, and Seminoles. The tragic "Trail of Tears" that brought the Cherokees to Oklahoma was marked by hunger, exposure, exhaustion, and death. But once there, they showed great pertinacity in taming the virgin territory which they were granted in perpetuity, "as long as grass shall grow and rivers run." Many Indians had white lifestyles – hence the adjective "Civilized" – and some were slave owners. Hence, it was inevitable that the Confederacy should seek their help in the Civil War. Some, like the Choctaws, Chickasaws, and some Cherokees, fought for the South, while others, including Cherokees, Creeks, and Seminoles, served in the Union army. After the War, partly as a reprisal against Indians who had aided the South, the tribal lands were reduced by nearly one-half, and from the late 1880s the Government bought much Indian territory for resettlement by whites who flooded into Oklahoma in their thousands. In 1907 the predominantly white-populated territory became the forty-sixth state of the Union. Today whites and blacks constitute more than 90 percent of the population, but Oklahoma still has more Indians and more tribes than any other state. This is evident in the obvious pride that Oklahomans take in their Western and, specifically, Indian heritage.

The terrain is varied. In the east are four regions that extend into Oklahoma from Arkansas: the Ozark Plateau; the Arkansas River valley east of Muskogee (former capital of the Creek nation); the Ouachita Mountains; and the West Gulf coastal plain in the southeastern Red River region.

As in Arkansas, the Ozarks strongly remind one of the forested plateaus of the southern Appalachians. There are clear blue, manmade lakes set like glistening jewels in wooded hills, sparkling rivers and steep-sided valleys, especially in the rugged Boston Mountains in the south, and lovely foliage displays in the fall. The Ozarks are Cherokee country and contain the former Cherokee capital, Tahlequah, whose former Capitol building now serves as a courthouse. Nearby is Tsa-La-Gi, the Cherokee Heritage Center, which contains reconstructions of an ancient Cherokee village and a late nineteenth-century Rural Museum Village, together with the Cherokee National Museum and an open-air theater. At the theater, visitors can see the impressive musical drama of *The Trail of Tears* which tells the story of the Cherokee nation from 1838 to 1907.

Right: Oklahoma City stands on an oilfield and its Capitol is unique in having an oil well on its grounds. The field began production in 1928 and wells soon spread throughout the city.

Winter wheat is the state's most valuable crop and hay, cotton, sorghum, and peanuts are also important.

The Arkansas River valley is also like its counterpart in Arkansas, containing wooded ridges and some magnificent manmade lakes. Not far from the Arkansas state line is the Spiro Mound State Park, which contains nine pre-Columbian Indian mounds built from about AD 1200 to 1350. They are now being excavated and yielding a fascinating array of grave goods.

South of the Arkansas River valley are the scenic Ouachita Mountains, which are so reminiscent of the ridge and valley regions of the Appalachians. One of the east–west ridges contains the Talimena Skyline Drive, which runs through the Ouachita National Forest. This is the only road in the country that was built specifically because of the superb views it provides.

The West Gulf coastal plain, bordering the Red River in the southeast, also contains a section of the Ouachita National Forest and a popular recreation area around the manmade Lake Texoma. Near this lake's northern shore are Tishomingo, which contains the Chickasaw Council House (the former Chickasaw Capitol), and a reconstruction of Fort Washita, which was built to protect the Civilized Tribes against the Plains Indians.

The central lowlands of Oklahoma cover about three-quarters of the state. This mostly hilly region is broken by escarpments, plains, and two small massifs, the Arbuckle and Wichita Mountains in the south. The state capital, Oklahoma City, which was founded in the land rush of April 1889 and incorporated in 1890, occupies a central location in the lowlands. Built on an oilfield, it has the only Capitol to have an oil well operating on its grounds. Places to visit in this leading financial and industrial center are the Oklahoma Historical Society Building, which contains much Indian material, the Oklahoma Art Center, and the impressive National Cowboy Hall of Fame and Western Heritage Center. Founded by 17 states and opened in 1965, this handsome museum commemorates the pioneers who tamed the West through such exhibits as life-size recreations of Indian and pioneer life, sculptures such as the poignant *The End of the Trail*, and works by great artists, such as George Catlin, Frederic Remington, and Charles M. Russell. These artists are also represented in the Gilcrease Institute of American History and Art in Tulsa, Oklahoma's second largest city northeast of the capital; this Institute also houses a fine collection of Indian artifacts. In addition, the Philbrook Art Center in Tulsa has another major collection of Indian art. More Western art can be seen at Woolaroc Museum, near Bartlesville north of Tulsa. Around this museum, on the former ranch of oilman Frank Philips, are buffalo, longhorn cattle, and other wild animals associated with the Old West. And just northeast of Tulsa, at Claremore, is the Memorial to Oklahoma's favorite son, the humorist Will Rogers.

East of Oklahoma City is the famous Seminole oilfield, while to the south lies the beautiful Chickasaw National Recreation Area. This unspoiled wilderness, with its forests, mineral and fresh springs, sparkling cascades, and low waterfalls, is in the heavily eroded Arbuckle Mountains. West of Oklahoma City is El Reno, standing on the historic Chisholm Trail that runs from south to north through the state, from Waurika to Medford. Southwest of the capital is another remarkable site devoted to Indian culture – Indian City USA at Anadarko. It contains accurate reconstructions of the villages of seven tribes, a museum, and a Hall of Fame. Spectacular ceremonials and dances are features of a week-long festival held in August. Near Anadarko are the rugged Wichita Mountains, which include a lovely wildlife refuge.

The northwestern central lowlands contain many scenic places, including the Glass Mountains, red buttes with strata of white gypsum that sparkle in the sunlight. The colorful Alabaster Caverns (alabaster is a form of gypsum) are the largest of their type in the world. And also worth visits are the Great Salt Plains in the far north, which provided salt for wildlife and pioneers, and the Little Sahara Recreation Area's high sand dunes on the Cimarron River.

Oklahoma's Panhandle, a no-man's-land and outlaw hideout in the late 1880s, belongs to the Great Plains region. In the far west, close to the New Mexico state line, it includes the lava-capped Black Mesa, Oklahoma's highest point at 4,973 feet (1,516 m) above sea level.

Lone Star State

"Brash, overwhelming, hospitable, larger than life," wrote Edna Ferber about Texas in her novel *Giant*, adding that "No visitor, casual though he might be, could fail to feel the almost fierce vitality that rocked the whole vast region." It is true that Texas, although it lost its claim as the largest

Indian City U.S.A., two and a half miles south-east of Anadarko, Oklahoma, has reconstructions of Indian villages and other exhibits that reveal the traditional life and culture of the Southwestern Plains Indians. The Indian guides and other Indians who work on the site are always ready to answer visitors' questions.

The National Cowboy Hall of Fame and Western Heritage Center was opened in Oklahoma City in 1965 in order "to honor the noble men and women who by their self-sacrificing toil and dauntless spirit pioneered that vast and rich empire known as the American West," in the words of Milward Simpson of Wyoming at the dedication ceremonies.

state to Alaska in 1959, might well be a country in its own right. It is more than twice as large as Italy, has nearly as many people as Australia, and its booming economy is the envy of many an independent nation. Between 1836, when it shook off Mexican rule, and 1845, when it became the twenty-eighth state of the Union, Texas was an independent republic.

In the nineteenth century, its economy was based on agriculture, with cotton reigning supreme in the east and the raising of cattle and sheep dominating the western prairies. From 1901, however, the discovery of huge oil reserves transformed the economy, and today Texas is the nation's leading mining state and one of the most important in manufacturing and agriculture. But, despite the Texan "dream of the longhorn steer and the unfenced horizon," as John Steinbeck expressed it in *Travels with Charley* (1962), four out of every five people live in urban areas, including a trio of contrasting cities that are among the most exciting in the country.

The northernmost of its great cities is Dallas, or "Big D" as it is affectionately known. Although founded in 1841 as a trading post, this sophisticated metropolis now shows few signs of its pioneering origins. Instead it is known for its impressive modern architecture, including the concrete and glass City Hall, the huge Market Center complex with its contemporary sculpture, the Hyatt Regency Hotel with its tinted glass exterior, and the Reunion Tower with its lighted, revolving dome. Dallas has elegant stores (such as the original Neiman-Marcus), a major symphony orchestra, a superb Theater Center (designed by Frank Lloyd Wright), museums, universities, and a dignified memorial to President John F. Kennedy. Dallas is the nation's sixth largest city, behind Houston which ranks fifth, but the Dallas–Fort Worth metropolitan area has a population of about three million which is more than that of Houston.

Between Dallas and Fort Worth, a distance of 30 miles, is a major tourist attraction, the 200-acre "Six Flags over Texas" amusement park at Arlington. (The six flags that have flown over Texas are those of Spain, France, Mexico, the Texas Republic, the Confederate States, and the United States.) Fort Worth is a modern city, the state's fourth largest, but its Western heritage is still evident in its stockyards, rodeos, the festivities during the Chisholm Trail Days, and the Log Cabin Village. It has also won a reputation as a cultural center, particularly for its great museums, including the Amon Carter Museum of Western Art with its Remingtons and Russells, the magnificent Kimbell Art Museum designed by the American architect Louis Kahn, and the Fort Worth Art Museum.

Vibrant, noisy Houston, 245 miles southwest of Dallas–Forth Worth, is the state's fastest growing city – its population increased by 830 per day

between 1970 and 1980. A boomtown that has been called the "Klondike of the Sunbelt," its soaring modern edifices, some graceful and some less so, symbolize its dynamism. A great industrial and commercial center, it is also the third busiest American port, being linked to the Gulf of Mexico by the 50-mile-long Houston Ship Channel. Energy and drive are also manifest in its cultural life – the Houston Symphony is one of the nation's greatest, there is grand opera, ballet, museums, and major educational institutions. Attractions for visitors include Astrodomain, which includes the Astrodome, an enormous, roofed, all-purpose stadium, and Astroworld, a "Six Flags" amusement center. Near Houston is the San Jacinto battleground, marked by an impressive 570-foot-high (174 m) Memorial. It was here that General Sam Houston's Texans, shouting the battlecry "Remember the Alamo," destroyed General Antonio Lopez de Santa Anna's Mexican army in April 1836 in a battle that decided the fate of Texas. And southeast of Houston is the Lyndon B. Johnson Manned Spacecraft Center, which played a central role in the space program and made an important contribution to Houston's prosperity.

San Antonio, the nation's tenth largest city located 197 miles west of Houston, is an entrancing mixture of the old and new. The old includes beautiful eighteenth-century Spanish missions, the Spanish Governor's Palace (1749) and La Villita, a charming restoration of the city's oldest buildings. The new is symbolized by the 750-foot-high (229 m) Tower of the Americas of HemisFair Plaza, site of the 1968 World's Fair. But it is that shrine of Texan independence, the Alamo, that draws most visitors. Here William B. Travis, Davy Crockett, Jim Bowie, and 184 others withstood the might of General Santa Anna's 5,000-strong Mexican army for two precious weeks in February–March 1836. San Antonio is a city that gives pleasure to those who

Dallas, Texas, was founded in 1841 as John Neely Bryan's trading post on the upper Trinity River and it was named for one of its early residents in 1843. Modern Dallas does not display its pioneering past; it is now a busy manufacturing, trading, and transportation center, with a rich cultural life.

usually detest urban life. There is much to enjoy and few can resist the lovely Paseo de Rio, a riverwalk on the San Antonio River overhung by cypresses, jasmine, live oaks, and willows. And, held annually in the week of San Jacinto Day (21 April) is the colorful Fiesta San Antonio, the equivalent of *Mardi Gras* in New Orleans.

Despite a common misconception that Texas is flat and featureless, it has varied scenery and many of its landscapes are as beautiful as any in the country. Topographically, there are four main regions: the West Gulf coastal plain; the north-central lowlands; the Great Plains; and the dramatic Basin and Range region in the far west.

The Gulf coast contains many industrial ports and oil and gasfields, but it also boasts magnificent beaches on its long, narrow sand bars that lie offshore beyond placid, shallow lagoons. The longest sand bar, Padre Island, runs south of Corpus Christi, a vacation center, industrial town, and seaport. The Padre Island National Seashore occupies much of the 113-mile-long island. This wilderness of sand dunes and beaches has no human settlements other than the tents of visitors, and here can be found more than 350 species of birds as well as coyotes, ground squirrels, kangaroo rats, and poisonous snakes. Another sand bar, South Padre Island in the far south, is a developed resort outside the protected National Seashore but it, too, has unspoiled areas. Galveston, near Houston, is another major coastal resort, with a ten-mile-long sea wall to protect the shore against high, hurricane-driven waves.

The broad, low-lying West Gulf coastal plain stretches inland between 150 and 350 miles. It is bounded to the west by an escarpment, roughly following a line joining Del Rio near the Mexican border to San Antonio and Austin to Dallas. The northern part of this coastal plain is fertile farmland, dotted with lakes and forests, which locals call Piney Woods. It includes the peaceful Angelina, Davy Crockett, Sabine and Sam Houston National Forests and the Big Thicket National Preserve. Austin, the attractive state capital, stands on the Colorado River, and is distinguished by broad, tree-lined boulevards and many handsome buildings, including the pink granite State Capitol Building (1888), the stately Governor's Mansion (1856), and the French Legation (1840). It also includes the Texas Memorial Museum, the Texas Archives and Library, and the Lyndon Baines Johnson Presidential Library. South of Austin, the climate becomes increasingly tropical and in the lower Rio Grande valley there is a patchwork of farms producing early vegetables, citrus fruits, avocados, and papayas, while the picturesque cities, such as Laredo with its Mexican flavor and Brownsville, the state's southernmost city, are ablaze with bougainvillea and oleander.

Cattle ranching is a major industry in the wide open spaces of Texas. Specially bred for their beef are the Herefords which originally came from the county of Hereford, in England.

The San José Mission near San Antonio, Texas, contains a lovely limestone and tufa church, Indian quarters, a restored mill, and a granary. The "Queen of Missions," it is the finest example of the early missions established in the Southwest by Spain.

The fertile north-central plains extend from the Red River, the northern border with Oklahoma, to the Colorado River above Austin, and the region includes the eastern part of the Texas Panhandle. The area was once the scene of conflict between the U.S. Cavalry and marauding Indians, as evidenced by the old Fort Richardson and Wichita Falls where there once was a large Indian tent village.

The Great Plains sweep in a broad arc down the western side of the Panhandle, through the Pecos River basin to Del Rio on the Rio Grande, and then across towards San Antonio and Austin to the south and east. The Texas Panhandle was once buffalo country; it is now a rich mineral producer and wheat flourishes in its extensive, irrigated farmlands. For superb scenery, there is the colorful canyon country in the Palo Duro Canyon State Park southeast of Amarillo, while the huge Amistad reservoir, near Del Rio in the south, is a leading recreation area. Tourists in that vicinity seldom fail to visit Langtry, the site of Judge Roy Bean's saloon–courtroom. The far southeastern corner of the Great Plains region, north of San Antonio and west of Austin is pleasant hill country where the LBJ National Historical Site near Johnson City is located.

West of the Pecos River the roads snake upwards into the mountains of the Basin and Range region, which contains bare mountains, precipitous canyons, whitewater rapids, and bleak, treeless landscapes covered by buffalo grass, mesquite, and sagebrush. Southwest of the town of Pecos are the superb Davis Mountains and that former outpost of civilization, Fort Davis, which was manned between 1854 and 1891 to prevent Apache and Comanche raids. Today the Fort Davis National Historical Site preserves the 50 stone and adobe buildings that made up the fort. South of Fort Davis, beyond Alpine, is the glorious Big Bend National Park, which encloses more than 700,000 acres of wild mountain terrain rising to more than 7,800 feet (2,377 m), and steep-sided, red sandstone canyons, the most accessible being Boquillas Canyon and the 1,500-foot-deep (457 m) Santa Elena Canyon. These canyons are arid and barren in summer, but they are adorned by wildflower displays in spring, when boating can be dangerous in the swollen torrents that sweep through them. The state's other national park, northwest of Pecos, is the Guadalupe Mountains National Park, which contains Guadalupe Peak, the state's highest point at 8,751 feet (2,667 m) above sea level, and a spectacular, 2,000-foot-high (610 m) escarpment called El Capitan. There are also limestone caves – these mountains are an uplifted portion of an ancient coral reef – and McKitterick Canyon is a wonderland for naturalists, containing, among many things, a species of columbine that is found nowhere else in the world.

The main city in the Basin and Range region is El Paso, the state's fifth largest. El Paso stands on the Rio Grande facing another tourist center, Ciudad Juárez in Mexico. El Paso itself only became American after the Mexican War of 1846–48, when the country's boundaries were pushed south to the Rio Grande. It is now a modern industrial city, but it still bears the imprints of Indian, Mexican, Spanish, and frontier American cultures. In the southeast of the city is Ysleta, the oldest town in Texas which was founded by Spanish Franciscans in 1682. A wonderful view of El Paso is obtained by riding the aerial railway to Ranger Peak which reaches more than 5,600 feet (1,707 m) in the Franklin Mountains which overshadow the city.

*Above left: This open-air theater stands in the glorious setting of the Palo Duro Canyon State Park, southeast of Amarillo in the Texas Panhandle. In summer the theater stages **Texas**, a musical drama of Panhandle history, with a cast of eighty actors, singers, and dancers.*

Land of Enchantment

Legacies of its Indian, Spanish, Mexican, and frontier Western heritage loom large in New Mexico, which did not become part of the United States until 1848 and which did not achieve statehood until 1912. As recently as 50 years ago, most people spoke Spanish and even today an estimated two-fifths of the population are of Spanish origin. Furthermore, many Pueblo Indians and Navajos have preserved ways of life much like their ancestors.

Historical sites, diverse and often majestic scenery, and a sunny climate attract millions of tourists to New Mexico every year. The climate and hence

Above: Hunter's Peak is one of several mountains in the Guadalupe National Park in western Texas. It reaches 8,362 feet (2,549 m) above sea level. This scenic region contains rugged uplands, steep-walled canyons, arid lowlands, and much wildlife including antelope, deer, and quail.

Left: Big Bend National Park, in western Texas, is bordered to the south by the Rio Grande. It contains some precipitous canyons whose walls soar 1,500 feet (457 m) above river level. More than 350 species of birds live in its varied habitats.

149

the vegetation vary greatly according to the altitude and there are places where one can drive through several distinctive natural zones in the space of a few miles. This is because the cooler mountains generally have about 30 inches of rain per year, while the hot, low-lying basins get only about 5 inches. The main altitudinal zones include the Lower Sonoran, or desert zone, which is mostly below 4,500 feet (1,372 m) below sea level; the mostly treeless Upper Sonoran zone, up to 7,500 feet (2,286 m), which supports low bushes, with *piñons* (pines) near its upper limit; the Transition zone, between 7,500 and 9,500 feet (2,286 and 2,896 m), which contains fir and pine forests; the Canadian zone, up to 11,000 feet (3,353m) which is rich in tree species, including ponderosas, spruce, and white and dark Douglas firs; and the Hudsonian (taiga) and Arctic–Alpine zones on the highest peaks. The Lower Sonoran zone covers around 15 percent of the state, the Upper Sonoran about 75 percent, the Transition zone 8 percent, and the rest 2 percent. In addition to altitudinal contrasts, the state is divided into four topographical regions: the Great Plains in the east; the Rocky Mountains in the north center; the Colorado Plateau in the northwest; and the Basin and Range region in the center and southwest. However, within each of these regions, there is much scenic diversity.

The highest parts of the Great Plains are in the northeast, at the foot of the Rocky Mountains. The general level of this plateau region is 5,000 to 7,000 feet (1,524–2,134 m) above sea level, although there are deep canyons, lava-capped mesas, and lofty volcanic cones. One such cone, the Capulin Mountain National Monument, is almost perfectly symmetrical; accessible by road, the rim of its crater offers a splendid view. The flattest part of the Great Plains is a 3,000 to 5,000-foot-high (914–1,524 m) plateau along the border with Texas. This plateau ends in the west in the 500- to 800-foot-high (152–244 m) Mescalero escarpment which overlooks the Pecos valley, parts of which are rugged, although there are rich alluvial plains in the south around Roswell and Carlsbad. Southwest of Carlsbad is the Carlsbad Caverns National Park, where are some of the world's most remarkable limestone caves, including the largest known cavern, the Big Room, which covers 14 acres and is between 80 and 255 feet (24–78 m) high. The Big Room and three miles of trails are electrically lit to enable visitors to admire the majestic natural sculptures of stalactites, stalagmites and waterfalls in stone. Between May and October, there is another awesome spectacle around sunset at Bat Cave when around one million bats soar outwards at a rate of 5,000 a minute.

The state capital, Santa Fe, stands on a high plateau and is a good base for exploring the north-central Rocky Mountains. These include the largely

Right: The El Morro National Monument, southeast of Gallup in New Mexico, includes a sandstone cliff on which early Spanish conquistadores and American pioneers carved their names to record their passing.

Left: Characteristic Pueblo Indian adobe dwellings are common sights in Taos, which stands on a high plateau in the Rocky Mountain region of northern New Mexico. Taos impressed the British writer D. H. Lawrence so much that he bought a ranch nearby. His ashes were brought to the ranch from France, where Lawrence died, by his wife Frieda who is also buried on the ranch.

forested Sangre de Cristo (Blood of Christ) range in the east, named for its blood red ridges, and the rugged, volcanic San Juan and other associated ranges to the west. Santa Fe was founded in 1610 as capital of the Spanish province of New Mexico and it is the nation's oldest seat of government. It has a lovely central Plaza, many fine old buildings, such as the Mission of San Miguel and the Palace of the Governors, museums, art galleries, Pueblo Indian markets, and an impressive open-air opera house. From Santa Fe roads wind up into the mountains through picturesque Indian villages to the impressive Wheeler Peak, the highest point in New Mexico at 13,160 feet (4,011 m) above sea level. North of Santa Fe is Taos, another old and delightful town which, like Santa Fe, contains an artists' colony. One artist, the British writer D. H. Lawrence, was so impressed by the "brilliant proud morning sunshine high up over the deserts of Santa Fe" that he bought a ranch above the town. Near Taos is the Taos Pueblo, an ancient Indian village, and a magnificent gorge carved by the vigorous Rio Grande. Northwest of Santa Fe is Los Alamos, where the first atomic bomb was made. South of here is the Bandelier National Monument, a wilderness area with cave dwellings and houses that date back to AD 1200 to 1580.

The northern part of the Colorado Plateau in the northwest contains many colorful outcrops of sandstones and shales, sagebrush flats, deep canyons and towering mesas. Near Shiprock, the administrative center of the Navajo reservation, is a famous landmark, Shiprock Butte, an ancient volcanic core capped by jagged pinnacles and exposed by erosion, rising 1,400 feet (427 m) above the surrounding plain. East of Shiprock is the fascinating Aztec Ruins National Monument, a large prehistoric Indian village built about AD 1100, while the Chaco National Monument, south of Aztec, was a huge Pueblo Indian center from AD 800 to 1250. The southern part of the Colorado Plateau is generally more rugged. Here are lava-capped mesas, rough lava fields and volcanic cores, such as the massive Mount Taylor, west of Albuquerque. South of Mount Taylor is an extremely spectacular Pueblo Indian village at Acoma, perched on top of a steep-sided, 357-foot-high

The beautiful adobe Santuario de Chimayo, a shrine associated with miraculous healing and known as the Lourdes of the Southwest, is near Espanola, north of Santa Fe, New Mexico.

Right: The Hall of the Giants with its Giant Dome and Twin Domes is in the magical subterranean world of the Carlsbad Caverns National Park in New Mexico. The Caverns are the home of millions of bats and the summer evening bat flights from the caves are among North America's most dramatic spectacles.

(109 m) mesa, that has been inhabited for about 1,000 years.

The Continental Divide winds through the Colorado Plateau into the adjoining Basin and Range region, which covers about one-third of New Mexico. It contains several dozen major mountain ranges that mostly run north–south, between which are deep basins. In the northern part of this region is Albuquerque, the state's largest city, which stands on the Rio Grande in the shadow of the beautiful Sandia Mountain. In the side of this mountain is a cave in which the earliest traces of man in North America, dating back 17,000 to 20,000 years, have been discovered. Albuquerque is a mainly modern city, but it has a handsome Old Town area with a delightful Spanish atmosphere. The Rio Grande flows south from Albuquerque and has several reservoirs along its course. Southwestern New Mexico is thinly populated and contains some pristine forests in its scenic mountains, notably the Gila and Lincoln National Forests. But between the mountains are arid basins, such as the Tularosa basin which includes the White Sands National Monument, the world's largest gypsum dune field. Not far away is the White Sands Missile Range, which is closed to the public, as is Trinity Site, about 30 miles west of Carrizo, where the first atomic bomb was exploded in 1945.

The Grand Canyon State

Arizona achieved statehood only in 1912, the last state to be admitted to the Union except for Alaska and Hawaii. For many years after it had become part of the United States in 1848, it was thought to be remote, valueless, and

This wall painting depicts the Santa Fe Fiesta on the Old Santa Fe Trail. The End of the Santa Fe Trail Marker can be seen in the southeastern corner of the city's pleasant Plaza.

The famous central Plaza of Santa Fe is surrounded by many fascinating buildings that recall New Mexico's Spanish and Indian heritage. This is a detail of an adobe building.

dangerous territory. But irrigation has enabled the farmers to tame the deserts and, recently, industrialization has brought the state much prosperity. Today four-fifths of the people live in attractive, modern urban areas – the largest cities are Phoenix and Tucson – and manufacturing and tourism are the state's leading sources of income. Tourists flood into Arizona to enjoy its sunny climate and recreational facilities and to admire its fantastic natural wonders. Their imaginations are also fired by its rich cultural heritage, evident in magnificent archeological sites, the substantial Indian population, the Spanish-Mexican lifestyles and architecture which are especially marked in the south, and the Old West atmosphere of such places as Prescott and Tombstone.

The Colorado Plateau covers the northern two-fifths of Arizona, except for a strip of land in the northwest, while the Basin and Range region makes up the rest of the state. The Colorado Plateau contains fairly level plateaus that are mostly in the Upper Sonoran zone, broken by deep (Lower Sonoran) canyons, occasional forested mountains, and some amazing desert landscapes with strange and colorful rock formations. The Colorado Plateau terminates in the south in the nearly 200-foot-high (61 m) Mogollon Rim, which extends across the center of the state, passing between Flagstaff and Prescott.

The most famous part of the Colorado Plateau is undoubtedly the northwestern Grand Canyon section, which has given the state its popular name. Much has been written about the Canyon, but nothing can prepare first-time visitors for their initial reaction to this glorious spectacle. First, the Canyon is enormous; the Grand Canyon National Park is more than 200

The Grand Canyon National Park in Arizona is an ever-changing spectacle as light and shade continually play on the rocks, subtly altering their colors and shapes. At the bottom of the canyon is the mighty Colorado River, which was responsible for wearing out this wonder of the world.

miles long, while the Canyon itself is up to 18 miles wide and 1 mile deep. Second, while it descends in a series of steps bordered by sheer cliffs, the inside of the canyon is complicated almost beyond belief by towering rock spires, majestic buttes, volcanic cones, and precipitous side canyons. Third, the canyon is remarkably colorful: above the dark and extremely ancient schists and granites at the very bottom are horizontal layers of red, lavender brown, gray, gray blue, yellow, and creamy white sedimentary rocks formed in primeval seas. These colors constantly change as the sun and clouds cause shifting patterns of light and shade. Imagination is needed to comprehend the origin of this great gash in the Earth's surface. Less than 10 million years ago, the Colorado was flowing sluggishly over a nearly flat plain, but forces beneath the crust have pushed up this plain to form a high plateau. The movement was extremely slow, but it gradually increased the river's gradient, giving it the power to carve out the Grand Canyon. And, because the climate is arid, rain and frost have not worn back the steep canyon walls into the conventional, gently sloping V shape. In the presence of one of Nature's masterpieces, most people agree with Theodore Roosevelt who said in 1903: "Leave it as it is. You cannot improve on it. The ages have been at work on it, and man can only mar it."

The most popular and accessible place from which to view the canyon is the South Rim, which is open all the year round and is approached from Flagstaff. The higher North Rim has magnificent overlooks, but it is usually closed by snow from late October to early May. Trips into the canyon can be made on horses or mules or on foot, though visitors worried by heights should be warned that some of the narrow, twisting trails are edged by sheer cliff faces. Intrepid boaters can also accept the challenge of the Colorado River's rapids, but the flow is now controlled at the Glen Canyon Dam near the Utah state line. Behind the dam is a national recreation area of great beauty.

Flagstaff, the largest city on the Colorado Plateau, is an attractive tourist center. Between it and the Grand Canyon are the volcanic San Francisco Mountains that include the state's highest point, Humphrey's Peak at 12,633 feet (3,851 m) above sea level, and the Arizona Snow Bowl, a popular winter sports area. The Colorado Plateau is largely Indian territory. There are large reservations, and the Navajo, Walnut Canyon, and Wupatki National Monuments with their fascinating ruins testify to past glories. Flagstaff's fine Museum of Northern Arizona tells the story of the state's Indian tribes.

The Plateau has other natural wonders besides the Grand Canyon. Near Flagstaff is the volcanic Sunset Crater National Monument where astronauts prepared for moon walks, and south of Flagstaff, near Clarkdale, is the

Opposite: This view looking down into the Grand Canyon was taken from Yaki Point on the South Rim. The South Rim, which is open throughout the year and is the most popular side of the canyon, is usually approached along a scenic road from Flagstaff.

Above: The Little Painted Desert, near Winslow, Arizona, is an arid, gullied landscape distinguished by the colorful banded rock layers that are exposed on the surface.

Left: Prickly pear and giant Saguaro cacti flourish in the Saguaro National Monument near Tucson in southern Arizona. The area is particularly glorious in spring when the Saguaro cactus, the state flower, is in bloom.

colorful Oak Creek Canyon which rivals the Grand Canyon in splendor. East of Flagstaff, near Winslow, is Meteor Crater, created in a huge explosion caused when a large meteorite crashed to earth. Farther east, beyond Holbrook, is the Petrified Forest National Park, a marvelous desert area littered with fossilized logs. The Painted Desert here and along the Little Colorado River is badland territory with colorful, glowing rock strata. To the northeast is the Canyon de Chelly National Monument, which contains superb desert canyons and ancient Indian cliff dwellings, while farther north near the Utah state line are the brooding Western landscapes of red buttes; mesas, towers, and pillars in Monument Valley which were immortalized by the great American director John Ford in nine of his movies, including *Stagecoach* (1939).

The northern and southeastern parts of the Basin and Range region below the Mogollon Rim contain rugged mountain ranges and basins that run generally northwest–southeast. The most marked basins (in the Lower Sonoran zone) are in the south-center and southwest, where the average rainfall plummets to four inches a year.

The Basin and Range region contains Arizona's largest cities – Phoenix, Tucson, Mesa, Tempe, Glendale, and Scottsdale – all of which, except for Tucson, form a prosperous cluster of manufacturing and resort centers. The development of this region has been made possible by the construction of reservoirs on the Salt and Verde rivers in the forested mountains to the north and east. Phoenix, the nation's eleventh largest city, has a striking modern skyline but it also takes pride in its heritage. It contains the Heard Museum

Cholla cacti east of Phoenix, Arizona, grow near the Superstition Mountains. These mountains contain the Lost Dutchman Gold Mine, a rich mine reputedly discovered in the nineteenth century. An old prospector, Jacob Waltz, left inconsistent clues concerning its location, and it has been sought ever since by modern treasure hunters.

which houses a wonderful collection of Indian artifacts, the Pueblo Grande Museum and Indian Ruins on the site of an ancient Hohokam settlement, and the Phoenix Art Museum which has works by modern Southwestern artists. North of Phoenix is some lovely mountain country stretching up to the edge of the Colorado Plateau, not far from which is Prescott, whose Old West atmosphere recalls the days when the first territorial legislature met there. To the east of Prescott are the thirteenth-century Sinagua structures in the Montezuma Castle National Monument, and the Tuzigoot National Monument which contains a Pueblo hilltop citadel dating from about AD 1400.

Tucson is the main center of the southeast; an attractive city, founded in 1776, it retains a Spanish flavor. It stands on the edge of a desert and at the foot of the pine-forested Santa Catalina Mountains, where winter sports are becoming increasingly popular. Near Tucson, however, is the Arizona–Sonora Desert Museum and the Saguaro National Monument, where huge saguaro cacti reach heights of 50 feet (15 m) or more, and to the west, on

the Mexican border, is the impressive Organ Pipe Cactus National Monument. Southeast of Tucson is Tombstone which recalls the tough Old West. Here are the Bird Cage Theater, the O.K. Corral where the Earps and Doc Holliday fought the Clantons, the Tombstone Courthouse State Historical Park, the Wells Fargo Museum, and the Boot Hill cemetery. Southeast of Tombstone is Douglas, which is not far from Skeleton Canyon where Geronimo surrendered in 1886. North of Douglas is the Chiricahua National Monument which is wild Apache country, while the scenic Coronado Trail, followed by the Spanish *conquistador* in 1540 in his vain quest for treasure, runs between Clifton and Springerville to the north.

The mighty Colorado River forms almost all of Arizona's western border with Nevada and it contains dams, reservoirs, and resorts along its course. The leading resort area, the Lake Mead National Recreation Area around the towering Hoover Dam, is shared with Nevada. In the far southwest, the historic Yuma district, a former desert, has been made green by the life-giving waters of the Colorado River.

Overleaf: The Montezuma Castle National Monument, south of Flagstaff, is a well-preserved ancient Sinagua Indian cliff dwelling. The apartments built in the face of a limestone cliff were accessible only by ladder. Nearby is Montezuma's Well, a limestone sinkhole from which the Indians got water to irrigate their crops.

The Western Mountain States

Rising above the vast expanses of the Great Plains west of the Mississippi River, the high mountain ranges of the Rockies run north to south across America, from Canada to the state of New Mexico, their crests forming the Continental Divide that separate the eastward- and westward- flowing rivers that drain them. Thrown up by great upheavals in the earth's crust millions of years ago, the Rockies are a geologically young mountain system, and volcanic activity is still taking place in such places as the lava beds of Idaho, the geysers of Wyoming's Yellowstone National Park, and the hot springs of Colorado.

The highest part of the Rockies is in Colorado, where over 50 peaks soar above 14,000 feet (4,267 m) above sea level. But throughout the range, lofty, snow-capped summits can be seen piercing the deep blue skies above breathtaking landscapes of rock-strewn crags, blinding glaciers, crystal lakes, and flower-speckled alpine meadows while, lower down the slopes, myriads of sparkling streams cascade through forests of deep green pine and spruce. Here grizzlies, elk, bighorn sheep, and many other kinds of wild animals wander through the remoter areas, providing a moment of excitement for the passing visitor. On the lowest slopes and in the valleys, cattle ranches, farms and mining enterprises add to the mosaic of color across the landscape.

West of the Rockies, in the vast, dry plateau region of southern Idaho, Utah, and western Colorado, the rivers have gouged colossal, steep-sided canyons and the forces of erosion have carved incredible landscapes of strange rock shapes, nowhere more spectacularly than in the amazing cluster of national parks and monuments of Utah.

For thousands of years this rugged mountain wilderness was known only to the Indians, whose way of life was perfectly attuned to the natural conditions. Even the first white fur-trappers, who wandered through the area from the late eighteenth century, posed no threat, but after the Louisiana Purchase of 1803 brought the western boundary of the United States as far as the Rocky Mountains, there came a time of sudden and drastic change. Explorers such as Meriwether Lewis and William Clark, Zebulon Pike, and others paved the way for an inrush of settlers from the east who believed that it was their "manifest destiny" to take possession of the whole continent as far as the Pacific. The epic story of their bitter struggle with the Indians – a classic clash of cultures – has been the subject of countless books and movies, and the main participants in the saga, particularly Colonel George Custer, the focus of considerable controversy.

As the white communities in the Mountain West grew up into statehood, the dispossessed Indians found themselves corraled into reservations; the old buffalo grazing lands were transformed into cattle spreads and sheep territory; and the high prairies that many people considered to be no better than barren desert were cajoled into producing oceans of amber wheat and barley. The mountains themselves gave up their treasures of minerals – gold, silver, and lead among them – to a burgeoning mining industry that survives today. Now tourism is also important, and every year thousands of people visit the region to marvel at its scenic wonders, to take part in such vacation activities as skiing, hiking, whitewater rafting, and fishing, to sample

Against the dark backcloth of the Rocky Mountains, the imposing City and County Building stands out in gleaming white splendor in the Civic Center complex at Denver, Colorado. Every Christmastime the building is spectacularly illuminated with lovely colored lights.

Western life on a dude ranch or thrill to the excitement of a real rodeo or a ceremonial Indian dance.

Top of the Nation

Looked at on a map the rectangular state of Colorado appears neatly parceled into a western half made up of the high Rocky Mountains and an eastern half extending into America's vast central plains. Yet this superficial geographical tidiness disguises an amazing variety of such stunning natural landscapes that a clearly impressed Theodore Roosevelt was moved to remark that "the scenery bankrupts the English language." For, apart from the eastern plains, this is a spectacularly rugged land of towering mountains, high flat-topped mesas and buttes, deep rock-cut ravines and canyons, swirling torrents and rapids, and even hot springs. The mosaic of color is further patterned with myriads of blue lakes and expanses of deep green pine and spruce forests, enlivened in the fall when the aspen trees turn to bright gold.

To those early pioneer families crossing the continent on their hazardous trek to find prosperity in California, Colorado's "Shining Mountains" of glistening rock were an impenetrable barrier which they were forced to bypass to the north and south. With more than 50 peaks over 14,000 feet (4,267 m) high and an average overall elevation of 6,800 (2,073 m) Colorado can justifiably claim to be the "Top of the Nation." Winding north to south across the state the Continental Divide watershed separates Colorado's westward-flowing rivers – principally the Colorado itself – from those entering the Mississippi and the Gulf of Mexico – the South Platte, Arkansas, and Rio Grande.

Lying at a height above 3,000 feet (915 m) above sea level, the dry, rolling plains of eastern Colorado, once judged by the explorer Zebulon Pike to be "incapable of cultivation" and sure to become "as celebrated as the sandy deserts of Africa," were once the grazing lands of vast herds of buffalo and an important hunting ground for Arapaho, Cheyenne, and other Indian tribes. But the coming of the white man brought drastic changes, and after the appalling massacre of Cheyenne families by the Army at Sand Creek in 1864 and the bloody battle at Beecher's Island four years later, Indian control of the high plains was irrevocably broken. Today this territory has been transformed over much of its area into a rich wheat- and crop-growing and cattle-raising region watered by manmade reservoirs and irrigation systems, the skyline broken here and there by huge grain elevators or

Nestling among the rugged granite peaks of southwestern Colorado's San Juan Mountains, the old mining town of Silverton got its name, according to tradition, when one early miner boasted "We may not have gold here, but we have silver by the ton."

windmill water pumps. In the north, nature has made one particularly dramatic contribution to the generally uniform landscape: a group of immense rock outcrops known as the Pawnee Buttes, which rise starkly out of the surrounding plain. In the far south, on the Arkansas River, is the restored Bent's Fort, one of the Old West's best-known landmarks, a trading post visited by travelers on the Santa Fe Trail and frequented by the area's fur-trappers and hunters, among them that renowned adventurer Kit Carson.

Along the foot of the Front Range of the Rockies, which rises abruptly from the plains, Colorado's three largest cities have grown up: Denver, the state capital, accurately labeled the "Mile High City"; the resort center of Colorado Springs; and the steel-making city of Pueblo. Denver grew out of a cluster of huts thrown up in 1858, when an over-rated discovery of gold in the area prompted a rush of fortune-hunters to flock in from the east to the cry: "Pike's Peak or bust!" Today the city's metroplitan area has over 1½ million inhabitants, more than half of Colorado's entire population. Despite its semi-arid climate, Denver has well-watered residential districts, beautiful green parks, and tree-lined parkways that make it a particularly alluring city. Of especial interest among its many attractions are the U.S. Mint, the mansion of the "Unsinkable" heiress Molly Brown and the state Capitol building, whose gold-veneered dome stands out in the downtown area against a distant backcloth of green mountain slopes and snowy peaks. A reminder of Denver's importance in the West's cattle business, the colorful National Western Stock Show and Rodeo attracts thousands of visitors to the city every January.

The hills and valleys of the Rockies behind Denver are scattered with old mining communities, some of them now ghost towns, that sprang up after

Rolling waves of sand up to 600 feet (183 m) high in Colorado's Great Sand Dunes National Monument echo the ever-changing forms of the billowing clouds that often form above the nearby Sangre de Cristo Mountains.

another, richer, gold strike was made at Central City in 1859. Their very names rich with historic associations, such colorful towns as Crystal City, Aspen, Dillon, Leadville, and that "300-million-dollar cow pasture," Cripple Creek, have retained much of the Victorian flavor of those tough pioneer days and can boast many fine examples of nineteenth-century architecture. But today miners and prospectors have been superseded by vacationers, for this is Colorado's major resort area, the location of such celebrated winter sports centers as Vail and of the popular hot-water spa town of Glenwood Springs.

Stunning natural scenery of all kinds characterizes Colorado's Rocky Mountains, where, in the words of an observer of 1865, "everything is sidehill and edgewise one way or the other." Among the most fascinating and beautiful features are the poetically named rock peaks of the Maroon Bells near Aspen, which reflect in the crystal-clear waters of a nearby lake; the strange Great Sand Dunes National Monument northeast of Alamosa; the lofty snow-capped summit of Pike's Peak with its extensive panoramas west of Colorado Springs; and, nearby, the curious Garden of the Gods, with its huge upright rocks believed by Ute Indians to be giant invaders turned to stone by an angry deity. But the gem of Colorado's scenic wonders is the Rocky Mountain National Park, a paradise of soaring mountain peaks, forests, lakes, valleys, and glaciers that provides an unspoiled refuge for a rich diversity of wildlife in the north of the state.

Gradually descending into Utah in the northwestern corner of Colorado is a vast, dry plateau region into which the Green and Yampa rivers have carved deep canyons, a harsh landscape that offered remote hideaways for

Right: A magnificent vista of the deep, winding canyon carved by the Green River in northwestern Colorado can be enjoyed from an overlook on the Harpers Corner Trail. A journey down the river in 1869 inspired John Wesley Powell to recall: "Its walls and cliffs, its peaks and crags, its amphitheaters and alcoves tell a story of grandeur that I hear yet."

Beautiful Alta Lake, near Telluride in the mountains of southwestern Colorado, lies beside one of the many jeep trails that provide access to this rugged part of the state.

such Wild West outlaws as Butch Cassidy and the Wild Bunch. But this is also grazing country, where sheep and cattle far outnumber human inhabitants and where sheepherders and cowboys still follow the traditional ways of their calling. In the crumbling rocks of this rugged territory, the fossilized remains of prehistoric dinosaurs are still being uncovered in the area designated as the Dinosaur National Monument. Farther south, the Colorado River and its tributary the Gunnison surge through snaking ravines across spectacular mesa country, the Gunnison's 55-mile-long, half-mile-deep Black Canyon northeast of Montrose offering one of the most awesome experiences in the area. Downriver at Grand Junction, the Colorado National Monument encloses a strange wonderland of eroded rock formations, and nearby the famous huge balancing stone known as Miracle Rock seems ready to topple at the push of a finger.

In Colorado's southwestern region, the Rio Grande and other southward-flowing rivers have helped to shape a land of beautiful mountains and valleys in which the jagged granite peaks of the San Juan Mountains rival the massive volcanic plugs of the Four Corners area in the extreme southwest corner of the state as the most interesting scenic wonders. In the Mesa Verde National Park, the mysterious, abandoned Pueblo Indian settlement nestling snugly beneath overhanging cliffs provides evidence that the area was inhabited many centuries ago. But it was not until more recent times that the vast mineral wealth of these southern mountains was tapped, leading to the sudden growth of raw mining towns such as Creede, whose booming prosperity attracted for a time such colorful Old West characters as Calamity Jane, Sheriff Bat Masterson, and Bob Ford, the youthful assassin of the legendary Jesse James.

Opposite: The lifegiving waters of the Rio Grande create a beautiful canvas of green and yellow vegetation in the San Juan Mountains of southern Colorado.

The impressive ruins of ancient dwellings built by Pueblo Indians centuries ago nestle beneath immense cliffs in the Mesa Verde National Park, southwestern Colorado. For reasons not fully known, the Indians had abandoned the settlement by the early fourteenth century.

The Land of Rainbow Canyons

When, one day in 1875, that down-to-earth cattleman Ebenezer Bryce looked down on the plunging multicolored canyons and towering rock buttes along Utah's Virgin River and uttered those unforgettable words: "Well, it's a hell of a place to lose a cow," he might well have been referring to the whole of that incredible state. For the breathtaking panorama in the southwest of the state at which he gazed, now better known as Zion National Park, is but one of the countless geological wonders fashioned by nature in this part of America's Mountain West. Here, much of the immense upland plateau lying to the west of Colorado's Rocky Mountains has been sliced into vast mesas of multicolored rocks by the canyons carved out by the Colorado, Green, and other rivers, and sculpted by the rain, wind, sun, and frost into fantastic rock arches, Gothic spires and pinnacles, and an array of astonishing shapes that tempt the imagination to create a strange world peopled by giants and goblins. Elsewhere there are vast salt-pans that disappear into the shimmering distance and sand-dune deserts that roll like petrified inland oceans. Yet, at the same time, Utah is also a land of lofty snow-capped mountains, green alpine meadows, immense forests, and cool blue lakes.

In the northwestern corner of the state there is an immense flat expanse of desert sometimes used for attempts on the land speed record and once covered by the shallow waters of historic Lake Bonneville, now shrunk to its present size as the Great Salt Lake. On tasting its briny water one day in the winter of 1824, the young fur-trapper Jim Bridger cried out with astonishment: "Hell, we're on the shores of the Pacific!" Faulty though his geography undoubtedly was, the trails that he and mountain men like him blazed through this territory were soon followed by others, and by the 1840s a route to the Far West had been opened up along the California Trail across the north of the state. In 1847, the ailing Brigham Young halted the great westward trek of the Mormon pioneers on the shores of the Great Salt Lake with that awesomely simple utterance: "This is the place." Then, in 1869, came another major event in Utah's history: In that year a final golden spike was driven into the soil of northern Utah west of Brigham City to link up the two sections of America's transcontinental railroad. Since those early days, northern Utah has become the most populous part of the state.

The gray granite Temple built by the Mormons in Salt Lake City, Utah, took forty years to complete after the foundations were laid in 1853. Dominating Temple Square in the center of the city, this six-spired building, together with the nearby Tabernacle, forms the symbolic heart of the Church of Jesus Christ of Latter-day Saints.

With over 175,000 inhabitants, Salt Lake City is Utah's largest city and its capital. Laid out by Brigham Young, its patchwork of broad, tree-lined avenues spreads out across the flat Salt Lake Valley. At the heart of the city is Temple Square, the spiritual center of the Mormons, or Church of Jesus Christ of Latter-day Saints, a ten-acre site dominated by the grey, six-spired Temple, the Tabernacle containing a particularly fine organ, and the Assembly Hall. North of the city the heavily populated lakeside counties of Davis, Weber, and Box Elder are also a rich farming region producing a bountiful harvest of fruit. Here, too, horses and rodeos are high in the popularity stakes.

In this part of Utah, the morning sun rises over the lovely forested mountains of the Wasatch Range, which provide excellent hunting, fishing, and skiing country, its valleys of lush green pastures supporting a flourishing local dairy industry known for its cheeses. Silently presiding over these comparatively recent human activities, the gnarled Jardine Juniper growing in the scenic splendor of Logan Canyon is claimed to be over 3,500 years old, although not as ancient as glorious blue Bear Lake, a paradise for water sportsmen on the Idaho line perhaps seen at its most beautiful from the breathtaking overlook at Bear Lake Summit.

Much farther south, amid the lovely green mountain scenery east of Orem and the freshwater Utah Lake, the delightful Heber Creeper steam train offers travelers continuously changing vistas over the surrounding country as it winds along the lush Heber Valley and Provo Canyon to the beautiful Bridal Veil Falls. Here, the landscape is crowned by lofty, snow-capped

Big Spring Canyon overlook affords an awesome panorama of the rugged terrain in Canyonlands National Park, Utah. The largest national park in the state, Canyonlands contains nearly half a million acres of fantastic landscapes around the confluence of the Green and Colorado rivers.

Mount Timpanogos, which soars to 11,957 (3,644 m) above sea level, and below the ground the three limestone caverns of Timpanogos Cave National Monument have been cleverly illuminated to create a glistening fairyland of delicate coral-like rock formations.

South of this area a series of high, forested plateaus, forming Utah's central backbone, run down to the Arizona state line. To the east, the wild and lofty Uinta Mountains turn away at right angles to the Wasatch Range – the only mountain chain to run in an east-west direction in the entire West – and accompany the Wyoming state line as far as the Green River in Utah's extreme northeast corner. In this vast mountain wilderness, enclosed in the solitude of the Wasatch and Ashley National Forests, Utah's highest peaks rise above 13,000 feet (3,962 m), topped by majestic King's Peak at 13,528 feet (4,123 m) above sea level.

Where the Green River enters Utah from Wyoming, beautiful Flaming Gorge reservoir, now a National Recreation Area, has been created by damming the river's canyon at Dutch John, and a spectacular view of the 91-mile-long lake can be obtained from Red Canyon Overlook far above the winding blue water. Below the dam, the river plunges down rapids in a surge of white water through the Dinosaur National Monument, which lies partly in Colorado and where the fossilized bones of prehistoric beasts are still being excavated from the rocks. Lifelike replicas of these awesome creatures are displayed at the fascinating Dinosaur Gardens at nearby Vernal. More recent inhabitants of Utah, the Ute Indians, occupy vast tracts of territory in the Uintah and Ouray Reservations set aside for them in this corner of the state. Beautiful painted pictograms and carved petroglyphs left on rock faces by their ancestors can be seen at various sites all over Utah.

Standing higher than a seven-story building, the celebrated Delicate Arch rises starkly above the surrounding rocks in southeastern Utah's Arches National Park.

Left: Multicolored pinnacles of weather-worn rock pierce the clear blue skies of southern Utah in Bryce Canyon National Park, inviting the imagination to create a fantastic cityscape of strange towering buildings lining the edge of the canyon.

From here the Green River flows on southwards through a dry scenic wonderland of indescribable beauty between the Colorado border and Utah's central plateau backbone. In the San Rafael Desert region to the west, that curious geological phenomenon known as Goblin Valley seems to come alive with fantastic rock shapes that are easily transformed by the imagination into elves, gnomes, and dwarves. And where the Green River meets the Colorado, the breathtaking Canyonlands National Park opens up a staggering variety of landscapes with deep ravines and gigantic rock pinnacles. Not far away, an unforgettable view over the Colorado's winding red canyon can be enjoyed from Dead Horse Point State Park before going on to Moab and to Arches National Park. Here, as the name implies, the forces of erosion have sculpted a whole collection of immense arches and bridges out of the living rock, the most impressive including Landscape Arch and the amazing free-standing Delicate Arch, irreverently labeled the "Schoolmarm's Britches" by local cowhands. Similar formations can be seen in Capitol Reef National Park with its multicolored rock cliffs and sheer-walled canyons on the edge of the high forested plateau region to the west, and in the Natural Bridges and Rainbow Bridge National Monuments farther down the Colorado. Before crossing into Arizona, the Colorado's surging

Colossal rock monoliths soar above the barren landscape in Monument Valley south of the San Juan River in southeastern Utah. A classic setting for many Western movies, the valley lies in the Navajo Tribal Park, which stretches into neighboring Arizona.

Above: Scuttling clouds mottle the green landscape with shadows in the Wind River Indian Reservation, the home of Arapaho and Shoshone Indians in western Wyoming. Livestock ranching and the exploitation of underground oil and natural gas resources are the major source of income for the reservation.

waters, now joined by the San Juan River, come to a halt in the deep blue stillness of Lake Powell, an outstanding recreation area created by a dam just inside Arizona and bordering the vast Navajo Indian Reservation.

The photogenic southwestern region of Utah, a favorite location for film-makers, is scattered with ghost towns such as Grafton, Frisco, and Silver Reef which are relics of long-past silver-mining days. But the main attraction of the area remains the rugged scenery, for this is the location of incredible Bryce Canyon, not a canyon at all and much better described by its old Indian name, "red rocks standing like men in a bowl," although it is named today for old Ebenezer. And of course there is Zion, that "land of rainbow canyons"...

The Cowboy State

> *Yipi ti ye, get along little dogies,*
> *It's your misfortune and none of my own.*
> *Yipi ti ye, get along little dogies,*
> *You know Wyoming will be your new home.*

The smell of leather, the scent of sage, the bellowing of complaining cattle in the dust-laden air – a taste of ranching in the wide open spaces of the Big Country, Wyoming. The old cowboy song recalls those tough pioneering days a century ago when great spreads were being established by the cattle barons across Wyoming's vast grasslands and herds of longhorns were being brought in along the well-worn trails from Texas to stock them. Often referred to as the "Cowboy State," Wyoming was recognized early on as profitable grazing country, even though the climate is dry and the winters bleak. Great herds of buffalo once roamed over the Great Plains that extend into the eastern part of the state, the hunting grounds of Sioux, Arapaho, Cheyenne, and other Indians, which they fiercely defended against white American encroachment under such charismatic leaders as Sitting Bull and Red Cloud.

West of the Great Plains, the craggy, high peaks of Wyoming's Rocky Mountains are a magnificent spectacle, towering into the sky to heights of over 13,000 feet (3,962 m) above sea level. In Wyoming, the various ranges are widely separated by immense rolling plateaus, or basins, at elevations between 4,500 and 7,500 feet (1,372–2,286 m), on which the short, tough grass gradually gives way to sagebrush and scrub in the driest areas. Rivers

Left: Defying attack by sun, wind, and frost, the weather-beaten "Lone Fir Tree" perches triumphantly, if precariously, on dry sandstone rocks in the serenity of Zion National Park, southwestern Utah. The oldest of Utah's national parks, Zion was named by the Mormons, as were many of its natural features.

The awesome Devils Tower is a celebrated landmark soaring 1,280 feet (390 m) above the Belle Fourche River in northeastern Wyoming. Consisting of a pillar of fluted rock columns, the tower was formed by the cooling of molten volcanic rock.

flow through these basins in all directions on either side of the Continental Divide, the North Platte and Sweetwater offering a comparatively easy route through the Rockies for the early pioneers struggling westward to their destinies – or death – along the Oregon and California Trails.

Northeastern Wyoming is rich cattle and sheep country enclosing the Thunder Basin National Grassland and, on the edge of South Dakota's Black Hills, the Black Hills National Forest. Rising starkly out of the surrounding landscape, the gigantic volcanic stump known as Devils Tower rises dramatically 865 feet (264 m) above the huge pine-covered mound at its base, an awesome sight whose chilling eeriness at night made it an ideal location for the science fiction movie *Close Encounters of the Third Kind*. West of here, in the foothills of the Bighorn Mountains beyond the Powder River, is the site of the notorious Fetterman massacre perpetrated by the Sioux under Crazy Horse in 1866, and not far away, near Buffalo, an astonishing shoot-out at the TA Ranch between enraged local citizens and mercenaries hired by the cattle barons had to be stopped by the U.S. Cavalry in the scandalous Johnson County War of 1892. This ranching country scenario was vividly immortalized in Owen Wister's classic western *The Virginian*.

The ranch owners' plush headquarters was far away in Cheyenne, a tough frontier town in the southeastern grasslands which sprang up when the Union Pacific Railroad reached the area in 1867. It was once nicknamed "Hell-on-Wheels" because of the rip-roaring celebrations of the cowboys whooping it up after a successful drive with their valuable herds along the Goodnight–Loving or Western Trails from Texas. The city is now a more peaceful place as the capital of the state, although every year the lively "Frontier Days" carnival commemorates those early Old West times.

Fifty miles west of Cheyenne, the university town of Laramie, also with a wild and woolly past, lies on the plain beyond the beautiful Laramie Mountains, which rise over 10,000 feet (3,050 m) above the encircling

Medicine Bow National Forest. Farther north is its namesake, Fort Laramie, another reminder of pioneer days, which was founded as a fur-trading post on the North Platte River in 1834. Now partly restored, the fort was also used as a military base where several peace treaties were negotiated with the Indians. Upriver, along the route taken by the Oregon, California, and Mormon Trails, is the oil center of Casper, Wyoming's second city, and farther southwest the isolated landmark named Independence Rock rises to 193 feet (59 m) above the flat surrounding country and is inscribed with the names of thousands of early pioneers. Their trails slowly climbed westward up the Sweetwater River north of the wide open spaces of the arid Great Divide Basin, then over the gentle slopes of South Pass before descending into the harsh rocky valley of the south-flowing Green River. Near the coal-mining and sheep-rearing town of Rock Springs, the river enters the lovely Flaming Gorge reservoir on the border with Utah. But its long journey begins much farther north, beyond the little resort center and cattle town of Pinedale, where it emerges from its source in the towering granite Wind River Range, Wyoming's highest mountains, where Gannett Peak rises to 13,804 feet (4,207 m) above sea level.

On the other side of these mountains a vast stretch of territory has been set aside for the Wind River Indian Reservation, occupied mostly by Arapaho and Shoshone. On a bend in the Wind River nearby, the uranium-mining town of Riverton sits amid irrigated farming country, beneath which are vast underground deposits of oil and natural gas. North of here the river

South Pass City, in western Wyoming, was founded in 1867 near the route of the old Oregon Trail after gold was discovered along the Sweetwater River. After a few years, however, the gold deposits ran out, and today the once-thriving community is a derelict ghost town.

Overleaf: Named for the lovely Shoshone Indian wife of an early fur-trapper, Jenny Lake, in northwestern Wyoming, mirrors the craggy peaks of Grand Teton and Mount Owen in its ice-cold, still waters. This beautiful section of Wyoming is enclosed in the scenic grandeur of the Grand Teton National Park.

has sliced a spectacular 2,000-foot (610 m) canyon between the Owl Creek and Bridger Mountains, before rushing on through Thermopolis, where the famous hot springs gush from the ground in a particularly attractive part of the Bighorn Basin. Changing its name to the Bighorn, the river then runs northward through irrigated farming country into the magnificent Bighorn Canyon on the Montana state line. On the western edge of this vast basin is the old frontier town of Cody, founded by Buffalo Bill, which is packed with mementoes of the colorful Old West showman.

The exceptionally beautiful Wapiti Valley road west of Cody winds through the huge Shoshone National Forest and the mountain country of the lofty Absaroka Range into the most spectacular scenery in all Wyoming. In this northwestern part of the state the Grand Teton National Park encloses a landscape of staggering ruggedness, dotted with gleaming glaciers and ice-cold lakes, in which the wild, jagged peaks of the Teton Range – the eroded eastern edge of a gigantic uplifted block of land – rise abruptly and dramatically above the beautiful flat stretch of the Snake River valley known as Jackson Hole. The valley teems with wildlife and has become a popular all-season vacation area with three internationally famous ski slopes.

Adjoining the park on the north side is the nation's number one national park – Yellowstone – once nicknamed "Colter's Hell" because of the astonishing descriptions brought back by its first white visitor, that doughty explorer John Colter. In this incredible mountain wilderness, filled with wild animals, the earth's primal forces can be experienced at first hand, for this is an awesome land of gushing hot springs, strangely colorful mineral pools,

Bison stand out sharply against the glaring winter snow at Black Sand Basin in Yellowstone National Park, Wyoming. Steam rising from the ground betrays the awesome thermal energy pent up below the ground, ready to burst forth in the many geysers dotted throughout the park.

and bubbling mudflats, where the air is filled with sulfurous fumes, steam hisses out of deep crevasses and jets of scalding water erupt into the sky. Of the many geysers in the park, the most visited is Old Faithful, which reliably shoots a tremendous spout of hot water up to 170 feet (52 m) into the air roughly every hour. Many of the park's wonders can be visited along the famous Grand Loop drive, which also takes in the huge, beautiful Yellowstone Lake and the spectacular, winding Grand Canyon and thundering falls on the Yellowstone River as it plunges on its way north into neighboring Montana.

Killed by the toxic effects of minerals in the water, dead trees stand bleakly in the strangely colored Opalescent Pool at Black Sand Basin in Yellowstone National Park, Wyoming. The park encloses countless hot pools tinted with various colors depending on the minerals they contain, the temperature of the water, and the tiny plant life that is able to survive in such apparently inhospitable conditions.

Left: The coral-like Minerva Terrace of the Mammoth Hot Springs in Yellowstone National Park, Wyoming, has been built up from limestone dissolved in hot water deep underground and deposited on the surface.

From the edge of a sheer 700-foot (213-m) drop to the floor of the Yellowstone River's Grand Canyon, the overlook at Artist Point, in Wyoming's Yellowstone National Park, offers a breathtaking view of the spectacular Lower Falls upriver. Here the water plunges 308 feet (94 m), twice the height of Niagara Falls, over the yellow rocks which give both the river and the park their name.

Big Sky Country

In the far north of the Mountain West, on Canada's border, the vast territory of Montana, America's fourth largest state, has been endowed with superb rugged scenery of outstanding beauty. Its western part rises up into the tingling cool air of the high forested ranges and green valleys of the Rockies bordering Idaho, while to the east the rolling prairies of the High Plains, crossed by the eastward-flowing Missouri and Yellowstone rivers, extend beyond the horizon into the neighboring Dakotas.

It was along the wide waters of the Missouri that Meriwether Lewis and William Clark, the first explorers to pass through this remote region, sailed on their historic journey to the Pacific from 1804 to 1806. For many years, fur-trappers opened up trails through the area, but it was the discovery of gold in the Rockies that brought in droves of settlers along the celebrated Bozeman Trail after 1862, despite the dangers of passing through Indian grazing lands. Clashes with the Indians were inevitable, but none so shattering as the massacre of Colonel George Custer's Seventh Cavalry by Crazy Horse's Sioux and Cheyenne warriors at the Little Bighorn in 1876. The Indian victory, however, was shortlived, and the following year Chief Joseph's Nez Percé tribe was forced to surrender in northern Montana after its unsuccessful bid for freedom in Canada. From then on, sod-busters, homesteaders, miners, and a motley collection of hopeful settlers, both good and bad, flocked in from the east, as the defeated Indians were herded into reservations, of which Montana today has seven.

Much of the state's eastern plains region is now covered with sprawling cattle ranches and farmland that yields enormous harvests of wheat, barley, and other valuable crops. There are also large areas of badlands, as well as extensive wilderness areas and wildlife refuges in beautiful, unspoiled country. Several of these refuges are located around the 1,600-mile shoreline of Fort Peck Lake, a huge reservoir created by damming the Missouri. Along the route upriver taken from here by Lewis and Clark is the landmark known as Citadel Rock, and some 65 miles beyond, the old trading post and military base of Fort Benton, which played a major role in opening up the West from 1860 to 1887. Farther on, where the Missouri has cascaded over spectacular falls, the aptly named industrial city of Great Falls grew up, and it was here that the cowboy artist Charlie Russell painted his famous pictures of life in the Old West. Not far from the city, an impressive sight can be enjoyed at Giant Springs, where 338 million gallons of sparkling water gush from the ground every day.

In the southern part of Montana's plains region, the state's largest city, Billings, stands conveniently close to several places of interest including the Custer Battlefield National Monument in the Crow Indian Reservation; Pompey's Pillar, a 150-foot (46 m) sandstone block on which Clark carved his name; Pictograph Cave, containing centuries-old Indian paintings; and the magnificent Bighorn Canyon, with its towering, craggy cliffs over the lake far below.

Farther west the Yellowstone River cuts its way through Montana's highest mountains, a rugged forested region crowned by Granite Peak, at 12,799 feet (3,901 m) the state's highest mountain. One of the most impressive sights in this vast wilderness area is the Natural Bridge State Monument south of Big Timber, where the Boulder River plunges through a deep chasm and over high falls, especially dramatic in spring. South of here is Wyoming's incomparable Yellowstone National Park, which can be entered through three gates in Montana. One of these is approached along the Beartooth Highway, which passes through breathtaking scenery on the way from Billings.

From the Yellowstone area, the Rockies run right across western Montana in a northwesterly direction into Canada, the mountains and forests containing an infinite number of beautiful landscapes and vistas. In the rugged country around the old copper town of Butte, now a major industrial

center, are two special atractions: the delightful recreation area of Lost Creek Canyon, with its soaring cliffs and 50-foot (15 m) falls, and the fascinatingly beautiful Lewis and Clark Caverns. Some miles east of here, at Three Forks, the mighty Missouri is born at the confluence of the Jefferson, Madison, and Gallatin rivers.

Reminders of the wild gold rush days over a century ago abound in the mountains of southwestern Montana, where the mining town of Bannack, now abandoned, became the state's oldest town and first territorial capital. The discovery of gold here in 1862 was soon followed by even richer strikes in Alder Gulch to the east, where the boom towns of Virginia City and Nevada City sprang up and attracted thousands of prospectors and fortune hunters. Among them, of course, were a certain number of disreputable characters, the most notorious being Henry Plummer, the leader of a gang of

The small year-round resort and recreation area of Big Sky offers a wide range of facilities for visitors to the Rocky Mountains of southwestern Montana. The village stands in flower-strewn pastures among the peaks of the Madison Range, where Lone Mountain soars to 11,166 feet (3,403 m).

outlaws (ironically nicknamed the "Innocents") who cleverly managed to get himself elected sheriff at Bannack before being hanged for his crimes by the celebrated Montana Vigilantes. Virginia City and its sister Nevada City have since been restored, and a flavor of those rip-roaring boomtown days can still be gained by a walk through their streets.

During those same years, at a spot that became known as Last Chance Gulch, some unlucky miners made a last despairing dig to find gold – and struck it rich. The site was soon swallowed up in the prosperous mining town that sprang up there and is now the Main Street of Helena, Montana's state capital.

Despite the invasion of gold-hungry humans, a rich diversity of wild animals and birds still abounds in Montana's rugged mountains. In the Flathead Indian Reservation north of Missoula, hundreds of bison, deer, and other animals graze in peace on the spacious grasslands of the National Bison Range. Protection is also given to a wide range of animals on Wildhorse Island in Flathead Lake, a large and beautiful stretch of water with especially delightful scenery along the eastern shore bordering the Mission Range. But the most impressive of all Montana's natural wonders are contained in lofty Glacier National Park on the border with Canada, an unequaled scenic panoramaland of high snowy peaks, sheer rock faces, awesome glaciers, dark blue lakes, bubbling icy torrents, and dark green forests crossed by the spectacular Going-to-the-Sun Highway.

Right: Distant peaks glowing in the sunlight contrast with dark rain clouds gathering over Kintla Lake in the breathtaking scenery of Glacier National Park, northwestern Montana.

Below: Lonely marker stones in the open grasslands of southeastern Montana indicate the spot by the Little Bighorn River where Colonel George Armstrong Custer and his Seventh Cavalry were surrounded and killed by Sioux and Cheyenne warriors led by Crazy Horse in 1876. The site has been designated the Custer Battlefield National Monument.

Left: Montana's vast grasslands in the eastern three-fifths of the state provide rich grazing country for the great numbers of cattle which are the state's biggest agricultural product.

A spectacular vista over the awesome Bighorn Canyon in southeastern Montana can be gained from the lofty Devil Canyon overlook. The 71-mile-long lake has been created by damming the Bighorn River near Fort Smith to the north.

As well as rugged mountains and churning rivers, Idaho has immense tracts of fertile farmland, irrigated by the waters of the mighty Snake River, where great quantities of grain and other crops are produced.

Wild Landscapes and Rivers

When space scientists wanted to give American astronauts an idea of the kind of terrain they would find when they landed on the moon, they could think of no better place to take them than to Idaho's incredible Craters of the Moon National Monument west of Idaho Falls, a stark, broken landscape of black lava and cinder pierced with huge, jagged peaks, all spewed out long ago during tremendous volcanic upheavals along a deep fissure in the earth's crust. Idaho's image as an impassable, remote land of unbearable harshness peopled by fierce Indian tribes took a long time to die, and even Abraham Lincoln had a tough time finding a governor willing to go there. Lying west of Montana in the high mountain ranges of the Rockies, Idaho does indeed have vast wilderness areas, clothed in thick forests and cut by deep canyons and racing torrents, yet there are also broad river plains with rich farming country, and today visitors arrive in their thousands to enjoy its scenic wonders and such leisure activities as skiing, fishing, backpacking, and many more.

The first white faces to appear in the territory, however, had a much more commercial purpose in mind. They were those intrepid fur-trappers and mountain men who wandered through the wilderness and, like Lewis and Clark in 1805, prepared the way for that flood of settlers who were to battle their way along the Oregon Trail from the 1840s. A strike of gold near Orofino in Idaho's northern panhandle in 1860, followed by another in the Boise area, brought an inrush of prospectors, and soon the mining of gold, silver, lead, and other minerals became a major industry, which it still is. Here and there ghost towns such as Bonanza, Placerville, and Silver City remain as reminders of those tough pioneer days. One of the major mining centers was the northern Coeur d'Alene area, where Noah Kellogg struck it rich, so he said, from a lode found by his donkey. Today the town of Kellogg is still the center of a rich silver- and lead-mining district surrounded by beautiful natural scenery. Nearby, at Cataldo, is the lovely Mission of the Sacred Heart, the oldest building in Idaho and affectionately known as "The Old Mission."

Of particular appeal in this part of the state is the flat, fertile valley of the Kootenai River, not far from those gems of fresh water, Lakes Priest, Pend Oreille and Coeur d'Alene, a fisherman's paradise in superb forested country. Unforgettably enchanting are the changing views of beautiful Lake Coeur d'Alene from surrounding overlooks on the scenic drive along the east shore, and not far south a lush green garden of forests, lakes, and cliffs can be enjoyed in Heyburn State Park.

Draining the forested mountains of central Idaho, the various forks of the Clearwater and Salmon rivers surge along in whitewater torrents on their way to join the majestic Snake River to the east, an especially spectacular course through rock-strewn rapids being taken by the Salmon's turbulent Middle Fork, the so-called "River of No Return." Above this wild, rugged area Borah Peak, Idaho's highest mountain, soars to a height of 12,662 feet (3,859 m) above sea level some miles east of the razor-sharp Sawtooth Mountains, the craggy silhouette of which bites into the sky like the jaw of some gigantic fossil monster. A sun-filled valley on the southern edge of these mountains shelters one of America's major all-season resorts, the renowned Sun Valley, where long-lasting powder permits superb skiing until late in the spring. Farther east, the Craters of the Moon National Monument marks the beginning of the extensive volcanic lava beds, riddled with caves and pierced by hot springs, which spread over the broad, fertile plain of the Snake River in southeastern Idaho.

The river enters this part of the state from its source in neighboring Wyoming and below the industrial city of Idaho Falls takes a long south-looping course right across southern Idaho to the Oregon state line, forming a natural route through the West's high mountain barrier followed by the famed Oregon Trail. Halted here and there by great dams, the river is harnessed to irrigate the farming country along its banks, where a varied harvest of vegetables and crops, including the famous Idaho potatoes, is produced. Elsewhere its waters surge through deep canyons or cascade over falls, and scattered throughout the country bordering its banks are countless places of interest and scenic beauty, only a few of which can be mentioned here.

Some of the best powder in all America brings winter sports enthusiasts from far and wide to the ski slopes of Dollar and Baldy mountains at Idaho's famous Sun Valley resort. Nearby is the old mining town of Ketchum, where Ernest Hemingway took up residence in his last years.

The internationally renowned ski resort of Sun Valley offers many pleasures other than skiing, including a lively and varied social life when the sun disappears over the mountains.

Just north of the industrial and railroading center of Pocatello is Fort Hall, once a post on the Oregon Trail and now headquarters of the Fort Hall Indian Reservation, where colorful ceremonies are a major annual attraction. Across the Snake, west of the city, there are several interesting natural features, including the Crystal Ice Cave, with its formations of ice, not stone, and farther west the Shoshone Indian Ice Caves, which curiously maintain a permanently constant temperature around freezing point. Some miles south, another subterranean wonder, Mammoth Cave, stretches like a tube for a mile through multicolored lava, and across the Snake River in the far south of the state, a 25-square-mile area of granite known as the City of Rocks has been worn into strange shapes resembling a city skyline. Scratched on the rock faces are initials and messages left by early west-bound pioneers, for at this point travelers following the Oregon Trail separated from those turning southwestward along the California Trail.

Along the rivers, too, there are scenic attractions. Just below the rich agricultural center of Twin Falls, the Snake plunges 212 feet (65 m) over the immense Shoshone Falls, a 1,000-feet-wide (305 m) cauldron even larger than Niagara. At Devil's Creek gorge stands Balanced Rock, a delicately poised 40-foot (12 m) mushroom of stone, and farther west the Bruneau River has carved a magnificent canyon 2,000 feet (610 m) deep and over 60 miles long, but narrow enough in places to throw a stone across.

In the fertile crop-growing and stock-rearing country where the Snake River turns north is Boise, Idaho's capital and largest city, which has a particularly impressive Capitol building conceived in the classical style and constructed in warm-colored sandstone. North of the city the Snake makes its last and most dramatic spectacle as it rushes through the breathtaking Hell's Canyon, a gash nearly 8,000 feet (2,458 m) deep along the Oregon state line, before turning west into Washington at the riverport of Lewiston.

The West

Beyond the Rocky Mountain states, the vast expanse of territory frequently referred to as the Far West takes in the varied landscapes of Washington, Oregon, Nevada, and California, among which Nevada stands alone without a shoreline along the Pacific Ocean. Behind the scenic magnificence of the rugged coastline, which mellows to long sandy beaches only in Southern California, the region is crossed from north to south by a series of thickly forested mountain ranges – the Coast Ranges followed by the higher, snow-clad Cascades and the Sierra Nevada – between which are immensely long and flat valleys intensively exploited for farming. Producing enormous quantities of fruit and vegetables, Oregon's Willamette Valley and California's vast Central Valley are blessed with some of the world's richest soils.

East of the high mountain ranges, all four states also encompass areas of land stretching over vast distances across the high interior plateaus comprising the Great Basin and the Columbia Plateau, a naturally arid region which almost completely encloses Nevada. Denied the rain-soaked westerly winds blowing in from the sea by the soaring barrier of the Cascade Range and the Sierra Nevada, this sun-seared land is also marked by the scars of huge volcanic lava flows and cinder cones thrown up by the awesome subterranean forces which also erupt from time to time through the volcanic peaks of the Cascade Range where, in recent years, Washington's Mount St. Helens has provided a terrifying reminder of their devastating power. Similar power lies pent up in that geological phenomenon called the San Andreas Fault, a sideways-slipping, gigantic crack between two of the immense plates that make up the earth's crust. Occasionally movement along the fault produces earthquakes of colossal intensity, such as that which destroyed San Francisco in 1906. Yet despite this, the West is a region of unparalleled beauty, a land of dramatic contrasts ranging from arid desert where only cacti can survive to rain-drenched forests of gigantic redwoods and sequoias, from sun-baked valleys dropping 200 feet (60 m) below sea level to towering mountain peaks wrapped in permanent snow, from silent, unspoiled wildernesses to the bustling, noisy streets of the great cities.

The appeal of the West goes back centuries, to the days when the Spaniards came here to look for gold and set up their colony, when British fur-trappers roamed around the wild mountains of Washington and Oregon, and when Russian ships trading in animal pelts plied off the coast around California's Fort Ross. Americans trickled into the region in the early years of the nineteenth century, the numbers becoming a flood from the late 1840s, when dramatic events overtook the entire West. In 1846 Washington and Oregon were finally wrested from British control; two years later, California and Nevada became American territory at the end of the Mexican-American War and gold was discovered in California's Sierra. Tales of Eldorado and the Promised Land filled the Oregon and California Trails for over 20 years with optimistic travelers determined to make good. Others came by sea, and years later the stragglers arrived in the comparative comfort of a railroad car. But out of their struggles in the extremes of the West the land was finally won and prosperity blossomed. The staggering beauty of the contrasting landscapes that make up this golden part of America is utterly breathtaking, an experience that remains in the memory long after a visit.

Evergreen Country

"Vancouver! Vancouver! This is it . . .!" As a watching geologist stood aghast, shouting into his radio transmitter, the bulging cone of Washington state's Mount St. Helens suddenly burst with a cataclysmic explosion of such force that it knocked 1,400 feet (427 m) of rock off the summit and hurled a billowing cloud of ash over 75,000 feet (22,860 m) into the sky. Over 500 times more devastating than the Hiroshima atomic bomb, the blast of hot gas and steam threw out a deluge of scalding mud and catapulting rocks over the beautiful forested slopes of the surrounding countryside, permanently scarring its face. The staggering events of 18 May 1980, in which 65 people died, hit the world's headlines and focused international attention on that deceptively tranquil and lovely part of America's far northwest.

Now cut down to a height of 8,300 feet (2,530 m), Mount St. Helens is one of several towering snow-capped volcanoes which, when seen from the air, seem to float above the haze and clouds covering Washington's Cascade Mountains, a magnificent range of thickly forested and snow-wrapped peaks that stretch right across the state from north to south like a rolling dark green wave splashed with white foam about to break over the land to the east. From the eternal color of these mountains has come Washington's nickname, the "Evergreen State." On either side there are two distinct climatic zones; the rainier, milder west, tempered by winds from the Pacific Ocean, and, belying the state's nickname, the drier, even semi-arid, east, with its more extreme temperatures influenced by the high Rocky Mountains. The resulting variety in its vegetation and landscapes makes Washington one of the most scenically beautiful in all America.

Once part of the vast Oregon Country that extended north into Canada, Washington was the subject of dispute with the British for many years before finally being won by the United States in 1846 and named for the first President on its separation from Oregon in 1853. During those early days Lewis and Clark had sailed down the Columbia River to an ecstatic sight of the Pacific Ocean that prompted Lewis to make his historic exclamation: "Ocean in view! O, the joy!" They were followed by others, among them that intrepid wanderer Jedediah Smith and John Charles Fremont, accompanied by Kit Carson, and then came those sturdy pioneer families on

Right: The majestic snow-capped peak of Mount Rainier in Washington soars above embracing wisps of cloud and the thick forests that cloak its lower slopes. Standing separately from the main range of the Cascades, the dormant volcano is enclosed in its own superb national park.

Glistening snow patches and myriads of wild flowers transform the high forested Cascade Mountains of Washington into an enchanting spectacle of color.

the last leg of their long epic journey to the West along the fabled Oregon Trail during the 1840s and 1850s.

In all these journeys, the 1,234-mile-long Columbia River provided an accessible, if terrifying, route through the mountains to the sea. Rising far to the north in Canada's Rockies, it enters northeastern Washington through the pine-forested ridges of the Okanogan Mountains, its waters soon broadening into the placid expanse of Franklin D. Roosevelt Lake, a snaking manmade reservoir and recreation area created by the immense Grand Coulee Dam downriver. The lake marks the northern edge of the vast Columbia Basin, a naturally arid plateau between 500 and 2,000 feet (152– 610 m) above sea level surrounded by mountains, where the terrain is marked by great stretches of bare lava called scablands and huge dry canyons known as coulees, which were carved by torrents from melting glaciers thousands of years ago. In more recent times however, irrigation has made the land here useful for farming, and rolling fields of grain crops and vegetables now cover much of the region, with the country along the Palouse River in the southeast transformed into a treeless, undulating ocean of wheat. And in the many broad river valleys running down the eastern slopes of the Cascade Range to join the Columbia River on its long, curving journey south, there are now cattle ranches, fruit orchards, and vineyards; from the Wenatchee and Yakima valleys, in particular, come the delicious apples for which Washington is famous. The main city of this region, the agricultural processing center of Spokane, lies in the far east of the state on the edge of the Rockies. Boasting several fine parks overlooking the Spokane River and its pretty falls, Washington's second city underwent some

Small sailing boats abound in the maze of channels and islands that make up Puget Sound, where Gig Harbor affords a tranquil haven across Colvos Passage from the bustling deep-water port of Tacoma.

renovation for the 1974 World's Fair, and has a fine shopping area in the downtown central plaza as well as many historic buildings.

About 60 miles south of the city the rugged Snake River winds along its scenic course westward from the Idaho border to meet the mile-wide Columbia River near the Tri-Cities of Pasco, Richland, and Kennewick. In this southeastern corner of the state, the forested slopes of the Blue Mountains alternate with irrigated valleys patterned with cropfields and cattle pastures, and just outside the town of Walla Walla are the ruins of the Whitman Mission National Historic Site, where Dr. Marcus Whitman, his wife and several others were killed by Indians in 1847. Below the Tri-Cities the Columbia River bends sharply westward to run along the Oregon state line through several big dams, cutting through the mountains of the Cascade Range in a wide, rugged gorge, where beautiful waterfalls plunge over the high, forested cliffs on either bank. It then flows on by the historic city of Vancouver, once the end of the Oregon Trail opposite the city of Portland, Oregon, before entering the sea in a broad estuary south of the Willapa Hills.

North of the Columbia River Gorge, the Cascade Range strides north across the state, offering beautiful and varied panoramas of thick undulating forests, snow-capped peaks, glaciers and lakes, crashing torrents alive with fish, and remote wilderness areas that are home for bears, elk, deer, and other wild animals. Above the general level of the mountains tower the snow-covered cones of several lofty, dormant volcanoes, among which 14,410-foot (4,392 m) Mount Rainier stands majestically aloof in its own national park, a magnificent sleeping giant visible for miles around, and

Evening sunshine tints the towering futuristic Space Needle in downtown Seattle, framed by the sculptural outline of "Changing Form" on Queen Anne Hill. A legacy of the 1962 World's Fair, the well-known landmark stands among the cultural and entertainment facilities in the 74-acre Seattle Center.

Sculpted by the hand of nature, an old dead tree trunk stands beside the still waters of lovely Lake Quinault on the forested western slopes of Washington's Olympic Mountains. This beautiful, remote part of the Olympic Peninsula, facing the Pacific Ocean, is among the wettest places in America, receiving around 85 inches (2.16 m) of rain a year.

awesome Mount St. Helens to the south provides dramatic evidence of the awesome forces of nature pent up deep below ground. Glistening amid the forested mountains of the north, Ross Lake and Lake Chelan are two particularly attractive, long, winding stretches of water which are popular national recreation areas. Nearby is the soaring peak of Mount Baker, which rises to 10,778 feet (3,285 m) to the west of the remote scenic paradise of the North Cascades National Park, the wild alpine beauty of which, seen in its jagged peaks and plunging canyons, its blinding glaciers and ice-cold streams, and its clear blue lakes, can only be described in superlatives.

On the timber-clad western slopes of the Cascades, sparkling streams and rivers, rich in salmon, tumble down, often through broad valleys, or to the huge farming plain that runs across the state from Puget Sound south to the Oregon border. At times shrouded in thick, rain-bearing clouds, at others blurred by blue haze, the mountains are an ever-present backcloth of dark green topped with snow-white behind the colorful tapestry of cropfields, dairy farms, and flower-bulb nurseries that covers much of this lush region. They are visible too from the bustling manufacturing cities of Seattle, Tacoma, and Everett that line the eastern shore of Puget Sound and make this region the most heavily populated part of the state.

Although the state capital, Olympia, is not far away, Seattle is by far the largest of these urban centers with around half a million people. Founded as a timber port back in 1852, the city took off as a boisterous boom town on the route to the gold camps of Alaska's Klondike in the late 1880s, before turning to manufacturing, especially for the airplane and aerospace industries centered around Boeing. Conscious of their history, Seattle's citizens have preserved and protected as much as they can of their architectural legacy, such old downtown places as Pike Place Market and Pioneer Square, where the city began, with the old brick buildings now buzzing with jazz clubs, boutiques, and restaurants. Nonetheless, bold new ventures have not been outlawed, and the World's Fair of 1962 left behind a wealth of newer buildings in the Seattle Center to enrich the city culturally: the Opera

The longest river of America's Northwest, the Columbia flows majestically through the state of Washington from Canada's Rockies to the Pacific Ocean. In places its waters are halted by huge dams which provide irrigation water for surrounding farmland.

House, Playhouse, and Pacific Scientific Center are just three of these, all placed in a park setting in the shadow of the towering 607-foot (185 m) steel Space Needle, which provides magnificent panoramas over the city and beyond. Reminders that Seattle is the "Gateway to the Orient" abound in the International District, where a host of fine restaurants serve superb Japanese and Chinese cuisine.

Across the maze of inlets and islands of Puget Sound to the west, the broad Olympic Peninsula points north across the Strait of Juan de Fuca at the forested cluster of the San Juan Islands and at Canada's Vancouver Island. Behind its shoreline, dotted with fishing ports, oyster farms, sawmills, and farmland, the land rises up thickly forested slopes into the rugged and remote wildernesses of the Olympic Mountains, where several high peaks wrapped in glaciers climb above 7,000 feet (2,134 m) in the breathtaking Olympic National Park, a silent, undisturbed refuge for elk, deer, bears, and a rich variety of birds. On the mild, rain-drenched western slopes facing the Pacific Ocean, the wettest spot in continental America, there are thick, eerie jungles of trees draped with moss, and below them huge ferns and fungi that seem to belong to another world. And along the rugged headlands, islands, and beaches of the Pacific coast, countless sea birds and seals feed on the bountiful seafood available in the waters just offshore.

Sea mist blanketing the sun often creates an eerie atmosphere along the Strait of Juan de Fuca between Washington's Olympic Peninsula and Canada's Vancouver Island.

The Pacific Wonderland

Around 1830 a Bostonian schoolmaster named Hall Jackson Kelly, an enthusiastic promoter of American settlement in the northwestern territories then disputed with Britain, declared that if Oregon were "improved and embellished" by white pioneer families it would become the "loveliest and most envied country on earth." A century and a half later, most Oregonians would claim that it has. Since Lewis and Clark explored the region in the winter of 1805/1806 and the first white settlers arrived some 30 years later after long sea voyages round the Horn or overland journeys along the fabled

Oregon Trail, the state has been transformed into the nation's leading lumber producer and a prosperous farming region growing vast quantities of wheat, orchard fruits, grapes, and vegetables, while at the same time preserving the outstandingly beautiful natural scenery that has inspired people to call it the "Pacific Wonderland." Lying to the south of its ruggedly attractive neighbor Washington, Oregon has similar geographical regions and climatic features. Bathed by rain-bearing winds from the Pacific Ocean, the western slopes of its mountain ranges are covered with deep forests dominated by Douglas fir, while to the east, basking under dry, sunny skies, open pine forests descend to the wheatfields and ranches bordering the desert country of the vast interior Columbia Plateau region.

As proof of their pride in this beautiful land, Oregonians have set aside the entire 400-mile length of their spectacular Pacific coastline as an unspoiled parkland for the "free and uninterrupted use" of everyone. Between the town of Astoria, Oregon's first permanent settlement, at the northern end of the coast, and the fishing port of Brookings, near the California state line, Highway 101 passes through a series of state parks and waysides offering breathtaking vistas of dramatic rocky headlands, sheer rugged cliffs, craggy offshore islets such as the celebrated Haystack Rock, and sandy beaches, pounded by white-capped surf and populated by sea lions, otters, and a multitude of screaming sea birds. Picturesque little fishing villages, where Oregon's renowned Dungeness crabs, clams, salmon, and other fish are landed, alternate with superb recreational resorts, among the finest of which are those along the "Twenty Miracle Miles" south of Lincoln City. And between the charming port of Florence, with its colorful rhododendrons and its famous sea lion cave, and the Coos Bay area, there is a spectacular 42-mile stretch of rolling sand dunes, designated a national recreation area and backed by large fish-filled lakes.

Behind this overwhelming scenic coastline, the land climbs up the forested slopes of the Coast Ranges, a line of low mountains rarely rising above 3,000 feet (914 m) above sea level. Through the southern section, the Umpqua and Rogue rivers have cut magnificent gorges and valleys on their way to the ocean from their sources in the higher mountains inland. On the Umpqua, surrounded by thick forests, is the lumbering town of Roseburg, famous for its nearby vineyards and its wild animal park. Farther south, the town of Grants Pass is the starting point for an exciting whitewater trip through an awesome canyon along the rushing Rogue River, and upstream one of the Rogue's tributaries flows through the fruit-picking town of Medford, seen at its best in the spring when the surrounding pear orchards become a sea of white blossom. Not far away is the restored old mining town of

Sandy beaches stretch for miles along Oregon's magnificent Pacific coastline, where the ocean surf has shaped a series of superb panoramas visible from Highway 101.

*The wreck of the **Peter Iredale** rests like the skeleton of a dead sea monster on the Pacific shore near Astoria, Oregon, a visible reminder that this beautiful coast can also be treacherous.*

Jacksonville, and farther south, enclosed in the forested Siskiyou Mountains, the little town of Ashland, with its celebrated Shakespearean theater built in the English Elizabethan style. The rugged mountains of this area also contain the Oregon Caves National Monument, a series of impressive underground chambers once called by a visiting poet the "Marble Halls of Oregon." Another favorite spot for visitors lies to the east, the lumbering and farming city of Klamath Falls, which offers sporting and recreational facilities amid beautiful forest and lake country abounding in wild animals and birds.

Extending northward from this mountainous southwestern region, the magnificent Cascade Range crosses the state to the Columbia River Gorge and on into Washington, a powerful backbone of snow-capped peaks towering over their covering of forests and their tranquil blue lakes to heights above 10,000 (3,048 m). Thousands of people drive up the roads through the beautiful forested valleys and over the high passes between these peaks to gaze at the magnificent panoramas at every turn. In the southern part of the range is one of America's most celebrated natural wonders, Crater Lake, whose brilliant blue water fills the collapsed six-mile-wide cone of an ancient volcano to a staggering depth of nearly 2,000 feet (610 m). Around the awesome 20-mile rim there are breathtaking views of its two mysterious islands, one poetically named Phantom Ship and the other Wizard Island, a newer tree-clad cone which rises from the water like some strange bristling monster of the deep.

Farther north, in a beautiful setting of alpine lakes and forests, is the much-photographed cluster of 10,000-foot (3,048 m) peaks known as the Three Sisters, attended by their aptly named Husband, who bows deferentially nearby to a mere 7,520 feet (2,292 m) above sea level. Then comes superb Mount Jefferson and, beyond, the magnificent spectacle of lofty Mount Hood, whose snow-white head rises through the clouds to 11,235 feet (3,424 m), the state's highest peak and a popular skiing area just south of the Columbia River Gorge, that tremendous gash through the Cascades on the Washington state line. From the top of the cliffs lining the gorge, beautiful wispy waterfalls such as the spectacular Multnomah Falls plunge hundreds of feet into the forested carpet bordering the river below, and superb panoramas can be enjoyed from vantage spots such as Crown Point.

Below the gorge, where the Willamette River flows into the Columbia from the south, the attractive seaport of Portland has grown up, a clean, graceful city that deserved its listing as first choice in a nationwide quality-of-life survey a few years ago. From high points in Pittock Acres Park, lovely Washington Park or the extinct volcano in Mount Tabor Park, the city can be seen stretching out below on either side of the Willamette River; moored to the jetties along its banks, seagoing ships stand out among downtown bridges. On the west side of the river are the downtown shopping area, the Pioneer Courthouse, the former business district now bustling with boutiques and craft shops and known as the "Old Town," and the spectacular Forecourt Fountain opposite the Civic Auditorium, in which many a sweltering citizen has cooled off on a hot summer's day. The many parks (and even a forest) within the city limits help to make Portland, the "City of Roses," a pleasant place in which to live, a city whose pace and quality of life have considerable appeal.

Portland stands at the northern end of the broad Willamette Valley, a rich agricultural region between the Coastal Ranges and the Cascades, where most of the state's population lives in a cluster of cities along the Willamette River, among them Salem, the state capital, Albany, Corvallis, and the twin cities of Eugene and Springfield. Around these cities a colorful patchwork of cropfields, fruit orchards, vineyards, pasturelands, and forests make up a peaceful rural landscape enhanced by rippling streams crossed here and there by charming covered bridges.

To the east, beyond the Cascades, the sunny high Columbia Plateau stretches across the state to the Snake River canyon on the Idaho border and southward into the desert country of Nevada. Once-active volcanoes have left behind vast lava beds, dead craters, and long lava tubes in this dry rugged country, a paradise for rockhounds hunting its rich variety of semiprecious stones. Elsewhere there are huge cattle spreads, vast wheatfields, tracts of pine forest, and old ghost towns dating back to pioneer mining days. Through this fascinating landscape two major rivers, the Deschutes and the John Day, have carved scenic courses, the Deschutes flowing north along the eastern edge of the Cascades past peaceful old towns such as Bend, Redmond, and Madras and the huge Warm Springs Indian Reservation before entering the Columbia River in the far north. The John Day also joins the Columbia, after meandering in broad sweeps past the

Curious black-topped Sheep Rock crouches on guard above the John Day River in the dry interior of central Oregon. Here the John Day Fossil Beds National Monument is a fascinating treasure trove of the fossilized bones of prehistoric animals.

Below: Bachelor Butte, a 9,060-foot (2,761 m) peak in Oregon's Cascade Range, is easily accessible via a scenic drive from the town of Bend, some 22 miles to the east. On its open slopes there are facilities for such recreational activities as fishing, swimming, and canoeing, as well as sites for picnicking and camping.

The unsurpassable beauty of Mount Hood, Oregon's highest peak, provides a superb backcloth for the glistening dark blue waters of Lost Lake and the dark green forests of the Cascade Range. Located not far from the city of Portland, the mountain is a center for recreational activities and has the only year-round downhill skiing slope in the country.

famous John Day Fossil Beds, but has its source in the beautiful forested Blue Mountains of the northeast. Rising above the wheat-growing and cattle-raising country around Pendleton, famous for its lively rodeo known as the Pendleton Round-up, the Blue Mountains and the rugged Wallowa Range to the east were once crossed by the renowned Oregon Trail and were the site of old mining towns, but in recent years they have become popular resort and guest ranch areas.

In the dry, silent cattle country south of the remote lumbering community of Burns, two large wildlife refuges alongside large lakes and marshes offer a chance to see migrating birds, deer, and other wild animals on the edge of the high sagebrush desert country that rolls south into neighboring Nevada.

Land of Silver and Sagebrush

It was almost as if the whole tide of human emigration to America's West had been thrown suddenly into reverse when, after the fabulous Comstock lode of silver and gold was unearthed in Nevada's western mountains in 1859, a flood of prospectors swarmed back over the high Sierra Nevada from California to try their luck in the overnight bonanza. Working as a newspaper reporter in the new boom town of Virginia City during those heady days, young Samuel Clemens, better known now as Mark Twain, was caught up in the excitement, later confessing: "I expected to find masses of silver lying all about the ground. I expected to see it glittering in the sun on

Overleaf: Time now stands still in Virginia City, a once-thriving community in the High Sierra of northwestern Nevada. Between 1859 and the 1880s the town was filled with miners and fortune-seekers – among them the young reporter Mark Twain – who followed the gold rush that resulted from the discovery of the fabulous Comstock Lode, a rich concentration of silver and gold unearthed by two Irish prospectors.

the mountain summits." Others, too, had faith in Lady Fortune, and mining camps mushroomed all over the territory, many of them to be deserted within a few years as the precious metals ran out. Today Nevada, the "Silver State," is dotted with ghost towns that recall those feverish times.

Yet the legend of Eldorado dies hard, and today 13 million visitors flock into Nevada every year in the search for rich pickings, not from rough digging but in the state's many gambling casinos, swelling the usual resident population of around 825,000 to considerable proportions. For gambling is still Nevada's major economic interest, even though now it is pursued in more salubrious surroundings amid the garish opulence of Las Vegas and Reno. There are those, however, who, content with their bank balances, prefer to spend their time in Nevada just admiring its magnificent rugged scenery.

Nestling in the high Great Basin desert region between the Rocky Mountains and the Sierra Nevada, the "Sagebrush State," as it is sometimes appropriately called, extends over a vast plateau wrinkled by short mountain ranges running in a north–south direction and rising here and there to heights over 11,000 feet (3,353 m) above sea level, many of them clothed in the green pine trees of the Toiyabe and Humboldt National Forests. Between these high ridges, there are broad, flat valleys sometimes interrupted by flat-topped mesas and buttes in which large herds of sheep and cattle roam over flower-speckled pastures. In places the stillness and silence is dramatically broken by the gurgling of steaming hot springs and geysers which spurt from the ground, providing evidence of the elemental forces deep below ground. In ages past those same forces threw out vast expanses of lava in the Columbia Plateau region of Washington, Oregon, Idaho, and northern Nevada, where seasonal torrents have cut deep, steep-sided canyons.

Because of the scarcity of rain and the nature of the terrain, there are few permanent rivers flowing out of this thirsty country. Some, like the Humboldt in the north, run for hundreds of miles across dry sagebrush country, only to fade away or vanish in depressions known as sinks; others, like the Truckee River in the west, are lucky enough to trickle into the safety of one of Nevada's beautiful permanent lakes, in this case Pyramid Lake. Some of the lakes are, in fact, seasonal, filling up shallow valley bottoms during the rains that fall between December and June and then drying up to leave either damp mudflats or chalky-white patches of parched, cracked earth. One of these lakes which, in the words of Mark Twain, "burned in the desert like a fallen sun," was ancient Lake Lahontan, which once covered a much larger area in the west, its remnants now gathered in the lovely Pyramid and Walker lakes. In the south is Nevada's only lake with a river outlet to the sea: manmade Lake Mead, created in the 1930s by holding up the turbulent Colorado River in a canyon behind the colossal

The gambler's paradise city of Las Vegas rises like an oasis in the desert of southern Nevada, defying the disadvantages of its natural setting to become a mecca for hedonists seeking excitement and entertainment in its many casinos and lavish nightspots.

Hoover Dam. The lake, 115 miles long, brought electricity and much-needed water to southern Nevada, at the same time providing a wonderful recreation area for the people of the now highly populated region nearby, centered on Boulder City, the industrial city of Henderson, and the "Entertainment Capital of the World," exciting Las Vegas, the state's largest city.

Glittering under the desert night sky like a million illuminated Christmas trees, "Vegas" is a breathtaking sight, an incongruous cluster of luxurious hotels, casinos, and neon signs concentrated in the downtown "Casino Center" and along that fabulous three-and-a-half-mile long boulevard known simply as the "Strip," all catering to the needs of every energetic hedonist who has a few dollars to spare. Incredibly lavish and spectacular shows performed by the world's leading superstars last well into the night, a relentless orgy of entertainment broken only by the seriousness of gambling, the real *raison d'être* of this amazing city. If, as someone has claimed, Las Vegas is "a city without clocks or conscience," it is nevertheless an unforgettable experience.

Dominated by the distant Spring Mountains to the west, Las Vegas stands like an oasis surrounded by desert, but trips from the comfort of its excellent hotels into the seemingly inhospitable country around do reveal spectacular scenic attractions and sites of historic interest. Not far from the city is the fascinating Valley of Fire State Park, with its Indian petroglyphs and fantastic rock formations carved by the elements in its red and pink sandstone. To the north are incredible Cathedral Gorge; the beautiful underground limestone formations of the Lehman Caves National Monument in the lovely Wheeler Peak Scenic Area; the awesomely huge hole scraped out of the earth in the Ruth copper pit near the town of Ely; and, beyond, the magnificent forested Ruby Mountains and their pleasant lakes southeast of Elko.

Northwest of Las Vegas, on the other side of the state, the road skirts round the huge nuclear testing area, now called the Desert National Wildlife Refuge, roamed by bighorn sheep, and on past the many old ghost towns that litter this region on the way to Nevada's other main population area, a group of cities around old Virginia City in the ranching country between Lakes Tahoe, Pyramid, and Walker. Here, on the edge of California's Sierra Nevada, Carson City subtly suggests its rank as Nevada's capital with a statehouse crowned with a dome finished in silver rather than the usual gold, while its much larger neighbor, Reno, the state's second city, has a neon sign

The red sandstone rocks of the sun-seared Valley of Fire northeast of Las Vegas display the scars of the desert heat and winter frost which have molded this harsh rugged landscape.

215

Opposite: Whittle's Castle stands on a wooded promontory bathed by the mottled blue and green waters of lovely Lake Tahoe on the Nevada/California state line. Cradled by the encircling peaks of the Sierra Nevada, the lake area is a year-round resort offering a wide range of recreational activities for visitors.

A sprinkling of winter snow provides cooling relief from the blazing sun which in summer scorches the rocks of aptly named Cathedral Gorge, near Pioche in eastern Nevada. Here the gray and yellowish bentonite clay has been worn into curious formations by the elements.

at its center bluntly – and somewhat confusingly – declaring that it is "The Biggest Little City in the World." Famous for its rip-roaring rodeo, Reno is also known for its liberal attitudes to divorce and gambling, and, as in Las Vegas, casinos, slot machines, and bright lights are much in evidence. But so are trees – cottonwoods, willows, elms, pine, and elder – all creating a beautiful spectacle throughout the city unsurpassed in the fall, so that some 60 years ago an appreciative songwriter was moved to call Reno the "City of Trembling Leaves."

About 35 miles from Reno that other gem of western Nevada, lovely Lake Tahoe, sits astride the California state line, a stunning natural creation which Mark Twain thought "must surely be the fairest picture the whole earth affords." Enclosed in its beautiful setting 6,200 feet (1,890 m) high in the tree-covered mountains of the Sierra Nevada, the lake stretches out invitingly beneath cloud-free summer skies, its sparkling clear water colored with patches of deep blue and shallow green. A spectacular drive around the lake affords beautiful views and provides access to its many recreational facilities. And in winter the mountain slopes of the area are transformed into a snowy

white wonderland enjoyed by lovers of skiing and other winter sports.

Although "Battle Born," in the words of the state slogan, during the Civil War, Nevada is a land where peace and enjoyment seem to come naturally.

The Golden State

Conjuring up images of golden sun-washed beaches, magnificent mountain scenery, glamorous alluring cities, and endless lines of laden fruit trees and grapevines, it is perhaps fitting that the "Golden State" of California should owe its name to one of those old romantic tales of knightly fantasy that turned the brain of poor Don Quixote. Scholars tell us that the name "California" was invented for an imaginary rugged island abounding in gold "west of the Indies and east of Eden," a fiction that became a reality when the explorer Juan Rodríguez Cabrillo borrowed it to label the land he visited north of present-day San Diego in 1542.

Three centuries of Spanish and, briefly, Mexican dominion over California left behind a host of Spanish place names and a string of Franciscan missions

Left: Looking south down North Virginia Street, in the northwestern Nevada city of Reno, the night-time reveler is left in no doubt as to where he is, though he may be puzzled by the motto. A haven for both gamblers and those who have already lost in the game of marriage, Reno has an astonishing pace of life for a small town.

Right: The lovely old Franciscan mission of San Carlos Borromeo near Carmel is one of the chain of such buildings established after 1769 along the Californian coast by Father Junípero Serra. The missions were an important element in the system of triple institutions – missions, military garrisons, and ranches – through which the Spanish colonial government sought to control the territory during their rule.

set up by Father Junípero Serra along the Camino Real, the King's Highway on the coast between San Diego and Sonoma to the north. But in 1846 American settlers, encouraged by John Charles Fremont, proclaimed their independence from Mexican rule, and two years later their Bear Flag Republic was acquired by the United States. In the years following the celebrated gold rush of 1849, "Go west, young man, go west" became a popular slogan as thousands of Americans and others flocked in to seek their share of the fabulous wealth to be found in this golden land, and through their endeavors California set out on the road to become the richest state in the nation today and its leading agricultural producer.

A land of dramatic contrasts of scenery and climate, California stretches south of the Oregon border for nearly 850 miles, its cool, rugged Pacific shoreline providing the setting for its three major cities: Los Angeles, San Diego, and San Francisco. Behind the coast, the land ripples eastward across the low green ridges and valleys of the Coast Ranges, down into the broad, flat expanse of rich farmland and orchards in the vast Central Valley, and then up forested slopes into the lofty, snow-capped peaks of the mighty Cascade Range and the Sierra Nevada, before finally plunging down into the dry interior plateau and desert region extending into Nevada and Arizona.

The gateway to this land from the sea has always been San Francisco, shaken from its slumbers as the tiny frontier village of Yerba Buena by the 1849 gold rush to grow into one of the nation's major ports and one of the

Left: The lovely drive along the
Californian coast south of Monterey to
Big Sur offers magnificent views of
rugged sea cliffs, rocky headlands and
offshore islands. Along this shoreline a
wide variety of sea birds, seals, and sea
otters thrive on the rich marine life that
lives in the cold water.

Below left: Probably the most
photographed tree in all America, the
Lone Cypress stands proudly on a rocky
promontory of the Monterey Peninsula
near Carmel. This species of cypress is
unique to the peninsula.

Below: Contrasting styles of architecture
add to the charm and visual excitement
of San Francisco's magnificent skyline.
Behind the colorfully painted old homes
of Steiner Street, the adventurous
modern designs of newer commercial
buildings create a dynamic skyline
expressing the city's great vitality and
confidence.

best-loved and most beautiful cities in the world. Nestling on one of the world's finest natural harbors, the city rolls across its hills on a narrow peninsula between the cold Pacific Ocean and San Francisco Bay, a fine modern metropolis whose charm and beauty never fail to captivate all who pay it a visit. Blessed with an even, fresh climate that rarely takes temperatures above 70 degrees Fahrenheit or below 55, the city is, however, known for its fog, which can often roll in from the sea to shroud the city streets in its thick woolly blanket, sometimes leaving the tops of the tallest buildings to bask in the brilliant sunshine. Clanging up and down the steep slopes of its streets, the beloved old cable cars offer constantly changing views of the city's countless sights: the old prison island of Alcatraz, brooding silently in the cold, churning currents of the bay; the red sweep of the celebrated Golden Gate Bridge and, farther round the bay, the elegant gray Oakland Bridge; the ships along the waterfront of the Embarcadero, where the old square-rigged steel sailing ship *Balclutha* lies moored alongside Pier 43, close by the fishing boats, seafood stalls, and restaurants of Fisherman's Wharf; the whimsical "Crookedest Street in the World," more properly referred to as Lombard Street; the high-class hotels and apartment buildings of Nob Hill; and, a landmark atop Telegraph Hill, the Coit Tower built 50 years ago as a memorial to firemen. There are also the newer sleek and tall commercial buildings which pierce the skyline behind the waterfront, among which the Transamerica Pyramid is immediately recognizable, contrasting with the old elegance of the city's many white Victorian-style houses and the colorful Oriental charm of the Chinatown district around Grant Avenue. Away from the everyday bustle and noise of

Market Street and the downtown business and shopping area, Golden Gate Park offers peaceful relaxation in its celebrated Japanese Tea Garden or an hour or two's intellectual stimulus in its planetarium and museums.

Across the Golden Gate Bridge, just north of the park, the magnificent rugged coastline of Northern California sweeps away for some 350 miles to the Oregon border, its rocky headlands, steep cliffs, and boulder-strewn beaches continuously pounded by the thundering, cold Pacific surf and frequently shrouded in mysterious banks of summer fog. Once claimed for England by Sir Francis Drake and frequented by Russian fur-traders based at Fort Ross, the coast is now a haven for sea lions, otters, gulls, cormorants, and other sea birds which compete with local fishing boats for the abundant fish below the waves, and inland there are majestic stands of soaring, age-old redwood trees, now protected in the silence of Muir Woods National Monument and the Redwood National Park.

Behind the shore, the ridges of the Coast Ranges rise eastward, in places reaching heights over 7,000 feet (2,134 m) above sea level and enclosing sheltered valleys producing cheese and, farther south, the famous wines of Sonoma and Napa counties. Northwards the Coast Ranges broaden into the high Klamath Mountains bordering Oregon, a beautiful region of high peaks, thick forests, swiftly flowing streams alive with salmon, trout, and steelheads, and, in the southern part, those three magnificent recreational lakes, Clair Engle, Shasta, and Whiskeytown.

East of this outdoor-lover's paradise, the dark-forested mountains of the spectacular Cascade Range emerge from Oregon, the highest summits capped in permanent snow. Towering to an imperious 14,162 feet (4,317 m) above them, the solitary volcanic peak of superb Mount Shasta looms, in the words of the Californian writer Joaquin Miller, like "a shining pyramid in mail of everlasting frosts and ice," and, farther south, the 10,457-foot (3,187 m) cone of Lassen Peak dominates the strange surrounding landscape of lava flows, cinder cones, gaseous fumaroles, spouting hot springs, and bubbling mud pools in the Lassen Volcanic National Park. Similar evidence of volcanic activity on a colossal scale can also be seen beyond the Cascade Range in the "Lonely Corner" of California, the dry northeastern plateau region bordering Oregon and Nevada, the location of the fascinating, rugged Lava Beds National Monument.

South of this remote corner, the Cascades hand over their role as California's eastern highland barrier to the mighty Sierra Nevada, which Californians prefer to call the "High Sierra," the towering, snow-covered mountains of which, snugly wrapped lower down in thick forests, march briefly across Nevada's border to enclose gem-like Lake Tahoe in their rugged embrace. In winter the snow that blankets the slopes around the lake transforms this part of California into a mecca for winter sports enthusiasts from across the nation and abroad. From here the High Sierra strides off southwards into the distance, its steeper rocky face towards Nevada, its gentler western slopes divided into bands of pearl-gray snow, dark purple forests, and aspen-yellow foothills. History has left its mark on this part of the Sierra, through which the weary overland pioneers trudged from the East along the fabled California Trail in early days, and where the ill-fated Donner party met disaster in the early snows of 1846. On the forested lower slopes farther west, the abandoned diggings of prospectors and now-restored gold rush towns such as Folsom, Nevada City, and Placerville recall the frantic times that followed the first discovery of gold at Captain Sutter's sawmill at Coloma in 1848, when, within two years, the population of the territory leapt from 13,000 to 100,000.

Into this towering southerly section the High Sierra has packed its most spectacular scenic treasures, enclosed in the breathtaking grandeur of three magnificent national parks. The most northerly, Yosemite, offers staggering vistas from the Yosemite Valley of gigantic vertical rockfaces such as the renowed El Capitán, and thundering waterfalls that include the spectacular Yosemite Falls, the highest on the American continent. There are also

One of the most famous manmade structures in the world, the elegant Golden Gate Bridge, spans the churning narrow channel at the mouth of San Francisco Bay to link the city of San Francisco with Marin County and the rest of northern California.

sweeping panoramas from atop Glacier Point and the sight of awesomely gigantic sequoia trees in Mariposa Grove. Other stands of immense sequoias are protected in the adjoining Kings Canyon and Sequoia National Parks farther south, a 65-mile-long area of impressively rugged gorges and high mountain scenery alongside continental America's highest peak, 14,495-foot (4,418 m) Mount Whitney. Beyond the parks the mountains gradually lose height as they veer almost imperceptibly westward to merge with the much lower peaks of the Tehachapi Mountains bending south around the oil town of Bakersfield before joining, in their turn, the Coast Ranges running down from San Francisco.

From Bakersfield the immense Central Valley of California stretches northward for 450 miles as far as the town of Redding and the Klamath Mountains, like a gigantic, elongated saucer reaching 80 miles across at its widest between the Coast Ranges and the High Sierra. Out of the catalogue of delightful sights that meet the eye in this agricultural Garden of Eden, John Steinbeck listed "the vineyards, the orchards, the great flat valley green and beautiful, the trees set in rows, and the farmhouses... The distant cities, the little towns in the orchard land... The grain fields golden in the morning, and the willow lines, the eucalyptus trees in rows... The peach trees and the walnut groves, and the dark green patches of oranges... And red roofs among the trees, and barns – rich barns." Among the many towns processing and marketing the abundant farm produce grown in the region's rich soils is the state capital, Sacramento, lying conveniently close to San Francisco in the heartland of the Valley. While fulfilling its role as the state's busy government center, the city has also recognized its importance as a guardian of the state's historical legacy and has set aside a large area of the downtown district for a fascinating reconstruction of a mid-nineteenth-century frontier town.

Away to the west the ridges and valleys of the Coast Ranges begin their long journey to the south from San Francisco Bay, following the sinister earthquake line of the San Andreas Fault which, having once destroyed San Francisco in 1906, looms like a permanent threat over this part of the state. Along the beautiful, rugged shoreline, edged by stands of wind-swept cypresses, the cold Pacific surf crashes over jagged rocks and islets shared by seals and countless sea birds, a seascape made accessible by the magnificent scenic road that runs along the entire coast. Around the bay beyond the lovely resort of Santa Cruz the historic town of Monterey sits comfortably on its peninsula, accompanied by those now-abandoned fish factories immortalized by Steinbeck, which "dip their tails into the bay" at Cannery Row. Across the peninsula the charming artists' colony of Carmel huddles behind its lovely bay of gleaming white sand, its quaint shops buzzing with tourists. Inland is the "Salad Bowl of America," the flat and fertile Salinas Valley, "a long narrow swale between two mountain ranges" which provided the setting for much of Steinbeck's writing. Farther south the twisting scenic road along the cliffs bordering the ocean passes beyond Big Sur, by the celebrated castle of William Randolph Hearst at San Simeon, and the much-photographed, 580-foot (177 m) volcanic spire which rises sheer from the sea at Morro Bay. From here, the coast road turns southeastward to elegant, attractive Santa Barbara and the sunny, sprawling cities and resorts of Southern California.

Beyond Malibu the vast metropolitan area of Los Angeles, California's largest city, spreads out like "fifty miles of suburbs in search of a center" between the Palos Verdes Peninsula and the San Gabriel Mountains, a conglomeration of indistinguishable, smog-bound urban communities linked by a complex web of fast concrete freeways on which the city's car-bound inhabitants spend much of their lives. But contrasting with the unflattering realities, the legend of L.A. is far more glamorous, for the city is surely the land of dreams for seekers of fame, wealth, and the good life under warm, blue skies. The fantasy was once made real by the movie stars who built luxurious mansions and swimming pools in the beautiful Beverly Hills area of Hollywood, that glittering fantasyland the name of which became synonymous with the movie industry and whose glamorous boulevards – Wilshire, Hollywood and Sunset – with that fabulous section known as the "Strip," are known the world over. Pressed into the concrete outside Mann's Chinese Theater (formerly Grauman's) on Hollywood Boulevard are the signatures and hand and foot prints of the movie stars who made Hollywood famous. The advent of television brought drastic changes to the great film studios that congregated here, but a trip around the sound stages and

Right: Vineyards in the Napa Valley, sheltered by northern California's Coast Range just north of San Francisco Bay, produce some of the world's finest wines.

Below: The glassy waters of lovely Mirror Lake reflect the towering rock faces and lush vegetation of Yosemite National Park in California, one of the most breathtakingly beautiful parks in the nation.

The starkly rectangular Union Bank and the futuristic rounded forms of the Bonaventure Hotel and Shopping Gallery rise like interlopers from another age behind the florid old street lamps of downtown Los Angeles. Beneath Atlantic Richfield Plaza is the nation's largest underground shopping center, with more than sixty shops and restaurants.

backlots of the Universal Studios still provides a fascinating nostalgic insight into movie-making both now and in its heyday.

North of Hollywood Boulevard, in a lovely hillside setting, is the famous Hollywood Bowl auditorium, where summer evening concerts under the stars are especially entrancing. In downtown L.A., where newly built hotels and offices now rise over 50 stories, the area around the old Plaza has been turned into a state historical park containing the site of the original Spanish settlement. Here the pedestrian mall of Olvera Street reproduces a Mexican-style village street with typical shops and restaurants, while not far away, the districts known as Chinatown and Little Tokyo catch a flavor of the Orient. Both downtown L.A. and Beverly Hills boast elegant shops and boutiques and a wide-ranging choice of international restaurants. Out of the city there are famous entertainment parks that never fail to enchant the visitor, young or old: Disneyland, at Anaheim; Knott's Berry Farm, in Buena Park; and Marineland oceanarium, on the Palos Verdes Peninsula.

South of Los Angeles and the nodding oil-well heads beyond Long Beach, the now warmer waters of the Pacific wash a series of superb beaches along the coast of wonderful Orange County, among them Huntington, Newport, and Laguna, where tanned surfboarders and vacationers relax in the idyllic climate. The warmth and sunny, clear-blue skies of this part of California have convinced the people of San Diego, the state's second city just by the Mexican border, that theirs is a paradise city offering a pleasant lifestyle unequaled anywhere. Less frenetic than Los Angeles, San Diego can justifiably claim to be one of the most livable cities in the entire United States. Basking behind its superb beaches and the magnificent natural harbors of San Diego Bay and Mission Bay, the city has grown beyond the original confines of the Old Town to extend across the surrounding hills and valleys, becoming a vast metropolis reflecting both its Hispanic past and its modern status as America's eighth-largest city and a major naval base. It was here that San Diego de Alcalá, the first of the Franciscan missions scattered across California by the Spaniards, was founded in 1769, one of many buildings in the city still surviving from Spanish colonial times. Balboa Park is one of San Diego's major highlights, a lovely enclosure of gardens, woods and lakes in the heart of the city, containing a Shakespearean theater, several fine museums and art galleries, and the world-famous zoo. Shamu the killer whale, dolphins, seals, and other sea animals attract thousands of visitors each year to the fascinating Sea World entertainment oceanarium in Mission Bay Park, while a wide range of facilities for fun and leisure are available on Harbor Island and Shelter Island in San Diego Bay.

Inland the ideal climate of San Diego turns into the searing heat of southeastern California's desert region. In the far south, however, irrigation water from the Colorado River has transformed the Imperial Valley in the Colorado Desert into a fertile agricultural area which stretches around the shimmering salty waters of the huge Salton Sea as far as the date-palm gardens of Indio. Not far away is the fashionable millionaires' city of Palm Springs, the "Golf Capital of the World," which stands like a green oasis amid rugged mountains and desert country. East of the city the Joshua Tree National Monument encloses a section of arid land where cacti, palms, and the rare species of yucca known as the Joshua tree grow on the edge of the vast, hostile expanse of the Mojave Desert.

Farther north, a series of dry, craggy mountain ranges and deep desert valleys extend eastward behind the Sierra Nevada, "a land," as the celebrated naturalist John Muir described it, "of desolation covered with beautiful light." Here is awesome Death Valley, a name that once sent a chill through the hearts of early westbound travelers, where sun-baked sand dunes, salt flats, and borax deposits sink to 282 feet (86 m) below sea level. This was the incredible setting chosen by Walter Scotty, a performer in Buffalo Bill's "Wild West Show," for a lavishly furnished, Spanish-style home now known as Scotty's Castle. It stands as a symbol of man's conquest of nature in a land which is teeming with extremes and surprises.

Right: Cacti, palms, and other kinds of desert vegetation grow undisturbed in the 360-acre Living Desert Reserve in the Colorado Desert area of southern California between Palm Springs and Indio.

Alaska and Hawaii

In 1959, Alaska and Hawaii became the forty-ninth and fiftieth states to be admitted to the Union, but superficially they have little else in common. Almost one-third of Alaska lies north of the Arctic Circle and ice, snow, or bleak, treeless tundra cover large areas. On the other hand, Hawaii is located in the tropics and its sun-baked beaches are major tourist attractions. Alaska is the largest state in the Union; it covers an area more than twice as large as Texas, although it has fewer people than any other state. Hawaii, by contrast, is small – only Rhode Island, Delaware, and Connecticut are smaller – and densely populated.

Alaska and Hawaii, however, share magnificent wild scenery molded by the ever-active forces of nature. Alaska lies on the unstable edge of the Pacific "ring of fire" and is subject to earthquakes and volcanic eruptions. Hawaii, "the loveliest fleet of islands that lies anchored in any ocean" according to Mark Twain, is a volcanic chain with two great active volcanoes in Mauna Loa and Kilauea. Alaska at present plays host to only about one-tenth of the number of tourists who flock annually to Hawaii, and yet Alaska's snow-capped mountains, brooding volcanoes, moving glaciers, steep-walled fjords, evergreen forests, abundant wildlife, and recreational facilities offer vacations with a difference in unspoiled and unforgettable landscapes.

The Last Frontier

The 1867 purchase of Alaska, popularly called "The Last Frontier," added yet more elements to that melting pot that is the United States, principally the cultures of Aleuts, Eskimos, and Indians, all of whom now constitute 18 percent of the state's population, and aspects of the Russian culture that predated American rule. But there were many who were quick to condemn the purchase, which cost $7.2 million (or two cents an acre), as "Seward's Folly" or "Johnson's Polar Bear Garden," after the Secretary of State and President who were involved. But the state's mineral resources alone, particularly oil, have made it one of the best deals in history.

In southeastern Alaska is the narrow Panhandle about which the much-traveled Scottish naturalist John Muir wrote: "Never before this had I been embosomed in scenery so hopelessly beyond description." This region contains about 11,000 islands that are blanketed by lush forests of cedar, hemlock, and spruce (now protected in the Tongass National Forest), an intricate network of glittering fjords, huge glaciers, dazzling mountain scenery, and a wide range of wildlife, with brown and black bears and many birds, including the bald eagle. The climate is mild and wet, the result of a warm offshore current. This ensures that harbors stay open in winter, but it also means that travelers must be prepared for drenching rain.

The best way to explore the Panhandle is by cruise ships or ferry services. In the south is Ketchikan, Alaska's fourth largest city, renowned for its salmon fishing and an abundance of totem poles that recall the city's humble origins as an Indian fishing camp. From Ketchikan ships maneuver through a

maze of ice-worn channels to Wrangell, a lumber port, and on to Petersburg, whose name evokes the splendor of imperial Russia but whose appearance is more like a Norwegian town. Not far from Petersburg is LeConte Glacier, North America's southernmost tidal glacier. West of Petersburg is Sitka which was founded in 1799 but destroyed by Tlingit Indians in 1802. In 1804 the Russian defeated the Tlingits in a battle commemorated in the Sitka National Historical Park, and established Sitka on its present site. In 1806 it became capital of Russian America, as Alaska was then called, and it witnessed the transfer of power in 1867.

Juneau, the state capital and third largest city, lies north of Sitka. This handsome port is overlooked by a huge icefield from which flows the Mendenhall Glacier, which is only about 13 miles from downtown Juneau. It was even closer 100 years ago but, like all glaciers on this coast, it has recently retreated leaving space for new city suburbs and an airport. Juneau is a mainly modern city, but it has some charming nineteenth-century buildings and ruins associated with the Klondike Gold Rush. From Juneau, a tranquil 60-mile-long fjord, called the Lynn Canal, leads northwards to Skagway where gold prospectors landed in the 1890s. Skagway contains buildings that are preserved in the Klondike Gold Rush National Historical Park, which is being developed in cooperation with Canada to preserve parts of the prospectors' routes. From Skagway, a road and a railroad lead visitors through some breathtaking territory to Whitehorse in Canada, and from here the Alaskan Highway, built during World War II, winds westward to Fairbanks. Some superb scenery also awaits travelers who land at Haines, on the Lynn Canal south of Skagway, because Haines is the terminus of another road that winds over Chilkat Pass before reaching the Alaskan Highway.

The Nenana River flows northward to the Tanana River, a tributary of the Yukon River. The Nenana River valley, which is on the Anchorage-Fairbanks road, is a popular fishing, canoeing, and hiking area. It is near the Denali National Park and Preserve which includes North America's highest peak, Mount McKinley.

West from Juneau, sea passengers pass the Glacier Bay National Park, where whales, porpoises, and seals cavort offshore, while virgin forests grow on coastlands only recently freed from thick glacier ice. But inland, the forests dwindle and barren landscapes presage the retreating glaciers. Turning northwest up the Pacific coast, ships pass Lituya Bay, scene of a landslide in 1958 which generated the world's highest wave; reaching a maximum height of 1,740 feet (530 m), it stripped bare the slopes around the bay. Beyond Lituya Bay is the Malaspina Glacier, which is larger than Rhode Island. This sprawling sheet of ice is sustained by glaciers that originate in the rugged St. Elias Range.

The lofty St. Elias Mountains extend from the Panhandle into south-central Alaska, a region of curving mountain ranges separated by lowlands. The ranges include the Wrangell Mountains northwest of the St. Elias Range, the coastal Chugach and Kenai Mountains, the Talkeetna Mountains behind Anchorage, and the mighty Alaska Range which forms a half circle running through the center of southwestern Alaska and is crowned by Mount McKinley, North America's highest peak at 20,320 feet (6,194 m) above sea level. In the far southwest are the rugged Alaska Peninsula and the Aleutian Islands, both of which are littered with volcanoes. In fact there are hundreds of volcanoes in south-central Alaska and earthquakes are common, too. These phenomena are the consequence of the fact that here, just south of Alaska, the Pacific Ocean plate, which is sliding past California along the San Andreas Fault, noses down beneath the North American plate in the

Evening at Mineral Creek, Valdez, on the eastern side of Prince William Sound. Earthquakes and volcanic action are features of southern Alaska which lies within the Pacific "ring of fire." As recently as 1953 Valdez was rained upon by ash that originated in a volcanic eruption 200 miles away.

Husky-drawn sleds remain an efficient form of Eskimo transport in the frozen wilderness of Alaska, such as here on the icy Bering Sea, near Nome. The powerful Eskimo dogs can travel up to 40 miles a day.

deep Aleutian Trench. The movements are jerky and cause tremors which, in turn, may generate tidal waves called tsunami. And as the Pacific plate descends, it also melts, providing molten magma for Alaska's volcanoes.

Anchorage, Alaska's largest city, lies at the head of Cook Inlet on the south-central coast. Like most settlements in the area, it suffered damage during the severe 1964 earthquake which originated in Prince William Sound to the east. The city has been rebuilt on a new site, but the ruins of the old city can be seen in Earthquake Park. Anchorage is a center of some of Alaska's finest scenery, including the Chugach National Forest. East of Anchorage is Whittier which has ferry services across Prince William Sound to Valdez, another town relocated after the 1964 earthquake, and Cordova, which was raised up by seven feet. The journey across the Sound affords marvelous views of the large Columbia Glacier and, from Valdez, roads lead up to sublime snowy mountains and deep blue glaciers.

South of Anchorage is Kenai peninsula which contains much unspoiled wilderness, and beyond is the scenic island of Kodiak, known to naturalists for its brown bears. The town of Kodiak, founded in 1792, was battered by a tsunami in 1964, when the death toll reached 70, and it also suffered in 1912 when hot ash rained down from the sky to a depth of about 1 foot

Gulkana Airport. Apart from the southeast, transport facilities are extremely limited in Alaska, and many places are best reached by air.

Nome is a port on the Seward Peninsula in northwestern Alaska. Founded in 1898 when gold was discovered nearby, it is near the Bering Land Bridge National Monument which includes North America's westernmost point on land.

(0.3 m). This ash came from volcanic eruptions in what is now the Katmai National Monument on the Alaska Peninsula. Near the volcano, a verdant valley was buried by deep ash flows, steam from underground water burst through countless holes in the hot ash and the valley was christened the "Valley of Ten Thousand Smokes."

North of Anchorage a road leads to Alaska's leading attraction, the Denali National Park and Preserve, which includes Mount McKinley, an unspoiled tundra wilderness supporting a fascinating range of plant and animal life. Mount McKinley is classed as difficult climbing, but experienced mountaineers can join climbing parties in summer. Northeast of the park, the road descends into the Yukon River basin and reaches Fairbanks, Alaska's second largest city, where there is a museum with an outstanding display of Eskimo and Indian cultures. Beyond Fairbanks, traveling becomes difficult. There is one road that runs north from Fairbanks to the Brooks Range (an extension of the Rockies) and the oil-rich Arctic Slope, reaching Prudhoe Bay on the Arctic Ocean, but most of this road is closed to the public.

The chief way of sampling the special charms of northern and northwestern Alaska is by air. There are regular flights to Nome on the Seward Peninsula, whose westernmost point on the Bering Strait is only 51 miles from the Soviet Union. For those who want to see the Land of the Midnight Sun, there are flights to Kotzebue, north of the Arctic Circle, and Barrow on the Arctic Ocean, where the sun does not set for 82 days every year. A place of special interest to naturalists is the Alaskan Pribilof Islands in the Bering Sea, a sanctuary for fur seals and many kinds of birds.

The Aloha State

Hawaii is not only an exquisitely beautiful state with a highly complex, interracial society, free from all taint of racism, it is also an extremely friendly one, as its popular name suggests. Indeed, *Aloha* means affection, kindness, or love and it is used in greetings and farewells. The first European contact with these Polynesian islands occurred in 1778 when the British Captain Cook arrived and named them the Sandwich Islands. At that time,

Kilauea volcano stages one of the most awesome of all natural spectacles when it erupts. The volcano is frequently active and news of its "quiet" (meaning non-explosive) eruptions sends people flocking to the Big Island of Hawaii to witness a natural firework display. Kilauea lies within the Hawaii Volcanoes National Park.

the islands had separate administrations, but from the 1790s they were unified under King Kamehameha I, who ruled until 1819. American influence was first felt in 1820 with the arrival of New England Protestant missionaries. The monarchy was overthrown in 1893 and the United States annexed the islands in 1898.

This volcanic island archipelago extends from southeast to the northwest over a distance of about 1,600 miles. There are eight large islands at the southeastern end of the chain with 114 tiny ones to the northwest. The large islands, from east to west, are Hawaii (or the Big Island as it is often called to avoid confusion with the name of the state), Maui, Kahoolawe, Molokai, Lanai, Oahu, Kauai, and Niihau. The 114 minor islands together cover a total area of only three square miles, the relentless sea having completely worn away most of them. All that appears on the surface are small patches of coral that have built up on the eroded volcanic stumps.

The Big Island, which is geologically the youngest of the islands – volcanic eruptions are periodically adding to its area – makes up more than three-fifths of the area of the state. It contains five volcanoes, including the dormant Mauna Kea in the northeast which rises to 13,796 feet (4,205 m) above sea level, the state's highest point. The intermittently active Mauna Loa and Kilauea volcanoes in the south are preserved in the Hawaii Volcanoes National Park. Geologists describe these two volcanoes as "quiet" in that neither discharges huge clouds of destructive hot ash into the air in violent explosive eruptions. Signs of possible volcanic activity are, in fact, closely monitored and news of likely eruptions attracts people to the Big Island to witness some of Nature's most spectacular displays, including fountains of lava that may form 80-foot-high (24 m) curtains of fire or, in major eruptions, fluid lava streams that plunge down the flanks of Mauna

Loa at speeds of 35 or 40 miles per hour until they reach the coast and turn the coastal waters into a steaming cauldron. The Big Island also contains many historical sites associated with various stages of Hawaiian history, such as the Puukohola Heiau National Historical Site, which includes a temple built by Kamehameha I in 1791, the Pu'uhonua O Honaunau National Historical Park, an ancient city refuge for fugitives and criminals, and a monument in Kealakekua Bay marking the spot where Captain Cook was slain in 1779. Hawaii has much fine scenery, with sparkling waterfalls, trails through dense tropical forest, rugged coastlines, and serene beaches, especially in the west. For those interested in seeing dazzling displays of orchids, there are two nurseries open to the public in Hilo, the Big Island's chief settlement.

Maui, the Valley Island, is the archipelago's second largest, and consists of two volcanoes connected by a broad isthmus. East Maui, the larger of the two sections, is dominated by the Haleakala National Park, which encloses

The imposing Iao Needle overlooks the Iao Valley on Maui. This quiet valley was the scene of a fierce battle in 1790 when the stream flowing through it was dammed by the bodies of the fallen.

the huge caldera (crater) of Mount Haleakala, which is 3,000 feet (914 m) deep and has an area of 19 square miles. Other attractions include colorful jungle, the Seven Sacred Pools, a beautiful series of interconnected pools and streams at different levels, and the dormant volcano's rim which provides breathtaking views of the four neighboring islands. The smaller West Maui contains more exceptional scenery and some enchanting golden beaches. It includes historic Lahaina which was Hawaii's capital from 1795 until 1843, when Kamehameha III moved his court to Honolulu. Another early settlement, Wailuku, is near the tranquil, forested Iao Valley, scene of terrible carnage in 1790 when Kamehameha I slaughtered his enemies here.

Near Maui is the uninhabited Kahoolawe, which is used by the U.S. Navy for target practice, and Lanai. Lanai is best known for its vast pineapple plantations, but it also contains some forest wilderness and delightful isolated beaches.

Molokai, which is called the Friendly Island, contains large cattle ranches in the west, a fertile central plain and, in the east, some dramatic mountain

and canyon country, as well as many secluded coves, beaches, and jagged cliffs. Some of the northern sea cliffs tower about 3,300 feet (1,000 m) above sea level, probably the world's highest coastal cliffs. A place of special interest on Molokai is the leper community of Kalaupapa on the Kalaupapa Peninsula, formerly an isolated spot where lepers were dumped and left to die in terrible squalor until the Belgian missionary, Father Damien, arrived in 1873 and dedicated the rest of his life, until his death in 1889 (of leprosy), to caring for the afflicted. Today the disease is under control and adult visitors are welcome. Molokai's economy was based until recently on farming, but tourism is becoming increasingly important.

Although it ranks third in area, Oahu contains nearly four-fifths of the state's population, most of whom live in the thriving state capital and chief tourist center, Honolulu. Oahu is the most popular vacation island and its white Waikiki Beach is a justly world-renowned playground. Honolulu, the nation's thirteenth largest city, grew up on a narrow coastal strip, but it has now spread inland up the forested mountain spurs and valleys that provide it with such a magnificent backdrop. It is a dazzling modern city with much of interest to visitors, including the Iolani Palace (1882), the modern State Capitol, the Bishop Museum which houses a huge collection of Hawaiian memorabilia, the Foster Botanic Gardens, and, most popular of all, the U.S.S. *Arizona* which was sunk with 1,102 men lost during the infamous attack on Pearl Harbor (a short distance west of Honolulu) on 7 December 1941.

Above: Honolulu on Oahu Island is Hawaii's principal tourist center, although the development of the area and its fine beaches is comparatively recent. Honolulu is a modern city but it has much of interest to anyone prepared to move off the beaches.

Opposite: Maui, the second largest island in the state of Hawaii, contains some lovely scenery and luxuriant plant life, as here in the Puaa Kaa State Park, which also contains sparkling pools fed by waterfalls affording visitors the chance of a pleasant swim.

Overleaf: Waikiki Beach on Oahu is a famous two-mile-long stretch of generally coral-free sand, with excellent swimming because the water is protected by an offshore coral reef.

241

Oahu has much fine scenery, both in its eastern and western mountains and along its coasts. One popular spot at the southern end of Waikiki Beach is the perfect, 760-foot-high (232 m) volcanic crater at Diamond Head. Farther east is Makapuu Point, the easternmost spot on the island, and some impressive surfing beaches. To the northwest a road leads past pleasant beaches to Kailua from which a road runs southwestward over the mountains to Honolulu providing some extraordinary views en route. The northeastern coast contains several notable beauty spots, including the splendid Sacred Falls State Park, while Laie in the north contains the Polynesian Cultural Center where the arts, crafts, and buildings of various Pacific Ocean peoples are lovingly preserved. Beyond Kahuku Point in the far north are more fine surfing beaches – the walls of water off Sunset Beach reach 35 feet (11 m) in height. Another famous surfing resort is Makaha Beach on the western, leeward coast.

Northwest of Oahu is Kauai, the oldest of the main islands. Kauai is a verdant island with a vast array of tropical plant life and some awesome scenery. It also holds a world record: Mount Waialeale is the world's wettest place – between 1920 and 1972 the average annual rainfall on this lofty peak was 451 inches. The mountain forms a barrier between the wet northern coast, which has between 60 and 80 inches a rainfall a year, and the leeward, southern side, which lies in a rain shadow zone and has only 15 to 20 inches. Possibly the most outstanding scenery on Kauai is along the northern coast, particularly the Na Pali coast and Hanalei Bay, where deep, lushly forested valleys cut through the mountains to the sea. Also not to be missed is the colorful, 10-mile-long, 3,600-foot-deep (1,097 m) Waimea Canyon, which is the home of mountain goats and wild boars.

West of Kauai is Niihau, the eighth of Hawaii's main islands. Called the Forbidden Island, it is privately owned and may not be visited without permission.

The Pu'uhonua O Honaunau National Historical Park on the Big Island of Hawaii contains the peaceful City of Refuge where, in ancient times, defeated soldiers, criminals, and other fugitives, could seek sanctuary amid the stately palms.

National Parks and Other Places of Interest

Below is a list of many of the national parks, monuments, historical sites, and other areas administered by the National Parks Service, not including those that are not yet ready for visitors. The following abbreviations have been used: MP Memorial Parkway; NB National Battlefield; NHP National Historical Park; NHS National Historical Site; NL National Lakeshore; NM National Monument; N MEM National Memorial; NMP National Military Park; NP National Park; NR National River; NRA National Recreation Area; NS National Seashore.

The Northeast

Maine

Acadia NP   Magnificent coastal scenery, including part of Mount Desert Island, the Isle au Haut, and Schoodic Point on the mainland.

St Croix Island NM   Site of a French settlement established in June 1604, but abandoned after a harsh winter.

New Hampshire

Saint-Gaudens NHS   The home of sculptor Augustus Saint-Gaudens (1848–1907), at Cornish.

Massachusetts

Adams NHS   The home, in Quincy, of four generations of the Adams family, including Presidents John and John Quincy Adams.

Boston NHP   Historic sites in central Boston, on the Freedom Trail.

Cape Cod NS   Beautiful sand beaches, dunes, woodlands, and marshes.

John F. Kennedy NHS   President Kennedy's birthplace in Brookline, a Boston suburb.

Longfellow NHS   Home in Cambridge of the poet Henry Wadsworth Longfellow from 1843 to 1882 and General Washington's headquarters in 1775.

Minute Man NHS   Revolutionary War site in Concord, including the North Bridge where the Minute Men fired the "shot heard 'round the world."

Salem Maritime NHS   Includes the Customs House (shipping center of Salem, 1760–1860), Scale House, Bonded Warehouse, and Derby House.

Saugus Iron Works NHS   Reconstruction, in Saugus north of Boston, of a seventeenth-century iron-producing village.

Springfield Armory NHS   Museum of firearms, 1795 to the present.

Vermont

Green Mountain National Forest NF Central and southern Vermont.

Rhode Island

Roger Williams N MEM   Commemorates Roger Williams, founder of Providence and pioneer of religious freedom.

Touro Synagogue NHS   A beautiful synagogue in Newport built in 1763, the oldest in the United States and a symbol of religious liberty.

New York

Castle Clinton NM   Formerly a fort built in 1812, which became the nation's main immigrant depot from 1855 to 1890.

Federal Hall N MEM   Site in lower Manhattan, New York City, of the first Capitol where Washington was sworn in as President in 1789.

Fire Island NS   Holiday resort south of Long Island.

Fort Stanwix NM   A reconstruction of a fort built in 1758 in Rome.

Gateway NRA   Beaches, marshes, and islands south of New York City.

General Grant N MEM   Popularly called Grant's Tomb, in Riverside Park, New York City.

Hamilton Grange N MEM   Home, in New York City, of the first Secretary of the Treasury, Alexander Hamilton.

Home of Franklin Delano Roosevelt NHS   At Hyde Park on the Hudson.

Martin Van Buren NHS   Retirement home of this president, south of Albany at Stuyvesant.

Sagamore Hill NHS   Impressive summer home of President Theodore Roosevelt, on Long Island.

St. Paul's Church NHS   Events at St. Paul's Church green, in Mount Vernon, led to the establishment of the freedom of the press.

Saratoga NHP   Site of an American victory in 1777 in the Revolutionary War.
Statue of Liberty NM   151-foot high (46 m) statue on Liberty Island in New York harbor, a gift from France.
Theodore Roosevelt Birthplace NHS   A four-story brownstone at 28 East Twentieth Street, New York City.
Theodore Roosevelt Inaugural NHS   Where President Roosevelt was sworn in, in Buffalo, after the assassination of President McKinley.
Vanderbilt Mansion NHS   50-room mansion built in 1895, north of Hyde Park.

The Middle Atlantic States
New Jersey
Edison NHS   The inventor's laboratory in West Orange.
Morristown NHP   Washington's HQ in the winter of 1779/80.
Pennsylvania
Allegheny Portage Railroad NHS   Displays an unusual method of transportation, near Altoona.
Delaware Water Gap NRA   Scenic area in northeastern Pennysylvania.
Fort Necessity NB   Where George Washington led Virginians and Indians in 1754 against the French, southwest of Uniontown.
Gettysburg NMP   Site of the Civil War battle in 1863.
Hopewell Village NHS   Restored iron-making village, near Reading.
Independence NHP   Located in Philadelphia, this includes the City Tavern, Independence Hall, and the Liberty Bell.
Johnstown Flood N MEM   Where 2,200 people died when the South Fork Dam broke.
Thaddeus Kosciuszko N MEM   The lodgings in Philadelphia of the Polish patriot who helped George Washington.
Valley Forge NHP   Where Washington's army wintered in 1777/78.
Maryland
Antietam NB   Site near Sharpsburg of a Civil War battle in 1862.
Assateague Island NS   Home of the Chincoteague wild ponies and many bird species, partly in Maryland and partly in Virginia.
Catoctin Mountain Park   North of Frederick, this includes scenic hiking trails.
Chesapeake & Ohio Canal NHP   The canal connects Washington, D.C. to Cumberland.
Clara Barton NHS   Home of the founder of the American Red Cross, in Glen Echo, three miles north of the District of Columbia line.
Fort McHenry NM *and Historic Shrine*   Where "by dawn's early light," the flag was still flying after heavy British bombardment in 1814. Three miles from the center of Baltimore.
Fort Washington Park   Downriver from Washington D.C., this includes a nineteenth-century fortress, rebuilt under the direction of Major Pierre L'Enfant.
Greenbelt Park   Forest near Washington, D.C.
Hampton NHS   Eighteenth-century mansion near Baltimore.
Piscataway Park   On the Potomac River.
Washington, D.C.
Ford's Theater NHS   Where Abraham Lincoln was shot in 1865.
Frederick Douglass Home   Where the nineteenth-century black abolitionist lived.
John F. Kennedy Center for the Performing Arts   For concerts, plays, movies, and operas.
Lincoln Memorial   Doric-style temple containing a huge statue of Lincoln.
Lyndon Baines Johnson Memorial Grove on the Potomac   White pines commemorating the thirty-sixth President.
National Capital Parks   Include more than 300 historical sites.
National Mall   From the Capitol to the Lincoln Memorial.
National Visitor Center   At the monumental Union Station.
Rock Creek Park   Beautiful city park.

Sewall-Belmont House NHS   Center for women's rights.
Theodore Roosevelt Island   A memorial in the Potomac.
Thomas Jefferson Memorial   A Roman-style, columned rotunda.
Washington Monument   A 555-foot high (169-m) marble obelisk.
White House   1600 Pennsylvania Avenue.

West Virginia
Appalachian National Scenic Trail   From Maine to Georgia.
Harpers Ferry NHP   Site of John Brown's raid in 1859. The restored town
looks much as it did then.
Spruce Knob–Seneca Rocks NRA   Spruce Knob is West Virginia's highest
point.

The South
Kentucky
Abraham Lincoln Birthplace NHS   A memorial building encloses the log
cabin in which Lincoln was born, near Hodgenville.
Cumberland Gap NHP   This park, in Middlesboro, follows the route of
Daniel Boone from Virginia to Kentucky.
Mammoth Cave NP   The world's longest cave system, discovered in 1799.

Tennessee
Andrew Johnson NHS   In Depot Street, Greenville.
Big South Fork NR *and* NRA   On a scenic arm of the Cumberland River.
Fort Donelson NMP   The site of an early Union victory in the Civil War
(February 1862), near Dover.
Great Smoky Mountains NP   Superb mountain scenery, virgin forest, and
abundant wildlife.
Meriwether Lewis Site   Marking the spot near Hohenwald where Lewis was
killed in 1809 under mysterious circumstances, on the Natchez Trace
Parkway (*see* Mississippi below).
Obed Wild and Scenic River   Cutting through the Cumberland Plateau.
Shiloh NMP   Site near Savannah of a Civil War battle ("Bloody Shiloh").
Stones River NB   Site of a Civil War battle, southeast of Nashville.

Virginia
Appomattox Court House NHP   The village where the South surrendered in
1865.
Arlington House (Custis-Lee Mansion): the Robert E. Lee Memorial   A
mansion in Arlington Cemetery.
Booker T. Washington NM   Log cabin birthplace of the black educationist,
south of Roanoke.
Colonial NHP   Includes Yorktown, Jamestown, and a 23-mile-long parkway
to Williamsburg.
Fredericksburg and Spotsylvania NMP   Includes four Civil War battlefields.
George Washington Birthplace NM   Pope's Creek Plantation, in
Westmoreland County.
George Washington MP   Highway along the Potomac River.
Manassas NB *Park*   Site of two Confederate victories in 1861 and 1862 (the
First and Second Battles of Bull Run).
Petersburg NB   Site of a series of Civil War battles, south of Richmond.
Prince William Forest Park   Near Washington, D.C.
Richmond NB *Park*   Where fighting for the Confederate capital occurred.
Shenandoah NP   Along the crest of the Blue Ridge from Front Royal to
Waynesboro.
Wolf Trap Farm Park for the Performing Arts   Outdoor theater in Vienna,
near Washington, D.C.

North Carolina
Blue Ridge Parkway   Superb driveway following Appalachian crests, with
magnificent overlooks.
Cape Hatteras NS   Includes the barrier islands of Bodie, Hatteras, and
Ocracoke, and 70 miles of oceanfront.
Cape Lookout NS   Lonely barrier islands south of Cape Hatteras NS.
Carl Sandburg Home   Home of the poet at Flat Rock.

Fort Raleigh NHS Every summer, the drama of the *Lost Colony*, telling of the disappearance of the settlers who landed on Roanoke Island in an attempt to found the first English colony, is re-enacted at the Waterside Theater.

Guilford Courthouse NMP The site of a Revolutionary War battle in 1781, northwest of Greensboro.

Moores Creek NMP Site of a Revolutionary War battle (1776), in the southeast of the state.

Wright Brothers N MEM Near Kitty Hawk, it commemorates the first flight at Kill Devil Hills.

South Carolina

Congaree Swamp NM Southeast of Columbia, this contains virgin bottomland hardwoods.

Cowpens NB Site of a victory over the British in 1781, northeast of Spartanburg.

Fort Sumter NM In Charleston harbor, where the Civil War began.

Kings Mountain NMP Site of a major victory by the colonists (1780), west of Rock Hill.

Ninety Six NHS Remains of the Old Star colonial fort near Greenwood.

Georgia

Andersonville NHS Site of the Confederate prison, near Americus.

Chickamauga and Chattanooga NMP Civil War battle site on the Tennessee border.

Cumberland Island NS Beaches in the southeast.

Fort Frederica NM Commemorates General Oglethorpe's first settlement in 1736, on St. Simons Island.

Fort Pulaski NM Supply center for the Confederacy until 1862, near Savannah.

Kennesaw Mountain NB *Park* Civil War battle site near Marietta.

Ocmulgee NM Prehistoric Indian mounds and archeological museum near Macon.

Florida

Big Cypress National Preserve Protected swamp region north of the Everglades NP.

Biscayne NM Marine world south of Miami.

Canaveral NS Wonderful beaches north of the Kennedy Space Center.

Castillo de San Marcos NM On the site of an old Spanish fort at St. Augustine.

De Soto N MEM At the mouth of the Manatee River, west of Bradenton, honoring the Spanish explorer, Hernando de Soto (c. 1500–42).

Everglades NP Magnificent marshy vegetation and wildlife (including more than 200 bird species, alligators, snakes, bears, deer).

Fort Caroline N MEM French Huguenot fort (built 1564), at Jacksonville.

Fort Jefferson NM Nineteenth-century fort built to guard the Florida Strait, west of Key West, but its guns never fired a shot.

Fort Matanzas NM Spanish fort built in 1742, south of St. Augustine.

Gulf Islands NS The northwest Gulf coast near Pensacola.

Alabama

Horseshoe Bend NMP Commemorates Andrew Jackson's victory over the Creek Indians in 1814, near Alexander City.

Russell Cave NM Caves near Bridgeport in the northeast that were occupied by Stone Age people.

Tuskegee Institute NHS Founded by Booker T. Washington in 1881.

Mississippi

Brices Cross Roads NB *Site* Site of Civil War cavalry battle (1864), northwest of Tupelo.

Natchez Trace Parkway Follows (approximately) an old Indian trail (trace) from Natchez to Ashville in Tennessee.

Tupelo NB Site of Civil War battle (1864), near downtown Tupelo.

Vicksburg NMP Large area covering the siege and defense of Vicksburg.

Louisiana
Chalmette NHP   Site of the Battle of New Orleans in 1815.
Arkansas
Arkansas Post N MEM   Site of the first white settlement in the lower Mississippi valley near Nady.
Buffalo NR   Wild river in northern Arkansas. Marvelous canoeing.
Fort Smith NHS   Former center of Oklahoma Territory on the Oklahoma state border.
Hot Springs NP   Thermal water (average 143°F) surfaces in the city of Hot Springs.
Pea Ridge NMP   Site near Rogers of the Civil War battle in 1862 that kept Missouri in the Union.

The Midwest
Ohio
Cuyahoga Valley NRA   Includes preserved parts of the Ohio & Erie Canal, south of Cleveland.
Mound City Group NM   Prehistoric burial mounds of Hopewell Indians near Chillicothe.
Perry's Victory and International Peace Memorial   Monument on South Bass Island in Lake Erie commemorating the Battle of Lake Erie in the War of 1812 (1812–15).
William Howard Taft NHS   The President's birthplace, Cincinnati.
Michigan
Isle Royale NP   Wilderness island in Lake Superior.
Pictured Rocks NL   Colorful cliffs lining Lake Superior near Munising, best seen from a boat.
Sleeping Bear Dunes NL   Scenic Lake Michigan region, west of Traverse City.
Indiana
George Rogers Clark NHP   Memorial at Vincennes on the site of a British defeat.
Indiana Dunes NL   Beaches and high dunes on Lake Michigan.
Lincoln Boyhood N MEM   Where the President grew up, near Lincoln City.
Illinois
Lincoln Home NHS   Lincoln's home in Springfield before he left for the White House.
Wisconsin
Apostle Islands NL   22 islands in Lake Superior.
Lower St. Croix National Scenic Riverway   On the Wisconsin/Minnesota border.
St. Croix National Scenic Riverway   Includes magnificent rapids.
Minnesota
Grand Portage NM   Recreation of fur post on the site, in the northeast near the Canadian border, of the first white settlement in Minnesota.
Pipestone NM   A quarry where Indians got red stone to carve ceremonial pipes (calumets), west of Pipestone.
Voyageurs NP   Beautiful woodlands and lakes in the far north.
Iowa
Effigy Mounds NM   Prehistoric Indian burial mounds on the Mississippi River, north of Marquette.
Herbert Hoover NHS   Birthplace cottage and gravesite of the President, east of Iowa City.
Missouri
George Washington Carver NM   Birthplace of the black agricultural chemist, south of Joplin.
Jefferson National Expansion Memorial NHS   A 630-foot-high (192 m) steel arch in St. Louis – the "Gateway to the West."
Ozark National Scenic Riverways   Scenic riverways, including the Current and Jacks Fork rivers.
Wilson's Creek NB   Commemorates Civil War battle (1861) near Springfield.

Kansas

Fort Larned NHS   Army fort built near Larned in 1859 to prevent Indian attacks on the Santa Fe trail.

Nebraska

Agate Fossil Beds NM   Exposed fossil bones in the northwest.

Homestead NM   One of the first sites, near Beatrice, claimed under the Homestead Act of 1862.

Scotts Bluff NM   Landmark on the Oregon Trail.

South Dakota

Badlands NP   Spectacular landscapes in the southwest.

Jewel Cave NM   Sparkling crystal formations, near Custer in the Black Hills.

Mount Rushmore N MEM   The gigantic faces of four presidents sculpted in a granite cliff face, south of Rapid City.

Wind Cave NP   Unusual honeycomb cave near Hot Springs. Nearby are herds of buffalo.

North Dakota

Knife River Indian Villages NHS   Five Hidatsa Indian settlements (1845), northwest of Bismarck.

Theodore Roosevelt NP   Includes the scenic Little Missouri River badlands in the far west of the state.

The Southwest

Oklahoma

Chickasaw NRA   South of Sulphur, this includes the Lake of the Arbuckles and mineral springs.

Texas

Alibates Flint Quarries NM   Prehistoric Indian ruins on Lake Meredith in the northwest.

Amistad NRA   Reservoir on Rio Grande, near Del Rio.

Big Bend NP   Magnificent canyons and rocky peaks in the southwest.

Big Thicket National Preserve   Conserves bayou, forest, and upland country near Beaumont in southeastern Texas.

Chamizal N MEM   Celebrates the settlement of the U.S.–Mexican border dispute, at El Paso.

Fort Davis NHS   In the southwest, where the fort was once the only safe place to be.

Guadalupe Mountains NP   In the west along the southern New Mexico border, this includes the four highest peaks in Texas.

Lake Meredith NRA   Behind Sandford Dam on the Canadian River, in the northwest.

Lyndon B. Johnson NHS   Birthplace, ranch, and gravesite of the President near Johnson City.

Padre Island NS   Narrow Gulf Coast island; marvelous birdwatching.

San Antonio Missions NHP   Four Spanish colonial missions.

New Mexico

Aztec Ruins NM   Ancient Pueblo (*not* Aztec) homes in the northwest.

Bandelier NM   Ancient Indian cliff-dwellings to the west of Santa Fe.

Capulin Mountain NM   Extinct volcanic crater in the northeast. There is a road up to the rim.

Carlsbad Caverns NP   In the southeast, this contains the Big Room, the world's largest cave.

Chaco Canyon NM   Sites of ancient Indian settlements south of Aztec.

El Morro NM   Ancient graffiti on mesa cliff face east of Zuni.

Fort Union NM   Remains of a fort on the Santa Fe trail, northeast of Las Vegas.

Gila Cliff Dwellings NM   Indian cliffhouses north of Silver City.

Gran Quivira NM   Ruins of Indian pueblo and seventeenth-century Spanish mission in the center of the state.

Pecos NM   Ruins of Spanish church and convent (built in 1617).

White Sands NM   Vast gypsum sand dunes southeast of Alamogordo.

Arizona

Canyon de Chelly NM   Scenic gorges and prehistoric Indian dwellings in the northeast.

Casa Grande Ruins NM   Four-story Indian adobe building, near Coolidge.

Chiricahua NM   Stone pinnacles, balanced rocks, and narrow gorges, north of Douglas.

Coronado N MEM   Trail south of Sierra Vista of the first Spanish explorer in the southwest (1540).

Fort Bowie NHS   HQ of campaigns against the Apache in the southeast.

Grand Canyon NP   One of the wonders of the world.

Hubbell Trading Post NHS   First private trading post on a Navajo reservation in northeastern Arizona, founded in 1876.

Montezuma Castle NM   Well-preserved prehistoric cliff-dwellings, south of Flagstaff.

Navajo NM   Thirteenth-century cliff-dwellings, near Kayenta.

Organ Pipe Cactus NM   South of Ajo, it contains rare flora and fauna.

Petrified Forest NP   Fossilized trees composed of many colored minerals, east of Holbrook.

Pipe Spring NM   Site of Mormon fort (built in 1869) in the northwest.

Saguaro NM   Enormous saguaro cacti that bloom May–June, east and west of Tucson.

Sunset Crater NM   Volcanic cone and bare, moonlike landscape, north of Flagstaff.

Tonto NM   Fourteenth-century Salado Indian cliff-dwellings, east of Scottsdale.

Tumacacori NM   Adobe mission built around 1691, near Tubac.

Tuzigoot NM   Remains of large Indian hilltop pueblo (built around 1400), near Clarkdale.

Walnut Canyon NM   Over 300 Sinagua cliff-dwellings, east of Flagstaff.

Wupatki NM   Twelfth-century Indian ruins, northeast of Flagstaff.

The Western Mountain States

Colorado

Bent's Old Fort NHS   Outpost of Santa Fe trail at La Junta.

Black Canyon of the Gunnison NM   A 2,700-foot-deep (823 m) canyon in west-central Colorado.

Colorado NM   Rocky landscapes near Grand Junction.

Curecanti NRA   West of Gunnison, this includes Blue Mesa, Crystal, and Morrow Point reservoirs.

Dinosaur NM   Dinosaur fossils in a rock face, in the far northwest.

Florissant Fossil Beds NM   Near Florissant, west of Colorado Springs.

Great Sand Dunes NM   At the foot of the Sangre de Cristo Mountains.

Hovenweep NM   Ancient Indian city on the southwestern border with Utah.

Mesa Verde NP   Ancient cliff-dwellings in the southwest.

Rocky Mountains NP   Snow-capped peaks on the Continental Divide, northwest of Denver.

Utah

Arches NP   Natural sculpture, near Moab.

Bryce Canyon NP   Colored rock pinnacles in the canyon country of the southwest.

Canyonlands NP   Gorges, mesas, buttes, cliffs, spires, and columns in reddish sandstone, near Moab.

Capitol Reef NP   Desert country and Indian remains, near Torrey.

Cedar Breaks NM   Spectacular canyons and cliffs east of Cedar City.

Glen Canyon NRA   Near the Arizona border, this includes Lake Powell, one of the world's largest manmade lakes.

Golden Spike NHS   West of Brigham City, this was where the first transcontinental railroad was completed.

Natural Bridges NM   Unusual rock formations and cliff-dwellings, in the southeast.

Rainbow Bridge NM World-famous 309-foot-high (94 m) natural bridge in southern Utah.

Timpanogos Cave NM Limestone caves in north-central Utah.

Zion NP Includes spectacular gorge of the Virgin River, in the southwest.

Wyoming

Devils Tower NM A volcanic pillar in the northeast (as seen in the movie *Close Encounters of the Third Kind*).

Fossil Butte NM Fish fossils, west of Kemmerer.

Fort Laramie NHS A military post in 1849–90, northwest of Torrington.

Grand Teton NP Impressive mountain scenery in the far west.

John D. Rockefeller, Jr. MP Highway between Yellowstone and Grand Teton NPS.

Yellowstone NP The first national park, established in 1872. Contains the geyser Old Faithful.

Montana

Big Hole NB Site of clash near Wisdom between U.S. troops and Nez Percé Indians in 1877.

Bighorn Canyon NRA Includes reservoir behind Yellowtail Dam on the Yellowstone River.

Custer Battlefield NM In the Crow Indian Reservation, tombstones mark where Custer and his men fell in 1876.

Glacier NP A beautiful mountain wilderness in the northwest.

Grant-Kohrs Ranch NHS Restored ranch, west of Helena.

Old Fort Benton Once an important outpost on the Missouri River north of Great Falls.

Idaho

Craters of the Moon NM Moonlike volcanic landscape in southern Idaho.

Nez Percé NHP Near Lewiston, this honors history of Nez Percé Indians and Lewis and Clark expedition.

The West
Washington

Coulee Dam NRA Includes the Franklin D. Roosevelt Lake.

Fort Vancouver NHS Reconstructed Hudson's Bay Company fur-trading post in the southwest.

Klondike Gold Rush NHP Depicts the embarkation point near Seattle of prospectors for Alaska.

Lake Chelan NRA In a glaciated valley, in the northern Cascades.

Mount Rainier NP A glacier-capped volcanic cone southwest of Tacoma.

North Cascades NP A superb wilderness in the northwest.

Olympic NP Unspoiled shorelines and spectacular mountain peaks, west of Seattle.

Ross Lake NRA Divides the two parts of the North Cascades NP.

San Juan Island NHP Northwest of Seattle, this commemorates the "Pig War" of 1859 and the eventual agreement on the U.S.–Canadian border in 1872.

Whitman Mission NHS Mission to care for local Indians, established near Walla Walla in 1836.

Oregon

Crater Lake NP A sapphire-blue lake in a vast caldera within Mount Mazama.

Fort Clatsop N MEM Winter camp of Lewis and Clark, November 1805 to March 1806, in the far northwest.

John Day Fossil Beds NM In north-central Oregon.

Oregon Caves NM Marble passageways and caverns festooned with stalactites, stalagmites, and other features, south of Grants Pass.

Oregon Dunes NRA Between Coos Bay and Florence on the coast.

Nevada

Lake Mead NRA Includes the waters behind the Hoover and Davis Dams.

Lehman Caves NM Marble passageways and superb caverns, southeast of Ely.

California

Cabrillo NM   At Point Loma near San Diego, this commemorates the Portuguese explorer Juan Rodríguez Cabrillo. Superb place to watch whales from December to April.

Channel Islands NM   Off Santa Barbara, this includes Anacapa and San Miguel Islands. Superb for viewing wildlife.

Death Valley NM   In the southeast on the Nevada border, this contains the country's lowest point, 282 feet (86 m) below sea level, and four mountain ranges.

Devils Postpile NM   Remains of lava flow and basalt columns, southeast of Yosemite NP.

Fort Point NHS   Civil War fort near the south tower of the Golden Gate Bridge in San Francisco.

Golden Gate NRA   Ocean beaches, woodland, and hills in San Francisco.

John Muir NHS   Honors the explorer-naturalist, near San Francisco.

Joshua Tree NM   In the south, here are protected Joshua trees, a species of the lily family, and various desert animals.

Kings Canyon NP   Adjoins Sequoia NP and includes rugged High Sierra country.

Lassen Volcanic NP   Around Lassen Peak, a volcano active in the 1910s.

Lava Beds NM   Volcanic landscape in the far north notable in the Modoc Indian War (1872–73).

Muir Woods NM   Coastal redwoods on the Marin Peninsula, commemorating the naturalist John Muir.

Pinnacles NM   Volcanic spires in west-central California.

Point Reyes NS   Beautiful coastlands northwest of San Francisco, including part of the San Andreas Fault.

Redwood NP   Contains some of the world's tallest trees, in the northwest.

Sequoia NP   Adjoins Kings Canyon NP and includes magnificent sequoia groves and Mount Whitney.

Whiskeytown Shasta-Trinity NRA   Manmade lakes surrounded by forests in northern California.

Yosemite NP   Glaciated scenery of enormous grandeur in east-central part of the state.

Alaska and Hawaii
Alaska

Large areas are being set aside in Alaska to preserve its magnificent wildernesses. Below are some of the most accessible of these.

Denali NP   Contains the nation's highest peak, Mount McKinley, tundra, and much wildlife.

Glacier Bay NM   Contains glaciers, fjords, icebergs, and rare wildlife, in the southeast.

Katmai NM   Includes "The Valley of Ten Thousand Smokes."

Kenai Fjords NM   South of Anchorage, this includes Harding Icefield, one of the four main ice caps in the United States.

Klondike Gold Rush NHP   Starting at Skagway, this includes Chilkoot Pass where the prospectors of 1898 went.

Misty Fjords NM   Beautiful glaciated scenery near Ketchikan.

Sitka NHP   Site of Tlingit Indians' last stand against Russian settlers in 1804.

Hawaii

Haleakala NP   A vast and dormant volcanic crater on Maui, containing rare plants and birdlife.

Hawaii Volcanoes NP   Includes the awe-inspiring Kilauea and Mauna Loa, active volcanoes on the Big Island.

Pu'uhonua O Honaunau NHP   This was a city of refuge for defeated warriors in ancient times, on the Big Island.

Pu'ukohola Heiau NHS   The ruins of King Kamehameha's temple on the Big Island.

U.S.S. Arizona NM   The ship on which 1,102 crew members lost their lives in the 1941 attack on Pearl Harbor.

Index